P9-CCZ-382

PIPE CLAY AND DRILL

By Richard Goldhurst

PIPE CLAY
AND DRILL
John J. Pershing:
The Classic American Soldier

Richard Goldhurst

READER'S DIGEST PRESS
distributed by
Thomas Y. Crowell Company
New York   1977

Manufactured in the United States of America

LIBRARY OF CONGRESS CATALOGING IN PUBLICATION DATA

Goldhurst, Richard.
    Pipe clay and drill.

    Bibliography: p.
    Includes index.
    1. Pershing, John Joseph, 1860–1948. 2. Generals—United States—Biography. 3. United States. Army—Biography. I. Title.
E181.P4695   1977   355.3'32'0924 [B]   76-44269
                    ISBN 0-88349-097-8

            10 9 8 7 6 5 4 3 2 1

Acknowledgments

Marie T. Capps, Map and Manuscript Librarian of the USMA at West Point, pulled everything I needed from her domains. Timothy Nenninger of the National Archives suggested documents and studies for my research. For several weeks I worked in the Special Collections Room of the Library of Congress, where each morning dutifully but reverently and quietly a librarian rolled out a six-shelved cart with the specific boxes of the Pershing Papers I requested. Stanley Crane of the Pequot Library in Southport, Connecticut, arranged for my acquisition of several theses from university libraries as well as summoned out-of-print books from other libraries.

I am indebted to William Abbott of Westport, Connecticut, who let me read and quote from his study *Who Dies in American Wars?* William Craig of Fairfield University and E. Allen McCormick of the City University of New York read the manuscript at various stages.

Bruce Lee of the Reader's Digest Press suggested Pershing as a subject and Steven Frimmer, Senior Editor, made sure the idea was more than a chronological report of Pershing's derring-do.

What are soldiers made of?
Pipe clay and drill,
All kinds of skill
That's what soldiers are made of.

Contents

EPILOGUE

Introduction

As a young officer this soldier was a figure in a Frederic Remington painting. We remember the General memorialized in bronze equestrian statues. John J. Pershing's career was long and colorful, but he himself was austere, an inexorable taskmaster rarely capable of inspiring affection among his troops. He seems not to have thought much about military philosophy, but he could quickly master the details of military organization, even amid the unprecedented, ever-expanding crisis of a great European war. He became the prototypical American soldier—nurtured and matured by republican institutions; a military man, but not a militarist; something of an evangelist; and above all a hero.

Americans have always been averse to maintaining a large standing military force. They have feared that such a force would produce a military aristocracy, that it would prove repressive, and that it would certainly demand heavy expenditures. Americans have somehow presumed that a militia would fight its wars, as the militia had fought the Revolutionary War.

Soldiers who grasped the nature of modern war began to worry about where and how they would be able to recruit speedily the gigantic masses of men they might need. This worry nourished American militarism—a system in which the influence of the pro-

1

fessional soldier would become predominant; a system that leaves a great military enterprise to a purely military judgment and decision; one that encourages preemptive strikes and preventative wars, and makes the military a coordinate branch of government.

But the majority of the American people have always wanted military institutions that are consonant with national purposes and constitutional provisions. They want a President as commander-in-chief of the armed forces, and under him a soldier who can take orders. John J. Pershing always inspired respect in his political superiors by virtue of knowing that he was a subordinate in matters of policy.

In at least one respect the American military man differs from other men who have commanded armies in modern war. The American has always fought under a stable and permanent democratic government. That government asks of its general that he muster the army, bring it into the line, and secure victory. For over a century the American government promised to wage war for steady and comprehensible ends—independence, Manifest Destiny, Union, and empire. But, in time, ends became more complex, harder to comprehend and harder to achieve, diplomatically or militarily.

This complexity of policy made the concept of morale ever more imperative. Morale, which makes sacrifice acceptable, is the conviction that victory is not only morally necessary, but *certain*. Morale is crucial when democracies fight wars instigated by a minority, or for ends that do not guarantee immediate salvation for the nation.

Civilian war leaders and wartime commanders have generated morale by relying upon the all-encompassing myth of the American mission. That mission is to bring the good news of democracy and Christianity to other peoples and thus assure a harmonious working of nations. It is an evangelical mission with exalted religious overtones. Christianity was often the motivating animus for our foreign policy in the past; Americans have vowed even to bring it unto places already Christian.

The missionary zeal of the frontier was one of the formative influences of Pershing's youth, and the American world mission was the central political fact of his adulthood. Pershing consciously participated in this mission and, behind the military facade, felt its Christian inspiration.

Of West Point he once wrote: "Cadets who enter it with the purpose of following a military career yield the hope of wealth and consecrate themselves to the service of country as completely as young men studying to take Holy Orders consecrate their lives to the service of the Church. A military man who enters onto his career in this spirit finds it gives him a sense of buoyant exaltation."

When John J. Pershing first reported to a cavalry outpost in Arizona, American foreign policy was the Monroe Doctrine. Thirty years later, Pershing commanded American forces in a war in which victory certified his country's world dominance. In that war Pershing was the one recognizable American hero. But the proportions of his heroism were hard to assess. He was an unloved disciplinarian, a humorless man in a profession noted for humorless men. And in a world beset with dislocation and disillusion he seemed to his countrymen a soldier tailor-made only for monuments. So the one honor Americans had always bestowed upon their victorious generals eluded him.

George Washington, Andrew Jackson, William Henry Harrison, who beat the Shawnees at Tippecanoe (of whom Andrew Jackson predicted "They will nominate him for they have orators enough"), Zachary Taylor, Ulysses S. Grant, Theodore Roosevelt, and Dwight D. Eisenhower all came to the White House adorned with military splendor.* The nation did not call upon a soldier after World War I, not because that soldier was Pershing, but because the nation was not sure that the war had secured a comprehensible political end.

---

*Rutherford B. Hayes, James A. Garfield, and Benjamin Harrison were also generals who came to the White House. William McKinley had been a major in the Union army. Franklin Pierce had been a general of volunteers during the Mexican War. Professional politicians were fond of nominating generals for the presidency because their military expertise promised the constituency facility in resolving intractable problems.

Political ends or, to put it another way, United States foreign policy is at the core of this book. It dictated the orders Pershing obeyed. In short, I suggest in this book that the way to uncover the thinking of the American military mind is to find out what the American military mind is asked to think about.

SHOULDER STRAP

HOTSPUR: Send danger from the east unto the west,
So Honour cross it from north to south,
And let them grapple: O, the blood more stirs
To rouse a lion than to start a hare!

William Shakespeare,
The First Part of Henry the Fourth
Act I Scene III

1

Hard Times in
the Show-Me State

Missouri, with its long Iowa border, its longer river boundary
opposite Illinois, and its railroad connections with the entire
northeast, momentarily considered secession in 1861. Then the
state came to the only reasonable decision it could support by
joining the Union. At the Battle of Wilson's Creek, however,
Confederate Sterling Price beat back the Union forces. These
forces had intended to occupy still disaffected areas, and their
defeat cost Missouri four years of bloody guerrilla war.

Irregular bands of Confederates roamed the state, raiding government posts, robbing post offices and paymasters, rustling cattle, and stealing horses. Union General Henry Halleck put the
state under martial law, suppressed free speech, censored newspapers, and levied heavy taxes on Southern sympathizers. As the
situation worsened, General Thomas Ewing arrested the wives,
sisters, and daughters of Confederate soldiers and bushwhackers.
He housed them in a Kansas City jail that collapsed in the spring of
1864, killing four women and injuring many more. That summer
Sterling Price moved up from Louisiana with a Confederate army
of 12,000 men, coordinating his attack with the guerrilla
movements of Quantrill's Raiders.

"Kill every man big enough to carry a gun," ordered Will Quantrill, who was crazy. His raiders took him at better than his word: they killed twelve-year-olds. One of Quantrill's detachments, led by Captain Clifton Holtzclaw, descended on the town of Laclede on the morning of June 16, 1864. They were after Union sympathizers, in particular John Fletcher Pershing, from whose home flew the biggest Union flag in the state, handsewn by his wife.

John Fletcher Pershing had been a sutler for the Eighteenth Missouri Regiment, which he helped supply at Shiloh and in the early stages of the Vicksburg Campaign. He was owner of a general store in whose safe was stored not only his own cash, but the cash and valuables of his neighbors.

Within minutes of Holtzclaw's arrival there were dead men in the street. John Fletcher fled from his store through the back alley to his home. He loaded his rifle, knelt, and prepared to fire through the window at Holtzclaw, who was haranguing cowed citizens while his men looted nearby stores. But Pershing's wife, Elizabeth, who was shielding their four-year-old son, begged him to put the rifle down. Firing at Holtzclaw was a gesture a family man simply could not afford. The father lowered his weapon and watched Holtzclaw and his bushwhackers ride off with $3,000 of his cash and as much of his goods as they could carry.

Whether or not the son, John Joseph Pershing, could remember the scene, there was no chance he would forget that the raid had occurred. The memory of Civil War brutality died hard in places where battles were fought. Vicksburg, which fell to Grant on July 4, 1864, did not celebrate Independence Day again until 1945.

Missouri may not have bled as much as neighboring Kansas, but it was still violent ground, the home state of the James brothers. With the railroads came the rough men who laid tracks and on paydays staged drunken brawls in the saloons; and, after them, outlaws who galloped through towns firing randomly. Violence often inspires a relentless civilizing as harsh as lawlessness itself. Young men raised in a violent society are rarely thoughtful and rarely ceremonious. Often they are tough, hardened, and combative.

With peace, Laclede enjoyed good times. Located in Linn County in north-central Missouri, the town took its name from the

French trapper who established the trading post on the site of present-day St. Louis. In the late 1860s and early 1870s it was a hard-working and pious community. Its Methodist Episcopal Church, with its gleaming white steeple and shiny white filigree along the roof slope, occupied one corner of the town square. Every summer, members of the Methodist Free Churches collected in and around Laclede in tents and shacks for their devotionals.

Methodism was the religion of the American frontier because it was both democratic and enthusiastic. The itinerant Methodist preacher who traveled to prairie towns that were flyspecks on the map gave many frontiersmen their only chance to worship. Methodist bishops and preachers welcomed the piety and industry of women, the first large Christian denomination to do so—it was from feminine offices that Methodism began to undertake its considerable achievements in education and social work. John Fletcher Pershing was superintendent of the Sunday School; his wife, Elizabeth, was a noted church woman.

Elizabeth Thompson Pershing was not so "unspotted from the world" that she wouldn't play the piano in the evenings. Her family sang along as they clustered around her. She bore nine children, three of whom died in infancy. Her first was John J., born on January 13, 1860.

John Fletcher Pershing was the great-grandson of an Alsatian immigrant who arrived in Philadelphia in 1749 as an indentured servant named Frederick Pfoershing. By the 1870s that great-grandson had become a wholesaler for smaller stores in the county, as well as Laclede's postmaster. He also bought a lumberyard and forty quarter-sections of farmland whose sod was turned by oxen yoked in teams of four pulling behind them the great breaking plows.

In 1873, however, the nationwide depression wiped out John Fletcher Pershing. He could not collect all that was due him nor could he pay all that he owed. He gave up the store, the postmastership, the lumberyard, and the quarter-sections.

These periodic depressions ravaged the American Midwest. The farmer sought redress and reform through the Farmers Grange, the Greenback Party, and Populism, but it took a generation for these movements to gain political leverage. In the meantime the fine houses in Laclede emptied as men went back to scrubbing dirt for a living or moved on to try their luck somewhere else. John Fletcher Pershing went on the road as a traveling salesman for a St. Joseph clothing house at $2,000 a year. He put the son he'd hoped to send to college to farming the one piece of land he hoped to salvage. Eventually he would lose that, too.

John J. Pershing hoed potatoes, baled timothy hay, and planted corn and wheat, losing as much money in falling markets as he ever made in rising ones. Grasshoppers ruined one crop and drought another. He was later to say that farming "was the best thing that ever happened to me—it taught me more, gave me greater confidence and a keener sense of responsibility than anything else could have done." This is a temporizing of sorts, for, if hard times and hard work made men better and wiser, earth would long ago have been a paradise. Kicking clods from behind a harnessed mule may put a man into a Biblical sweat, but it doesn't elevate him any more than clubbing his head reforms him. In fact, young Pershing abandoned farming with a noticeable lack of regret.

Hard times did not diminish the hopes Pershing's parents nourished for him, nor did they dim his own ambition to become a lawyer. He was interested in the law not because he saw in it a chance for political advancement or money, in neither of which was he ever particularly interested, but because he recognized early on that he lived in a violent, capricious society in which law represented stability.

He was a strong boy, tough and somewhat cheerless, but obviously intelligent. Farming made him as well muscled as a boxer. And he was also the fastest boy in Laclede (in another age he would have been the perfect fullback). Square-jawed, gray-eyed, he had regular if not handsome features made glorious by perfect dimples when he smiled. Whatever humor was in him he tended to suppress; years later, as a general officer, he would be glacial, as remote as George Washington, whom no one ever dared slap on the back.

To supplement farm work, Pershing became the winter-time janitor of Laclede's two public schools, one black and one white. When the principal of the black school either embezzled money or was lynched, probably both, the Board of Education asked Pershing to take over the classes. The school was little more than a shack of sun-varnished clapboard with a chimney, coal box, two windows, and tar-paper roof. It was little enough, but more than blacks in the neighboring Southern states had. And Pershing, who carried little philosophical baggage around with him, was remarkably free from race prejudice. He had a way with blacks and, as he would later demonstrate, with black soldiers. Pershing said this was not so amazing, after all, since he grew up with them in Laclede.

Because of this experience, Pershing got a job in 1878 as an elementary school teacher in Prairie Mound. Every Sunday afternoon he rode on horseback seven miles south into Chariton County and two miles west to the small settlement where he boarded with a farmer. On the following Friday he rode home. He earned $40 a month for the school year, which lasted from November through March. Some of his students were older than he was. They tested his mettle only once. With the born instinct of the commander, Pershing walked up to the biggest of the boys and spoke directly to him, saying that he had to run the school the Pershing way and they would have to obey. The boy backed down, and when the big boy backs down, the others automatically decline.

Pershing spent two years at Prairie Mound. He saved enough money to enroll in the small normal school at Kirksville, forty-five miles east of Laclede. The term lasted ten weeks and the tuition was $50 plus room and board. In the early spring of 1882 he was graduated with the degree of Bachelor of Elementary Didactics.

Pershing was of the opinion later that he was marking time. But teaching was far from a meaningless pursuit. By the time of the Civil War public school education was widespread policy in the populous states of the North, though it was by no means the accepted method of education in the South or the sparsely populated West. Paradoxically, after the Crimean and Franco-Prussian wars, the professional soldiers of Europe had come to the conclusion that the critical need of the large modern army was officers who were intelligent and independent, ordinary men with common sense, who could think out military situations on their own and seize the initiative, such men as were to be found among the democratically educated.

In the late spring of 1882 Pershing heard that Congressman A. B. Burroughs was sponsoring a competitive examination for the appointment to West Point from the district. The examination was held at Trenton, and Pershing was one of eighteen applicants. He had to answer written questions in arithmetic, the history of the United States, civil government, and English grammar, as well as demonstrate proficiency in reading and orthography. Those who passed were examined orally by a board of examiners and gradually weeded out. Pershing and one other applicant were left. When the other could not parse the sentence "I love to run," Pershing won the appointment.

He had started to read Blackstone in the hope West Point would provide him with an education that would equip him for the law. In 1882, he was neither romantically nor patriotically inclined toward soldiering. He went to the Academy as hundreds of other boys went, either because their fathers pushed them into it or because the opportunity for a free education was better than any other they saw. In June, he willingly left Laclede.

It was farmboys like Pershing who became the professional soldiers of his day—and who, in some respects, still do. During the Vietnam War, more young men from West Virginia than from Connecticut died in action, although Connecticut is a more populous state and had more efficient draft machinery. Out of a male population of one and a half million, 480 Connecticut men (.033 percent) died in Southeast Asia. Out of a male population of less than one million, 575 West Virginians (.068 percent) lost their lives.*

*As a matter of fact, industrialized New England lost .039 percent of its male population in the war, while the equally populous but rural East South Central states of Alabama, Kentucky, Tennessee, and Mississippi lost .054 percent.

Whatever else these statistics may indicate, they help reveal the traditional composition of the United States Army; small-town, rural America has always furnished more soldiers proportionate to its numbers than the big cities. Not surprisingly, the military hierarchy comes from the small town.

On the occasion of its centennial celebration in 1902, the United States Military Academy published a list of the occupations pursued by the fathers of every cadet who had ever entered West Point: 1,149 were the sons of farmers (or planters); the next most popular paternal profession was banking, in which there were 92; this was followed by the ministry with 84, and so on down the list to the profession of detective, of which there was one.

Of the ten cadets in Pershing's class from New York, only one came from New York City; of the five from Illinois, none came from Chicago; and of the three from Missouri, none was from St. Louis. They came instead from the typical small towns of Massena, Hastings, and Farmington, and from towns just like them in Ohio, Pennsylvania, and California.

Though European armies were still led by titled aristocrats with vast property holdings to preserve, the contrary was true in democratic America. Professional army officers in Pershing's day were for the most part men without property. They were from small towns, where it is difficult to amass property. Small-town America is provincial; its life is never anonymous; its opportunities are limited; its young men are apt to feel that military service offers romantic and adventurous possibilities.

For these reasons small-town America furnished the army with professional soldiers who could accept the almost imperceptible advancement of a military career. While it is true that some of our Presidents came from such remote communities as Caldwell, New Jersey, and West Branch, Iowa, they are better remembered as sheriff of Buffalo, New York, or wartime food administrator in Brussels. The generals remain small-town boys, remembered as coming from Georgetown, Ohio, or Abilene, Kansas, or Laclede, Missouri.

2

No Horse, No Wife,
No Moustache

The founding of the United States Military Academy at West Point resulted from an act of Congress in 1802. This act provided that the Corps of Engineers stationed at West Point should constitute an Academy, and it shortly transformed that Academy into the national school of civil engineering. Until 1835, West Point was, in fact, the nation's only school of civil engineering. Until the Civil War, it was the preeminent engineering center of the new republic.

Such a school, of course, filled one of the central needs of frontier America. After the Louisiana Purchase and the War of 1812, the government saw that the crucial need of the country was to break down geographical barriers between localities and thus facilitate agriculture, commerce, and industry. Congress passed an act in the 1820s that enabled military engineers to construct roads, canals, bridges, and railroads; to map and improve rivers; to drain swamps; and to construct lighthouses. West Point was built on a rock and the rock was mathematics. It was for thirty years the only American college that concentrated on mathematics, which earned it a reputation as the citadel of learning in the ever-emergent new country.

The two men principally responsible for fashioning this citadel were Sylvanus Thayer, the Academy's second Superintendent (1817–1833), and Dennis Hart Mahan, an Academy graduate of

14

1824 who, after a course of study in Europe, prepared the curriculum of civil and military engineering. Soon the Academy displaced the divinity schools in prestige. Hundreds of its graduates, after fulfilling their obligations, resigned from the army to go into law, banking, or politics. Along the frontier, former West Pointers were usually the only educated professional men.

But by the 1880s, the Academy had lost this preeminence. Even before the Civil War, American education had begun transforming itself from an aristocratic, church-dominated institution to a democratic and secular one. Private endowments helped the growth of older universities, and the Morrill Land Grant Act of 1862 provided government money and support for the new ones. Many universities established technical and professional schools. Teachers introduced experimental and innovative pedagogy in classrooms and laboratories. This, combined with a hunger for education among a burgeoning middle class pushed colleges and universities toward flexibility. But the West Point alumni, high-ranking army men, wanted the Academy kept the way it was.

While scientific study became the animating purpose of the American university after 1860, West Point insisted on teaching primary engineering techniques. As a consequence the Academy changed slowly. In 1882 Cadet John J. Pershing found it observed nearly the same customs, habits, and traditions it had when his Commanding General, William T. Sherman, attended it forty years before. The Academy never had a succession of young men from prominent families, which characterized Harvard and other prestigious schools. Even if the Academy had inclined toward such nepotism, the system of entrance by congressional nomination doomed it. But West Point did have an unbroken line of regular army faculty, all of them Academy graduates and all wanting to preserve the school's prestigious past. Because the Academy never exchanged chairs with other neighboring schools, and never recruited or encouraged minority or controversial viewpoints, its faculty was virtually a cabal.

As an entering plebe, therefore, Pershing was matriculating at a school that the growing nation, with its changing role in world affairs, had left behind. The great technical school of pre-Civil War days was still a national school, but one devoted only to the education of professional army officers. The Academy was not even producing the new commanding generals; in the next decade most of them would be either old Indian fighters or surgeons. Much of the instruction was irrelevant to the needs of the army. Pershing and his classmates, for example, spent hours taking instruction from Antone Lorentz, the master of the sword at West Point. Cadets dueled with buttoned Solingen foils in an age when Krupp was mass-producing the machine gun and French artillerists had developed the 75 cannon.

From 1865 until 1902, West Point was typified by Peter Smith Michie, professor of natural and experimental philosophy. Michie,* who had been born in Scotland, was an 1863 graduate of the Academy and served with the Engineers in the Army of the Potomac. Colonel Michie claimed he could read a man's character in his face on his first official contact. He also believed that his course in physics proved conclusively the existence of God. He liked to interrupt his lecture on the relationship between matter and force with the comment, "All that shows, does it not, that there is a creator who set the hosts of the skies and determined their motions?" Cadets who remained unpersuaded of this proof, according to Michie, did not deserve to be graduated.

Complicating this academic distress was the fact that the Academy was under constant congressional criticism. Senators and Representatives charged that "wasp-waisted vampires were sucking the nation's blood." Congress also leveled the charge of prejudice against the Academy. One reason was that it had failed to commission more than three black officers since 1865, though it had easily assimilated the sons of Confederates.† Another was that the custom of hazing had precipitated several scandals.

*He was the father of Dennis Michie, Army's first football captain, who died in action in Cuba and for whom the athletic stadium is named.
†That the army and Academy hierarchy tried and failed to commission black officers is best explained by noting that the country itself, far from being aware of the military advantages of black officers, was not even aware of the essential

Two congressional committees had investigated the practice of hazing and condemned it, a condemnation echoed by the War Department. The brutal practice continued despite the attempts of several Superintendents and Commandants to end it. Hazing, once an upperclassman's casual mischief, had by the 1880s become a covert part of the Academy's regimen. It is still, for that matter, part of the Academy's regimen, though now it is subdued and physical torture is prohibited.

The third and major cause for congressional disquiet was jealousy. In the 1880s the House and the Senate were populated by men who were Civil War veterans, several of them excellent battleground leaders. But none had ever succeeded to one of the top commands. Though the old army numbered less than 20,000 in 1860, and though its officers were but a small fraction of the commanders who led the massive Union formations, by the end of the war West Pointers were in universal ascendancy.* Having been denied the commands they thought they merited, these politicians yearly reduced the army's budget, cut Commanding General William Tecumseh Sherman's salary and expenses, and, through the politically powerful Grand Army of the Republic, insisted that in a democracy the professional soldier can have no exclusive claim to the privilege of command.

So Pershing's military education came at a time when the Academy and the army itself were at a remove from the people.

With his own and some of his parents' savings, John J. Pershing

---

humanity of black citizens. Moreover, the almost nonexistent educational facilities available to blacks made a contingent of black officers illusory. Finally, the system of congressional appointment to West Point was hardly conducive to realizing such a prospect.

*Between the Civil War and World War II roughly one-third of the graduates of each West Point class became general officers. In 1885, 12 of 39 graduates became generals; in 1886, Pershing's class, 27 of 77; in 1887, 28 of 64; but in 1905, only 18 of 114. The class of 1915, "the class the stars fell on," which included Eisenhower, Omar Bradley, and George Van Fleet, produced 57 generals of 164 graduates; yet the class of 1918 produced only 35 generals of 227 graduates. Three of the first four five-star generals, Eisenhower, Bradley, and MacArthur, were West Pointers.

enrolled in May, 1882, for a month's preparatory study at the Braden School at Highland Falls, New York. This school prepared appointees for the West Point entrance examinations. Students went over and over and over the questions from old tests and learned and practiced the rudiments of drill. There were several of these schools located near the Academy (and still are) of which the Braden School, also called "The Rocks," was the most proficient.

It had been founded by Caleb Huse, a graduate of the West Point class of 1851. Although a New Englander, Huse had married a Southern girl and sided with the Confederacy during the Civil War. He spent the war years in England, purchasing arms for Robert E. Lee. Considering himself a renegade after Appomattox, Huse had founded the preparatory school to expiate his *mea culpa*, an enterprise that eventually won him the affection and respect of his former West Point classmates and a future generation of officers.

In late June, Pershing, along with 182 other appointees, presented himself at the Academy for the written and physical examinations. Each congressional district at the time was entitled to one Academy appointment, which was made by the Secretary of War at the request of the district's Representative. An additional ten at-large appointments were made by the President. But alternates did not replace appointees who failed admission. The army was small and virtually impoverished, promotion was almost nonexistent, and neither the Secretary of War nor the Commanding General wanted too many second lieutenants milling around for twenty years. Accepting an appointment therefore entailed a heavy responsibility; if a boy failed he deprived his district of a cherished opportunity.

An applicant was refused admission if he had the "loss of many teeth, a varicose state of the veins, or ulcers, or unsound cicatrices of ulcers likely to break out afresh." He also had to explain "the nature of prime number and the nature of fractions, common or vulgar; explain why and when the Constitution of the United States was formed; give the names of the Presidents in order along with the leading events from each administration" and promise to serve eight years-after his graduation.

One hundred and twenty-nine of the appointees of 1882 were admitted as "plebes"—the word is a shortening of "plebians"—of which 77 would be graduated, Pershing ranking thirtieth among them. He qualified for entrance only by lying about his age. Twenty-two was the statutory limit and he had turned twenty-two on January 13. He changed his birthday to September 13, which got him in under the wire. He was six years older than the youngest of his classmates and four years older than most. Twenty-two is hardly an advanced age, but it gave Pershing certain advantages. He had reached his full growth, about 5 feet 10 inches and 170 pounds,* and hard work and hard times had matured him early. In each of the four years he was at the Academy he was elected class president, an office for which a cadet may not campaign nor the faculty exercise its influence.

Cadets lived in the only American institution where cash didn't count or circulate and its possession was punished. They earned $540 a year in credits. From this, they were to provide themselves with uniforms, books, recreation, and "at least one broom which fit the Superintendent's specification." They were not allowed to receive money from home, nor could they own a horse or keep a wife, and they had to answer reveille clean shaven.

The Academy of 1882 was built of wood. Fireplaces provided the only heat, and free time was spent by the cadets in fire drills. In the winter hydrants froze, so the cadets did without water much of the time, but in the fire drills they simulated water. They never removed their stiff-necked gray tunics, which memorialize the Regulars who fought at Chippewa and Lundy's Lane in 1814. The tunic served a practical military purpose for the cadets. The only way the jacket looked presentable was when they stood up ramrod straight. The Academy remedied bowlegs by teaching the cadets to depress their toes in marching.

In its Regulations, the Academy recommended that all officers and cadets "diligently" attend divine services. Church attendance

---

*For some unexplained reason, Academy records list him as 5 feet 9 inches and 155 pounds, a fact every photograph taken of him at the time belies.

was then considered a military, not a moral, duty. Officers always attended in full dress. Upperclassmen patrolled the pews to make sure the plebes took notes during the sermon. The Corps of Cadets worshipped in a stone chapel built in 1821. It contained an organ set below a painting, commissioned by Congress, representing "a church without a bishop, a state without a king." On the wall was a tablet with the names and dates of the Revolutionary War generals, one blank space for Benedict Arnold.

West Point archivists called these the "Years of Iron" and they are epitomized in the character of Wesley Merritt, who became the Academy's Superintendent in 1882. Gallant, romantic, handsome, Merritt had been graduated from West Point in 1860, fought at Gettysburg, and at twenty-eight commanded a brigade in Phil Sheridan's cavalry of the Army of the Potomac. Merritt was also a sophisticate. He invited Mark Twain to lecture to the cadets, was the first Superintendent to encourage the unofficial visits of ex-Confederate alumni, and saw to it that William Tecumseh Sherman always handed out the diplomas at graduation. The cadets adored Sherman; Pershing, in fact, once walked a mile out his way for the chance to salute him.

But for Pershing and his classmates Merritt was a fearsome disciplinarian. He did things by the numbers, and he wanted things done in perfect, orderly sequence. When he was in charge of the troops handling the details of the Oklahoma land rush he settled disputes summarily—once honoring the claim of a woman who, having lost her stake, tied her bloomers to a landmark tree.

He was never as flexible with the cadets, but he was as summary. Avery D. Andrews of the Class of 1886, later a prominent New York City lawyer, a brigadier, and a Pershing biographer, wrote that his close friend Pershing deeply admired Merritt and fashioned his own notions of command upon this exemplar. Serving with Pershing in France, Andrews was struck by how much he mirrored the old Superintendent's style.

T. Bentley Mott, the class intellectual, saw in Merritt everything that was wrong with the Academy, a place where discipline wasn't taught, but rather enforced. West Point, he later wrote, had been founded in a time when the world, including Napoleon, drew inspiration from Frederick the Great. Will marks the great commander, but in Merritt will had become confused with inflexibility. "This automatism," Mott went on, "gave the cadet a false idea of how to exercise discipline as an officer when he had to deal, not with other cadets, but with privates and noncoms who would display the variety of human nature found in a company of soldiers."

Another who thought Pershing learned from Merritt was classmate Robert L. Bullard, who later commanded the Second Army of the AEF. "Pershing's exercise of authority was then and always has been since of a nature peculiarly impersonal, dispassionate, hard and firm. This quality did not in him, as in many, give offense; the man was too impersonal, too given over to business and duty. His manner carried to the minds of those under him the suggestion, nay, the conviction, of unquestioned right to obedience."

Pershing himself wrote, "The West Point under Merritt, Michie and Hasbrouck was still the West Point of Grant, Sherman, Sheridan, Schofield and Howard, a hallowed place."

Tales about the American university experience have two heroes: one is Frank Merriwell and the other is F. Scott Fitzgerald. West Point rigidity to the contrary, there is a folklore about its cadets that is genuinely American and filled with dramatic irony and humor. One remembers George E. Pickett, who left his native Virginia to win an appointment to the Academy from a compliant Illinois Congressman. Debonair and self-willed, Pickett refused to wear the stiff leather collar. The demerits he earned for this insubordination made him the "goat," the lowest ranking member of the Class of 1846. Nevertheless, the Congressman, Abraham Lincoln, now out of office, wrote Pickett congratulating him on his perseverance and wishing him luck in his chosen profession.

William Tecumseh Sherman, fourth in his class academically, was noted as the best "hash-maker" at the Point, adept at stealing butter, bread, potatoes, and meat from the mess and cooking it up for classmates after lights out. Years later, when he came back as the ranking United States general, he visited his old room in the company of the Superintendent and the Commandant. Poking with his cane in the fireplace, he noted that it was in here that he had hidden the makings for midnight hash. As luck would have it, the cane dislodged a cache of delicacies which rolled across the floor as two cadets turned eyes skyward. Allowing as the inspection was unofficial, Sherman suggested that no one saw anything.

Every day he was at the Point, Douglas MacArthur met his mother at 4:30 P.M. on the bench in front of the Sylvanus Thayer Hotel. He was the son of a famous general, and he and Ulysses S. Grant III, the grandson of another, were unmercifully hazed. One night other cadets almost choked MacArthur to death. Before a Senate investigating committee, however, he refused to name his tormentors, explaining to the Senators that he had often suffered choking attacks.

The Academy Yearbook nominated Dwight D. Eisenhower as the superior Mexican athlete of the Corps—the one who could sling the bull the farthest. He was graduated from West Point only after the authorities extracted from him the promise not to apply for the cavalry, because he had badly damaged his knee in football.

No such story attaches to Pershing. Anecdotes about him center on his ability to command. At the conclusion of the targetry course in 1883, Pershing had the highest score. "Well," said one cadet, "that big plebe, Mr. Pershing, has a cinch on a corporal's chevrons when the 'makes' are out in June." Indeed, the cadet was right. In June Pershing was made senior corporal of cadets. As a third-year man he was top sergeant; and as a senior he was First Captain of the Corps. "No promotion," he later wrote, "was ever as sweet." Three decades later, when Pershing had to put the Forty-second Division under heavy marching orders after months in the line, he told its brigadier, Douglas MacArthur, who was stunned by the orders, "We First Captains must never flinch."

There was never much that was boyish about Pershing. Avery D. Andrews, for example, who was made company clerk by Pershing their second year at the Point, was delighted because the position exempted him from guard duty. As Pershing's appointed battery clerk in his senior year, Andrews could keep his lights on after taps. But Andrews noted that Pershing wasn't interested in these indulgences, he was interested in giving orders. After graduation, when the cadets celebrated at Delmonico's in New York City, Pershing was reelected class president, an office he held until he died.

Pershing would attempt anything on a horse that required grit, strength, and skill, but never the spectacular. He was also, according to an old classmate, neither nervy enough nor crazy enough to have made a good aviator. He excelled in gymnastics and at exercises that required strength of arms and shoulders. Hazing appalled Pershing as a plebe, but he became proficient at it when he was a yearling. He invented the "jumping jacks" discipline in which he drilled plebes who marched at his command like marionettes.

One attribute that impressed not only his fellow cadets, but fellow officers throughout his career, was that the dance floor transformed him. He was courtly, and in his uniform, in a waltz, he was grace personified. He was cold, formidable, remote, and he could be vindictive and hard; but he always had an easy felicity with women, which, to the numberless men who do not have it, seems a mysterious talent, even a God-given gift.

Pershing studied algebra, geometry, trigonometry, analytic geometry, and calculus; chemistry, mineralology, and physics; history, geography, and ethics; topography, surveying, and drawing; French and English, the latter from an unduly complex and antiquated primer. Despite its help, he could not define a "pseudometaphor," and gave the feminine of "sultan" as "harem."

West Point in the 1880s was a place where cadets studied everything but war. The Academy did not offer a course on the Napoleonic campaigns principally because French military strategy had been discredited during the Franco-Prussian War. It offered seniors only a one-year course in the Civil War. The cadets studied more mathematics than they needed and had no instruction at all in the history of native military institutions. The four-year course in tactics was only close order and mounted drill with instruction in firearms. Cadets never commanded a platoon, nor did they learn the intricacies of a flanking movement or any of the detail of supply and administration. The Academy did, however, teach leadership, which it defined as "the art of influencing and directing people to an assigned goal in such a manner as to command their obedience, confidence, respect and loyal co-operation." It instilled leadership, the Academy believed, because it insisted upon character as the most precious component of an officer. Character, or honor, was associated with discipline, firmness, and intrepidity, which gave a military force superior weight and execution in attack.

No one can gainsay the Academy's success, but it is worth noting that this concept bears out the truism that soldiers are romantics. The soldier's quest for perfection of command is also the quest for an ideal, perfect obedience to perfect law. War is destructive and cruel, yet soldiers seek what virtues can be realized from its pursuit. Standards of soldiering are standards of morality.

Despite his considerable accomplishments, Pershing looked beyond the army for a possible livelihood. A plan to develop an irrigation project in Oregon, in partnership with four other cadets, came to naught. Nor did he give up his ambition for the law. Service in the regular army was, as far as he could see, not only unpromising but uneventful. "No one," said Pershing to his brother, Jim, "expects to hear a gun fired in anger for one hundred years."

The one story of symbolic proportions that does attach to Pershing's cadet years occurred in 1885, with the death of Ulysses S. Grant at Mt. McGregor, New York. As First Captain, Pershing led the cadets from West Point across the Hudson, the only time the Corps left the reservation, to salute Grant's funeral train as it proceeded to New York City. When the train had passed, and the cadets had shouldered their weapons, the sky grew black and lightning and thunder crashed down the Hudson from Storm King Mountain.

Ulysses S. Grant's death marked the end of a military era. William Tecumseh Sherman had already retired as Commanding General and Phil Sheridan, who had succeeded him, was to die within three years. These were the generals who had stormed and taken Troy. The American *Iliad* ended on that August day along the Hudson, and the American *Odyssey* was about to begin. Its first Odysseus would be the young cadet captain who brought the Corps to present arms.

3

Sheriffs Keeping Promises

In September, 1886, Pershing reported for duty with Troop L of the Sixth Cavalry at Fort Bayard in the New Mexico Territory. He wanted the Sixth principally because it was warring against the Apaches and, he later wrote, "the possibilities of rapid promotion were not overlooked."*

Bald mountains rimmed the horizon, through which rock-strewn canyons cleaved. The flat lands were blistering stretches of alkali. The sun was tropical, the night air arctic. Trails were elusive and worse—often they led nowhere. Water was scarce, so scarce that when the troopers came upon a spring they had to beat their horses off with the butts of their carbines.

"Fort" was a misnomer. The stockaded stronghold had long ago given way to the military post, principally because the Indians never attacked armed cantonments. The so-called fort was built out of indigenous materials at hand—Bayard was adobe. It was as much a fort, a general remarked, as a prairie dog village is a fort. It consisted of two-story enlisted men's barracks, officers' quarters, stables, corral, warehouse, mess hall, armory, blacksmith shop,

*"I don't believe I would say this," noted his editor in 1936. "Right," appended Pershing in pencil.

26

and headquarters, set in a square around a flat parade ground, over which the wind sometimes exploded billows of blinding dust. To the rolling of the same drum and the boom of the same small cannon, troops raised the flag every morning and dipped it in retreat every night.

Since the Civil War, the United States Army had eliminated the threat posed by the French-supported Emperor Maximilian of Mexico; had occupied Southern states during the Reconstruction; and had suppressed dissident Plains Indians. The test of muscle, sinew, and brains had been these 943 Indian campaigns, which occupied the postwar army for over twenty years. This campaigning army consisted of 2,153 officers and 23,254 enlisted men divided into five regiments of artillery, ten of cavalry, and twenty-five of infantry. Most of it was stationed in eighty-two such places as Fort Bayard, down from almost two hundred installations that had dotted the West a decade before. Then there had not been two million settlers past the Mississippi. In 1886 there were almost eight million, and four railroads spanned the continent. Still, it was a hard life for the horse soldier and a harder life for his enemy, the red man.

As a newly commissioned shavetail—a term derived from the cavalry's practice of shaving the tails of recently acquired (hence more stubborn) mules, to mark them for the pack walloper—Pershing earned $125 a month. He could expect to retire as a major in 1924, when he would earn $4,640 a year.

If he entertained notions of adventure and excitement, he was soon set straight. The life of a lieutenant in garrison was one of barely endured monotony. "Quarters were tumbled down," wrote Pershing to his brother, "the winters severe and it is always bleak and the surrounding country is barren absolute." Young line officers policed 1,400 miles of cattle trails, spent months checking on the heliographs, which were set up on mountains ten and fifteen miles apart. They spent Saturdays putting the troops through drill and the manual of arms, and often supervised a detail ordered to clean the dead pigeons from the post water supply.

Pershing made all the mistakes shavetails make. He took out a scouting party with some of the men so drunk they stampeded their own horses at the first dismount, stranding themselves and their officer for a day in the desert. On his first charge against a small Indian band, he galloped recklessly ahead of his troop. A brave stepped from behind a rock and felled him with a blow from his war lance. The brave had the choice of killing the unconscious Pershing or stealing his pistol, which had gone clattering. The brave stole the pistol. While the men revived Pershing, the Indians disappeared. Pershing also borrowed a first lieutenant's bedroll and forgot to return it punctually, which led to a dressing down: "Mr. Pershing, the first thing a man learns in this army is courtesy. It starts from the day you learn to salute."

The men Pershing commanded were Confederate officers, now serving in the ranks; Irish immigrants with an affinity for horses and fighting; Germans who, through their precision and rigidity, usually rose to sergeant major; and misfits, criminals, and bankrupted mechanics. The regimental band was composed of Italians; the bandmaster, named LaGuardia, was destined to father a colorful son. There were band concerts every evening. When the colonel said he didn't like the tune "Hard Times," a lieutenant listed it as "Other Days" with no one the wiser but the bandsmen.

These troopers were "bummers, loafers, and foreign paupers" as a New York newspaper once characterized them. Privates made $13 a month, sergeants $22, and they received their pay, when they received it, in currency which they had to convert to specie at a discount. An average of three thousand men deserted every year. Those who remained subscribed to the credo that a trooper should never drown, get kicked to death by a mule, or die of sickness—a trooper should bleed.

They wore heavy woolen tunics, blue flannel shirts, and light blue pants supported by suspenders. Their boots came from lasts in the Leavenworth Military Prison. The forage cap, which resembled the French kepi, offered no more protection from the desert sun than a clam shell and was harder to wear. Troopers discarded it in favor of their own white, brown, or black Stetsons, until the Ordnance Department authorized the Kossuth, later the standard campaign hat of the Spanish-American War. Officers and men wore white leather gauntlets for parade. All that distinguished Pershing's uniform from that of an enlisted man were the shoulder straps of the blouse and tunic. Along with "shavetail," "shoulder strap" was a synonym for a green West Pointer.

Pershing cleaned his uniform with benzine, when it was available, otherwise with alcohol or spirits of hartshorn. He cleaned his uniform often. He was always soldierly and the first business of a soldier is to look like one.

The cavalry was armed with single-shot, .45 caliber Springfield '73 carbines, while many Indians had come into possession of Winchester repeaters, which could be loaded on horseback. The Indians did not possess the Winchesters in quantity, and ammunition was scarce, which was fortunate for the cavalry; nevertheless, the troopers always took careful aim. Men also carried the single-action Colt '72 revolver, the noted "Peacemaker," which gave them an advantage in close fighting. They carried their ammunition in a standard belt to which leather loops were sewn, an invention of cavalry Captain Anson Mills, who made himself wealthy when his prairie belt became the forerunner of webbed equipment issued to armies throughout the world. And of course, cavalrymen were issued sabers, "cold steel" to the old army men. The saber had a curved blade three feet long, a triple-branched brass guard, a leather wired grip, and a steel scabbard; it weighed five pounds. Polishing the saber gave the troopers something to do.

Fort Bayard kept a ready-packed supply of ten days' rations for emergency calls. These rations could be buckled onto the mules within minutes. They included sowbelly, flour, beans, coffee, sugar, salt, and 120 rounds of ammunition for each man. Ten days' hard riding was the limit the horses and mules could sustain.

Apaches had been known to travel a hundred miles in one day. They could traverse a mountain at a killing gallop, steal fresh horses in the next valley, cut cattle out from a herd for subsistence, and if they had to, raid isolated ranches. The only way to trap these marauding bands was to use the troopers in relays, one troop picking up the chase from another, in the hopes this pursuit would wear the Indians down. It was by the use of dozens of these relays that the cavalry hunted down Geronimo, the last Apache chief. Though Pershing did not participate in that expedition, he was part of another that went over seven mountain ranges before it trapped Mangas, Geronimo's second-in-command.

Pershing quickly became a toughened Indian fighter and more. He learned Apache and other dialects so that he could converse with Indians with some facility. And he mastered the Indian hand signals, the *lingua franca* of the Great Plains. His superiors found him always proficient. Once he took out 36 mules for 140 days and brought back every one of them.

When horse thieves made off with a herd from the Zuni reservation, the Indians gave chase. The rustlers shot three of them, but the Zunis stayed on the track and eventually besieged the white men in a mountain cabin. Lieutenant Pershing was ordered to disperse the Indians and escort the criminals back to the post for trial. Pershing found the Zunis, and after protracted argument, persuaded the Indians to let him approach the cabin alone. He kicked in the door and told the three men they were under arrest. He signaled for the sergeant, who trotted up with the rest of the detachment and a buckboard. Pershing ordered the detachment to ride quickly through the ring of angry but momentarily confused Zunis. "We mean business," he said to the sergeant. The Zunis let them pass, then followed them to the post. Pershing noted later that one of the men escaped from the post stockade and the other two were subsequently released unpunished.

In his first hitch Pershing served in two more posts, Fort Wingate and Fort Stanton, both in New Mexico. Though desolate places, still a man could pull two hundred fish a day out of a mountain stream and the riding and the hunting were unsurpassed. And Pershing was invariably able to tell his replacement the best places on the post to make love to a girl. He became adept at high-stakes poker, playing with such a passion that he reproduced poker hands in his sleep. He gave it up before the passion consumed him, being too thrifty for poker.

There were other breaks in the routine. Pershing went to a plains reunion with eight members of his West Point class. Afterwards he wrote idiosyncratically: "It would have been more pleasant had two or three or four of the boys not gotten a little too full, one of whom I am which. I never went to a reunion yet that I did not wind up full as eighteen goats."

It was a hard life, and if it made men tough, it also made them brutish; if it taught them the virtues of discipline, it often made them vindictive, too. The raw demands of this life, however, instilled in the young officers who would become the mature generals of the twentieth century one valuable lesson: that an army is tested best by what it can do when it is exhausted. The frontier cavalry constantly traveled past exhaustion. Exhausted men followed the officers who cared for them, who kept close watch over their food, equipment, living quarters, and sanitation. Pershing was far from loved by his men, though they knew what to expect from him and what he expected from them. The men must be cared for, he was to insist, they must be trained to fight, and they must be led by a man willing to fight; and then, sometimes, they will do anything.

"The white man made us many promises," said an old Sioux chief, "more than I can remember, but he never kept but one: he promised to take our land and he took it." Simplistically, this sentiment describes the causes and objectives of the Indian campaigns. It serves as well as the theme of the atonement literature which has enjoyed a widening vogue since the mid-1960s. The white man was the aggressor, but he was an aggressor bewildered by the Plains Indian whose presence presented insuperable economic and cultural problems.

The Indian claimed vast lands as his own, all of it ill used. An Indian tribe of five hundred members often needed five thousand square miles to support itself. The Indian lived on the buffalo, depending on it for food, clothing, and shelter, and the buffalo needed an entire shelf of the earth for its grazing. The Sioux believed certain waters were sacred—rivers which ran for hundreds of miles—and could not be desecrated by any man's fording or crossing them. There were Shoshone mountains whose timber could not be felled because they were the hunting grounds of gods.

Some Indians tried to accommodate the new settlers by granting rights-of-way and selling off packets of the land. But accommodation is always a dangerous game. When the Indian said he could do with less, the white man made him do with nothing. The United States was not the first nation to push a people off the land, but it has become the first to indulge in a long and perhaps meaningless self-recrimination about it. For the Indian was not the sole target of post-Civil War cruelty. The mores of the entrepreneur and the industrialist toward employees were simply barbaric. Young children worked eighty hours a week as a matter of course. The Reconstruction stripped the South of its resources, its chances for the future, and its pride. And the South itself, through the convict-lease system, perpetrated against blacks and poor whites every conceivable outrage against the flesh and spirit that had made slavery hideous.

The troopers who directly engaged the Indians were themselves subject to summary punishments liberally administered. They were tied to wagon wheels for getting drunk, and tied upside down for getting very drunk. Captain Gerald Russell, an Irish immigrant whose colorful language and courage lent themselves to a myth of heroic size, welcomed new recruits with the statement that he was a fair and lenient commander who had never hung a man by his thumbs unless he missed roll call.

The Indian bewildered the white man; but Christians are always bewildered by a people who have no rationale for their savagery and no complex metaphysics for their supernatural. The Indian did not celebrate the vices of greed and ambition as virtues; he lived in a tribal society where such attitudes were destructive. The vice the Indian celebrated as a virtue was brigandage, and nothing could have been more annoying to the devotees of enterprise. The Indian thought of himself as a single member of a single tribe, of which there were many on the Great Plains; the white man made war on him as a people, transforming him and all his tribes into an aborigine who had to be exterminated or Christianized.

Commanding General William Tecumseh Sherman ordered the United States Army to bring war to the entire Indian population, to villages and encampments, aware that in conducting such a strategy women and children would get in the way, but contending, as he had contended in proposing the March to the Sea, that this warfare was humane because it brought a speedy and definitive end to the argument. General Phil Sheridan put it more succinctly: "The only good Indian is a dead Indian."

Though the Civil War had slowed the push westward, it had not halted it. The Union needed soldiers to facilitate settlement of the West, but it was hard to recruit men for plains duty when world-shaking events were transpiring at Vicksburg, Atlanta, and Richmond. So the War Department invented the concept of the "warpath" and found it encouraged enlistments. In the beginning the cavalry found easy pushing, but as the pushing became more determined so did Indian resistance. By 1876, when Sitting Bull wiped out 266 men of George Custer's Seventh Cavalry at Little Big Horn, the push had become stalemated.

The Indian Campaign called for different tactics, and these were devised and implemented by General George Crook. The war had been waged intermittently and only during the summers, but Crook determined to go after the Indians year-round. He dressed troopers in layer upon layer of heavy clothes, doubled rations, and led cavalrymen into canyons and over peaks where horned rams died from exposure and bad falls. He supplied troopers by mule rather than wagon, which increased mobility—Crook was a genius with mules. And he enlisted Indians as scouts. Called "hostiles," they were recruited from already pacified tribes or from tribes at war with other tribes. Crook destroyed Indian villages and habitations, scattered whole tribes, and, in short, made the Indian a refugee.

Nevertheless, the Indian took a toll. The campaigns cost the army two thousand soldiers, as against the lives of six thousand braves. (The number of white settlers and Indian noncombatants who died is unreckoned.) A better horseman, wily, inventive, and brave, the Indian never mastered guerrilla war, but he proved one of the most effective terrorists in history.

The United States Army made war against the Cheyenne, the Sioux, the Apache, the Kiowa, the Comanche, the Ute, the Shoshone, the Nez Perce, the Medoc, the Brule, the Bannock, the Hunkpapa, the Navajo, and the Paiute. The mythopoeic elements of the Indian culture, the legend fostered by the War Department about Custer, and the conditions under which the campaigns were waged on plains of unending natural glory lent these wars a poetry of epic proportions that obscured the military objectives. These were to defeat, round up, and concentrate the Indians on a reservation any place the Indian Bureau determined. When the lands of these reservations yielded unsuspected riches, the army resettled the Indians again, until finally the Indian people were asked to subsist on scrub land even snakes and lizards found uninhabitable.

The army was ordered to suppress the Indians and secure peace. But, as often as the soldiers secured peace, the federal government, the Indian Bureau, and the white settlers fomented war. Timbermen, ranchers, merchants, and mining operators wanted the Indians stirred up so white men could dispossess them of their lands. Easterners demanded justice for the red man, charged the cavalry with wanton butchery, and had no idea of the harsh realities of climate and soil that conspired against Indian reservation farming.

The frontier army was responsible neither for winning the West nor for the virtual extinction of Indian culture. It was, according to Robert Utley, in his definitive history, *Frontier Regulars*, "a conventional military force trying to control by conventional military methods, a people that did not behave like a conventional enemy and, indeed, quite often was not an enemy at all." This state of affairs was further complicated by the fact that Congress never declared conventional war on the Indians.

Over a period of twenty-five years plains duty transformed the army into something other than a purely military force. William

Tecumseh Sherman called the frontier regulars "the sheriffs of the nation." One of his successors, General John M. Schofield, described the 2,500-man cavalry as "a police force, not an army." And in 1910, General William A. Kobbé said that, aside from *maintaining the law*, the experience a large number of officers got at frontier posts between the Civil War and 1890 was militarily worthless. Pershing himself wrote:

> ... the belief was general that we were not likely to have any more war. The strength of the army was so reduced—2,100 officers and 25,000 enlisted men in 1895—that it was no larger than was needed as a national police force available for possible domestic disturbance.

The police role has become ingrained in the U.S. military tradition. In asking the American soldier to make the world safe for democracy, Woodrow Wilson in actuality was asking the army not to seize and consolidate military objectives, but to restore law and order to Europe. Ex-Artillery Captain Harry S Truman dispatched an American force to Korea in a "police action," and Presidents Dwight D. Eisenhower and John F. Kennedy sent military detachments to escort blacks into tax-supported public schools.

Other colonial nations never considered the military apparatus as a police apparatus. They recruited police forces in their colonies, invariably staffed by natives, but commanded by colonials. The policeman demands respect and cooperation because he is an integral member of his community—which the soldier is not. When the soldier undertakes police duties, he is repressive, even when he undertakes duties far from his community.

In December, 1890, Pershing and the Sixth Cavalry made the long train ride from Albuquerque to the Rosebud Indian Agency on the Sioux Reservation in South Dakota. They were dispatched to help suppress the "Ghost Dance Rebellion," the last full-scale uprising of the Great Plains Indians.

The rebellion was the inspiration of an ideologue named Wovoka, who had some years before converted to Christianity.

Wovoka proclaimed a vision: there was a messiah the Indians could summon, by prayer and a ritual dance, who would bring back the buffalo and send the white man away.

What started as an eclectic religious advent, however, gave signs of developing into a national Indian movement when Sitting Bull, the most influential and admired of all the old chiefs, embraced it. Members of the Sioux, Cheyennes, Gros Ventres, Utes, Shakes, Piegans, Bannocks, and Piutes traveled as far as 1,400 miles to dance with the Ghosts.

Alarmed Indian Bureau agents and settlers in Nebraska and South Dakota demanded the presence of the army to protect them from the seven thousand Indians. Reservation police sent to arrest Sitting Bull, which the army hoped would tame the Ghost Dancers, unfortunately shot and killed the old chief. In outrage and indignation, braves charged off their reservation, commandeering herds of cattle, replenishing their horses from ranchers' corrals, and stocking up on ammunition from small trading stores. Three thousand Indians from the Rosebud and Pine Ridge reservations moved into the Badlands, camping out on the high mesas, waiting for the Red Messiah. Indians elsewhere prepared to join them in the vigil.

The army threw a wide cordon around the area, from the South White Fork River, in the east, to Custer, South Dakota, on the Cheyenne River, in the northwest. On the perimeter of this cordon, Major Samuel Whitside of the Seventh Cavalry intercepted Chief Big Foot, who was leading a tribe of the disaffected. Whitside persuaded Big Foot to consent to a military escort, which would accompany him back to the reservation. On the evening of December 28, 1890, four cavalry troops and Big Foot's people made camp by Wounded Knee Creek. During the night, Colonel John Forsythe came upon the encampment with more troops of the Seventh and a battery of cannon from the First Artillery. In the morning the Indians found themselves surrounded by five hundred soldiers who were pointing four Hotchkiss cannons at their camp from low hills to the north.

Forsythe demanded the Indians surrender their Winchesters.

When they refused he sent troopers to strip the lodges and tents. In a fight between a brave and a trooper, someone fired. The Indians leveled their rifles at the soldiers and the soldiers blasted away at the Indians. As women and children sought refuge in the ravines, the cannon shelled them. After thirty minutes the firing broke off. Big Foot was dead, along with 150 of the tribe. Another 50 writhed with wounds. Twenty-five soldiers died and 39 were bleeding. Wounded Knee marked the end of the Indian campaigns, and remains what Thomas Macauley called the most frightful of all spectacles, the strength of civilization without its mercy. It also coincided with the announcement by the Bureau of the Census that there was no longer a picket line of settlements in the West to demarcate the frontier.

Within the cordon, Indians kept trying to break out. The sound of guns at Wounded Knee stampeded four thousand red men. It took General Nelson Miles two months of tightening the circle until the surviving Sioux chief, Kicking Bear, handed over his rifle.

Pershing's troop was part of the cordon. The men shivered in the bitter cold, forded icy rivers, slept tentless in the snow, made forced marches, and rode patrol duty in subzero weather that often incapacitated the horses by freezing their nostrils. They devoured enormous quantities of food. Pershing said, "I couldn't eat in four days what I did then in one." Food was the only insulation, and Pershing put on twenty pounds in the two months of the rebellion.

Guarding a trail that ran along Little Grass Creek, Pershing beat off an attack by Kicking Bear. The troopers killed four of the band and drove the rest back toward the epicenter. When the last of the Indians was corralled, General Miles held a review of the troops at Pine Ridge. In a heavy snow, troopers gave the salute to the strains of "Garryowen." An audience of impassive Indians, heads white with flakes, watched the soldiers pass by. "It occurred to me," wrote Pershing, "that these Indians must have been thankful that they were wise enough to surrender without fighting."

Immediately afterward Pershing was ordered to lead troops of the Sixth Cavalry to Fort Niobrara, fifty miles distant from Pine

Ridge. By noon of the first day, Pershing saw the ominous gathering of storm clouds and heard the branches swish like whips as a rising wind lashed them. He was the sole officer and he stopped the line of march. Going up and down the dismounted column, he instructed each trooper to peg his tent securely. These were conical tents that held sixteen men. He sent a mounted detail to nearby railroad tracks to haul back ties for firewood. He warned the troopers to wrap towels over their mouths and noses because the gale often blew so hard it left a man unable to catch his breath.

Winds shook the tents like a housewife shakes a sheet. Snow piled against the encampment as though heaped by a giant hand. It was impossible to keep fires burning in the Sibley stoves, small conical sheet-iron heaters with stovepipes extending through the top of the tent. With ropes around their waists, troopers crawled to feed and check the horses and mules. For thirty hours the wind howled and tried to ravage the small encampment. Then it blew away, leaving the men to dig out. Snow had climbed to the lowest branches of the trees. The forest groaned with its white weight.

To weather a Badlands storm is half the risk surmounted; the other half is to find shelter in that vast white land before another night. Pershing ordered his troop to saddle and move out into the glistening white plain now barren of landmarks. They started early in the morning. Every gulch and ravine was made level by the snow. Two men on horseback plunged into these and tried to batter their way on rearing mounts as far as they could go. When the horses could take no more, two more troopers relieved the first, pushing the path forward. Once they came upon a frozen soldier, a messenger who had been caught in the storm. He was in a crawling position. It took Pershing's troop until dusk to reach Niobrara, every man safely riding in on his horse.

4

Cornhuskers and
Buffalo Soldiers

After Wounded Knee, Pershing wanted to attend the School of
Application for Infantry and Cavalry at Fort Leavenworth. He
failed to win the appointment. He did succeed, however, in winning an assignment as Commandant of Cadets at the University of
Nebraska, and he reported for duty in Lincoln in September,
1891.

In 1862, Congress had given away public lands for the establishment of colleges and universities by passing the Morrill Land
Grant Act. Among other requirements, the act provided that these
land-grant schools train a student battalion in military science and
tactics, a provision not taken seriously. Not until 1865 did the army
authorize an officer to accept a professorship at a college other
than West Point. By the 1890s fewer than one hundred colleges
offered military instruction. One-third of the officers in the army
were without formal education. Many of them knew only how to
saddle a horse. The year Pershing accepted his appointment the
army requirements for the first time specified that new recruits
had to be able to read and write.

Military instruction languished at the college level in part because the students were unreceptive, in part because the universities concentrated their energies and resources in burgeoning ath-

letic programs, and in part because the army did not keep a record of who was graduated from these courses.* Nor did the army insist on a single standard at these schools. Training and equipment furnished the students varied from one institution to the next, and the excellence or indifference of the program depended upon its particular commandant.† Many professional officers assigned to the schools found the duty a vacation, some even found it a life-long sinecure. They could drill students once a day, if they chose, or once a month, which was more likely.

When Pershing first saw the University of Nebraska, it was a collection of Gothic buildings, each of which looked like a railroad station, all clustered on the prairie. The university was just twenty years old and its quality of instruction was unsophisticated, makeshift, and mediocre. But it had a new chancellor, an American, James H. Canfield, recruited from the Sorbonne, who came to it with revolutionary vision. The university was quickening along with the small prairie city that housed it. And Pershing, whose parents had moved to Lincoln, was quickly persuaded of its charms. Lincoln itself was the last of the gateway cities to what remained of the American West and it had attracted a professional class of adventurous men from the East. Twenty years later, when George MacAdam interviewed them for his biography of Pershing, these men were as proud of Pershing's relationship to the university as they were of William Jennings Bryant's residency in the city.

The course in military science and tactics was in a sorry state when Pershing took it over. The faculty were no friends to the program, the community lacked all comprehension of its importance, and the students railed against demands. These students were not at all malleable schoolboys; they were rough young men who earned their own living, most of them providing for their own education. The program consumed valuable time and demanded a needless expense, for they had to purchase their own uniforms. At

---

*There is the right way to do things, the wrong way, and the army way.
†The universities did not have an efficient Reserve Officers Training Corps until 1920, when Congress passed the National Reserve Act.

the first roll call, the ninety boys in the program fell in wearing white duck trousers, which billowed like sails, second-hand moth-eaten jackets, and shoes of questionable and varied quality. They stood inspection for a thirty-one-year-old commandant who was undeniably handsome, intelligent, knowledgeable, tough, and, in his uniform and shiny boots, resplendent. For his part, Pershing was impressed. He told Chancellor Canfield he could do anything with these boys.

He importuned the War Department to supply the university with sixty-five new Springfield rifles and fifty cavalry sabers, and he succeeded in requisitioning from the quartermaster at Chicago regulation army blues. He had the cadets convert a basement in the armory into a target range, and when he marched them to it for practice they stepped out like soldiers. Having learned to hit a target, the cadets followed him into a cornfield where they fired their rifles at a simulated battery.

"Load. Ready. Aim!" Pershing commanded.

He touched the heel of a prone cadet and whispered, "Fire your piece."

Every cadet promptly sent off a round in response.

One by one he dressed them down. "Did you hear the command to fire? Why did you fire? Do you always do what others do? Do you know what fire discipline is? It is waiting for the command."

A more humorous man might have seen the futility of such exercises. But a more humorous man would not have had his cadets pull an old, useless cannon onto the field and emplace it with the fervidity of troops momentarily expecting attack over the crest of a nearby hill. Playing soldier amuses little boys, and old men have thrown away their canes to join in the glory of a parade. So Pershing won them. They polished their shoes and buttons, tightened their belts, and stood with ramrods down their backs for his inspection. When they approached his desk they never slouched, but saluted smartly and in a military manner stated their business. They wore their uniforms to classes and to the hops. At the beginning of the next semester there were 192 boys in the program. Before Pershing left the university there were four hundred. They called him the "Loot" and they wanted, as one of them later recalled, "to walk like Pershing, talk like Pershing, and act like Pershing."

During his second year, when he was promoted to first lieutenant, Pershing entered a picked company of cadets in the National Competitive Drills at Omaha. He drilled this select company from 7 A.M. until classes commenced and from 4 P.M. until it was too dark to continue. In preliminary competition before the governors of several states, the contingent forgot to stack arms. Pershing told them afterward that a man wasn't worth the powder to blow him up if he does not always, under all circumstances, give the very best that is in him toward doing what he has set out to do. The next day, the cadets fell into their column of fours and determinedly set off for the field past the grim Pershing, rigidly erect, silent, formidable. As the last of the fours passed by, he stepped behind them and in his clear voice said, "Boys—I think you're going to *win*."

They did. The Nebraska drill team won the Maiden Competition, which brought their school $1,500 prize money and so excited Cornhusker spectators that they surged from their seats to the field and carried off the proud cadets. These cadets constituted themselves as the Varsity Rifles, later changing their name to the Pershing Rifles, an organization which spawned hundreds of chapters on other campuses in the coming decades.

The captain of that company, George L. Sheldon, later governor of Nebraska, said of Pershing, "His personality and strength of character dominated us. We loved him devotedly." Another cadet, William Hayward, who was to command the Fifteenth New York Infantry as a colonel in World War I, said, "Pershing was as severe a disciplinarian as a kindly man can be. He was always just. He had no pets. Punishments came no swifter than rewards."

Cadets also noticed that on occasion the "Loot" held drill with a hangover, though he issued commands clearly enough.* Chancel-

*Before he was forty, however, Pershing was noted for his temperance. He was a one-scotch and one-scotch-only man. When he took command of the Punitive

lor Canfield also recognized the symptoms and wisely surmised that Pershing needed more fulfilling occupation. He suggested that Pershing enroll in the new law school. Pershing had read Blackstone and Kent, and consequently was able to finish the three-year course in two. He received his law degree in June, 1893. One of his professors later recalled that Pershing had a clear, analytic mind. Charles E. Magoon, a fellow student and lifetime friend, and himself an eminent legal administrator, held the opinion that, while Pershing would never have made a good jury lawyer, "for grasp of legal principles, for power to discern the relation of one group of facts to another, I believe, had he followed the law, he would have stood in the forerank of the profession."

Charles Gates Dawes, later Calvin Coolidge's Vice President, was already in practice in Lincoln when he and Pershing became good friends. They bought ten-cent pancake dinners at Don Cameron's Restaurant and together borrowed law books from William Jennings Bryan, who served the district in the House of Representatives. When he was graduated, Pershing suggested to Dawes that they set up a partnership. Dawes said, "Better lawyers than you or I can ever hope to be are starving in Nebraska. I'd try the army for a while. Your pay may be small, but it comes regularly."

Another Lincoln lawyer, George D. Meiklejohn, who had served as lieutenant governor and was to serve as Congressman, also advised Pershing to stick with the army. Pershing took the advice to heart, and made application to the Quartermaster Corps, where there was a vacant captaincy. He explained his motives to a West Point classmate: "I am, as you know, considerably older than the average man of my rank and will never be able to serve in the higher grades of my own corps." His application was denied in 1893 and he stayed on at the University of Nebraska for another tour.

Chancellor Canfield offered Pershing the chance to teach two remedial classes in mathematics, which paid $650 a year. These

---

Expedition into Mexico, he told his subordinate officers that whiskey stopped at the border and that order held for all ranks from the privates through the colonels.

courses were offered to entering students to acquaint them with the rudiments of algebra and geometry. These students did not revere Pershing the way his cadets did, but he left a lasting impression on some. One was Alvin Johnson, later the editor of the *New Republic* as well as a founder of the New School for Social Research in New York City and its first director. "All movements, all play of expression [in Pershing]," wrote Johnson in his autobiography, "were rigidly controlled to a military pattern. His pedagogy was military. His questions were short sharp orders, and he expected quick, succinct answers.... Pershing's soul appeared to have been formed on the pattern of 'Present—arms! Right shoulder—arms! Fours right! Forward march!'"

Willa Cather was one of his students and so was Dorothy Canfield, the Chancellor's twelve-year-old daughter, later Dorothy Canfield Fisher, the novelist. Pershing doubted that his courses inspired their bent for literature and Dorothy Canfield confirmed this. But Pershing was for many years afterward a familiar figure to the Canfield family. In 1919, when she had established her popular reputation, Dorothy Canfield Fisher described her wartime meetings with Pershing in Paris, where she was a volunteer Red Cross worker. But even dealing with this episode, her memories of Pershing in Nebraska remained her vivid ones.

"He taught a living subject like geometry as he would have taught a squad of recruits how to drill—that is by telling them what to do and expecting them to do it," wrote Mrs. Fisher. "He never gave us any idea of what geometry was about, and now I have the impression that he didn't know himself there was any more to geometry that what was on page 32 and following." He swung along the college pathways, she wrote, with the cadenced rhythm of a man who marches no matter how hard he may try to walk.

On a ceremonious occasion, the cadets formed on the drill ground and Pershing emerged from the armory, where he usually changed from his pepper-and-salt civilian suit into his uniform. He had forgotten, however, to substitute his forage cap for his brown derby. He walked the length of the drill ground and took the salute from the cadet captain before he was aware of the oversight. Nobody laughed. When he returned the salute, he did an immediate about-face, marched back to the armory with face impassive, reappeared in a moment and, without hurrying his step, returned to his position where the drill ground echoed, "ParADE AT-ten-SHUN."

"I say without the slightest reserve," wrote Chancellor Canfield to the War Department in 1895, "that [Pershing] is the most energetic, industrious, competent and successful officer I have ever known in a position of this kind. . . . He is thorough in everything he undertakes, a gentleman by instinct and breeding, clean, straightforward, and with an unusually bright mind; and particularly just and true in all his dealings. . . . He is a man of broad outlook who desires to know and be more than he is."

After the last drill at Nebraska, a group of cadets approached and asked if they could have an old pair of his pants.

"What in the world for?" asked Pershing.

They intended to slit the trousers down the yellow stripe including some blue on both sides. This strip they would cut into smaller swatches to make a campaign ribbon for the chest of every cadet.

"I will give you the very best pair that I own," said the commandant.

Pershing was infinitely more at home in the university than on the prairie. He was a country boy, notes biographer Donald Smyth, one who "spent his first twenty-two years in a small town in Missouri, his next four in the confining, almost seminary-like routine of West Point, and his next five in isolated army posts on the frontier. His only contact had been with country people and soldiers." At the university he was introduced to not only a civilian society, but an urban society. The Nebraska experience was a crucial and broadening one, one that he hoped other officers would find rewarding, because it would give them "an understanding of the young men who would form the nation's citizenry in peace and her leaders in war."

This was a key phrase for its time. American military men, absorbing the lessons of the Civil War, saw that at the outbreak of hostilities the Union army had not been ready, that it had taken two and a half years to make it ready. In the event of another war, they realized, the present army was even less ready than it had been in 1861.

This worry nourished American militarism, whose first articulate and most influential spokesman was General Emory Upton. Upton was graduated from the Military Academy in 1861, joined his regiment at Bull Run as a second lieutenant, was wounded several times, and emerged at the war's end a brevet major general with a reputation as the Union's most innovative tactician. He was Commandant of Cadets at West Point in 1876 when General William Tecumseh Sherman sent him through the Orient and Europe to see what lessons the American army could learn from other armies.

Upton was inspired by the organization of the Germans, who had beaten Napoleon III six years before at Sedan.* In 1870, Germany had put 400,000 troops into France eight days after the declaration of war. Upton noted that a similar feat had taken a year in the United States in 1861, at a cost of $800 million, by which time the force was unequal to the military task at hand. In his report, published as the *Armies of Asia and Europe,* Upton urged the United States to adopt a modified form of the German cadre army, essentially a skeletonized force whose paper formations were fleshed out by citizen-soldiers in war.

The idea was not new. Such an army had been proposed by John E. Calhoun when he was James Monroe's Secretary of War. Calhoun called it the "expansible army." But it had not worked in practice. In both the Mexican and Civil wars, the volunteers swamped the regular army at great cost to themselves, the Treasury, and the strategy that could have produced a quick, decisive military result.

Upton presented a remedy in *The Military Policy of the United*

---

*German military efficiency inspired many American military men. The army in fact adopted the spiked helmet as officers' headgear.

States, which remained unpublished in his lifetime. Nevertheless, it circulated in mimeograph and carbon copies among regular officers in the late 1880s. Upton noted that a reliance upon the militia system had wreaked devastation on men and resources in the beginning of every war. This devastation was offset only by the nation's wealth, the inherent valor of its soldiers, and the weakness and folly of its enemies. Upton proposed to do away with this prodigality by abandoning the militia system altogether. He wanted to consign military preparations and expansion to the regular army, to have it formulate strategy and implement the means by which that strategy achieved objectives, and to do this without excessive expenditure or delay. This could be accomplished, Upton argued, only by removing the military institutions from coordinate civilian command, by removing the army from congressional purview, and by divorcing it from the command of the President. He insisted there was no alternative. "The student of modern history," he wrote, "cannot fail to discover that the principles of organization, like those of strategy, are of universal application, and that no nation has violated them except at its peril."*

Upton perpetrated a pernicious influence on military men by his insistence that national institutions accommodate military expediency.

Not all military men agreed with Upton. Many pointed out that what worked for Germany was not relevant for the United States. Germany had to depend upon speedy mobilization because her disadvantageous geography left her open for war on two fronts.

---

*It is a mistake to think of Emory Upton as a proto-fascist or revolutionary, for he had no political, economic, or ideological program. He was, however, a solitary brooder. He married in 1868. Two years later his pretty young wife died. Depressed, Upton worked for a decade until a brain tumor made concentration impossible. He resigned his commission in 1881 and shot himself. His unfinished manuscript was put in order by his friend, Colonel Henry A. DuPont, and in 1885, Peter Smith Michie of West Point published a biography of Upton that included a lengthy and admiring critique of his views. Secretary of War Elihu Root came across this in the 1900s and had it printed at government expense, himself providing the introduction. Root was interested solely in Upton's plan for a General Staff.

Others pointed out that Upton failed to do justice to the militia system. Some felt that he had suppressed an essential element to indulge his argument. That element was the militia itself, the able-bodied males between eighteen and forty-five. Upton had not assessed their qualitative worth, which was immeasurable. But officers generally could not make this assessment, because their duties made them remote from the society. It was the rare officer who could gauge the moral readiness of the potential citizen-soldier, to see that he was competent, intelligent, and trustworthy.

"It is not as pleasant as college duty," wrote Pershing of his new assignment, "but I had gotten tired of that." He had just reported to Fort Assiniboine in Montana Territory. The time was October, 1895, and he was now commanding the black troopers of D Troop of the Tenth Cavalry. Whereas the Cornhuskers had called Pershing the "Loot," the troopers called him "Ol' Red." There was an expression among them: "You better git at it, feller, or Ol' Red'll knock you in the river."

On an expedition to Great Falls, Pershing had to ferry the supply wagons across the dangerously swollen Marias River. The men covered the sides and the bottoms of the wagons with canvas, making them into boats. A horseman took a cable made of lariats tied together across to the other bank. The troopers put their shoulders to the wheels to launch the wagons into the river.

Ol' Red kept his eye on a notorious goldbrick who, though he put his shoulder to the wheel, made no real exertions. He was also dry where the others were wet. "I want you to get your feet wet," Pershing ordered. When the trooper made no move to comply, Pershing laid him out in the water with a right cross. "I do not approve such methods in general," he said, "but there are times when an example is necessary."

Black units had been part of the regular army since 1862 when Colonel T. W. Higgenson of Massachusetts took command of the First Regiment of South Carolina Volunteers, composed of escaped slaves. By the end of the Civil War, 180,000 blacks had served in the Army of the Potomac, 33,380 of them falling in battle. On July

28, 1866, Congress authorized six regiments of black troops, four of infantry, two of cavalry, commanded by white officers. The cavalry regiments were numbered the Ninth and the Tenth.

The first commander of the Tenth was Benjamin Grierson, who had been kicked in the face by a horse when he was eight years old. He remained skittish of horses ever afterward, though not so skittish that he could not lead a famous thirteen-day-long diversionary raid through Mississippi while Ulysses S. Grant tightened the noose around Vicksburg. Under Grierson, the Tenth Cavalry had fought on the plains of Kansas, in Indian Territory, in the vast expanse of west Texas, along hundreds of miles of the Rio Grande, in Mexico, in the deserts and mountains of Arizona, in Colorado, and in the rugged grandeur of the Dakotas.

The black regiments had also controlled the Boomer invasions—the encroachment of settlers onto Indian reservations hoping for boom times. Black troopers had built or renovated dozens of posts, strung thousands of miles of wire, escorted stages, trains, cattle herds, and railroad crews whenever ordered. They were called "buffalo soldiers" by the Indians, who said the soldiers wore buffalo coats and, when they took off their hats, had buffalo hair. A buffalo head decorated the Tenth's regimental crest and its motto was "Ready and Forward."

Although Custer refused command of the Ninth Cavalry on the grounds he was too glorious to command blacks, other officers vied for the assignment because they hoped promotion would come quicker. They hoped in vain. The assignment was arduous. Black regiments were never relieved from tough sectors and they endured discrimination in both quantity and quality of supplies, horses, and equipment. Many of these troopers, moreover, were illiterate, which forced more paperwork on the officers. Few possessed the mechanical skills that eased the daily life of a military unit. Black troopers often lacked resourcefulness, initiative, and responsibility. They were much more dependent upon competent leadership than white regiments. Yet, without question, these buffalo soldiers excelled in discipline, morale, patience, good humor in adversity, physical endurance, and sobriety. The rate of reenlistment was high and the incidence of desertion low. And they performed well in the field and bravely in combat.

Officers like Pershing appreciated that, where many enlisted men found a refuge in the army, these black men found in it a promising and rewarding career. At Fort Assiniboine in lonely Montana Territory, where the Tenth was stationed, the temperature once dropped to 60 degrees below zero. The winter winds were knife-edged and the blizzards maelstroms. The only activity the troopers dared was the exercise of the horses, which were swaddled in heavy blankets. Sometimes it was too cold for that.

Fort Assiniboine was thirty miles south of the Canadian border in the midst of the Crow, Blackfoot, and Flathead reservations. The nearest town was Havre, in the center of Montana. The Tenth had no trouble keeping peace with the reservation Indians, but it had spent years tracking a mobile band of Crees that had slipped over the border after staging an uprising against their Canadian keepers. Led by a halfbreed named Louis Riel, these six hundred Crees rustled cattle, stole horses, camped wherever it suited them, and got drunk now and then. It took the State Department several years to negotiate their repatriation.

In 1896, Canada said she would resettle all the Crees the cavalry delivered to Coutts Station on the border. Some Crees went docilely, some hired a lawyer, and a sizable number got away from their Montana village near Great Falls and made for the plains in Idaho and North Dakota. Pershing was ordered to round up these fugitives and diplomatically and bloodlessly shepherd them to Coutts Station, where the Northwest Mounted Police would take over.

It was a difficult pursuit. The Indians traveled fast and often took refuge in the coulees, the steep-walled, trenchlike ditches that scored the plains. Pershing's troop rode 600 miles in 62 days before they flushed 107 Indians from these fugitive encampments. The soldiers traveled over the Rockies by the trail Lewis and Clark had followed, scaled mountains past the timberline, and followed streams that had washed their beds a pure white. On the march back, one Indian died and one was born. But at Coutts Station a Mountie refused to pass the Crees because some of the children had measles. An argument over non-negotiable issues was Pershing's meat. He convinced the Canadian Mounties it was easier to repatriate Crees with measles than it was to tell his troopers they couldn't go home.

He had left a university for the command of regulars who knew only limited advantages and whose ambitions were restricted. But he knew that "fairness, justice and due consideration of their welfare would make the same appeal to them as to any other body of men. Most men of whatever race, creed, or color want to do the proper thing and they respect the man above them whose motive is the same."

These attitudes were no lip service. Pershing left an extensive correspondence—four hundred boxes in the Library of Congress alone—and yet in none of it does he ever remark on whether a man is Irish or Italian or an Easterner or a Westerner. He was able unself-consciously to take men as they came.

Pershing said he got along with black troops because he was brought up among blacks. Missouri, the state that gave its name to the compromise of 1820, was the only slave state whose constitution guaranteed freed slaves their constitutional rights. Nor was it apparently as ideologically bound to the concept of race as other Southern states. Henry Blow of St. Louis, a millionaire lead miner, financed the case of Dred Scott through the courts to advance the cause of abolition. Mark Twain, from Hannibal, was expressively and effectively liberal on the question of race. Harry Truman, from Independence, was the first presidential candidate to insist on a civil rights plank in his party's platform.

If Pershing had a professional "home" in the army, it was with the Tenth. He was to fight with it in Cuba, it would be under his command in the Philippines and accompany him on the Punitive Expedition. When he was in his seventies, on each of his birthdays, the Tenth Cavalry stood his inspection.

Upon his return to Assiniboine, Pershing had his first chance to do some politicking on his own behalf. General Nelson A. Miles, the new Commanding General of the Army, arrived at the post, ostensibly for an official inspection, actually to do some shooting. Miles was accompanied by a panoply of officers, politicians, and civilian free-loaders, among whom was the artist Frederic Remington. Pershing took the party to Bear Paw Mountain, where the pheasant and duck were so thick Miles often brought down two and three with a single shot.

5

Politicians and Cadets

In the fall of 1896, Pershing took a leave to visit his parents, who had moved from Lincoln to Chicago. The nerve center of the restlessly growing Midwest, Chicago was also where Pershing's friend Charles Dawes was directing the Republican Presidential campaign in seven Midwestern states. Pershing visited Dawes at Republican campaign headquarters on LaSalle Street. He also met Mark Hanna, the grocer turned political king-maker, and the candidate himself, William McKinley, supremely dignified in swallow-tailed coat and hollow-eyed gaze. A later historian was to remark that together Hanna and McKinley made one politician.

Like many military men, Pershing had an aversion for political partisanship. Professional army officers knew that, if the army hadn't factionalized in 1860, the Civil War would have been impossible. Professionals were also aware that administrations changed every four years and the sympathy overtly expressed for the politics of one administration inhibited a soldier's employment by a second.

The first election he could remember was that of 1872, when Ulysses S. Grant campaigned as the "Galena Tanner" and his running mate, Henry Wilson, as the "Natick Shoemaker." And he used to recall wryly the stumping of a candidate for Linn County sheriff: "I have no doubt that my opponent would make a good sheriff but my wife thinks I would make a better one." But he remembered best, and thought more about, the election of 1896, not only because its machinations were revealed to him by Dawes (it launched Dawes's political career), but also because (along with Lincoln's election in 1860 and Franklin D. Roosevelt's in 1932) the election of 1896 was a watershed election.

While Pershing was in Chicago, William Jennings Bryan, the Democratic candidate, stumped the city streets. Pershing saw a heckler throw a rotten egg at Bryan's carriage, and later stood on the corner of Michigan Avenue and Randolph Street watching an immense procession of torch-bearing Democrats, all wearing white hats and white shoes to dramatize their demand for Free Silver. Pershing did not catch their enthusiasm, and only commented that the demonstration was "composed of all the riffraff of Chicago." It was a mean-spirited remark, because those men represented his father. For they had failed in the same way John Fletcher Pershing had failed.

Yet it is a remark characteristic of the American military mind, which is universally regarded as politically conservative and invariably Republican. If, indeed, the military mind is Republican and conservative, it is because its makeup was sealed in 1896. Andrew Jackson had been neither conservative nor Republican; General George B. McClellan was the Democratic candidate against Lincoln in 1864; and General Winfield Scott Hancock, who repulsed Pickett at Gettysburg, ran as a Democrat in 1880 on a platform so liberal it inspired devotion in his adherents. Other generals vied for the Democratic nomination after 1880, but never after 1896.

William Jennings Bryan had won the nomination with the support of Populists, small farmers and urban workers, a coalition that was to become infinitely more powerful in the twentieth century. Bryan, campaigning on their behalf as the "Great Commoner" and the "People's Tribune," staked out positions that were polar extremes from those of the Republicans. For the first time since

Appomattox, an issue other than the tariff divided the constituency.

Bryan was campaigning for an eight-hour workday, for the abolition of child labor, for universal suffrage, for the right of working men to organize for their own protection. He was also charging that it was the great merchant who needed a navy, not the farmer, and the capitalist who needed an army, not the poor man—and the merchant and the capitalist ought to pay for them. These were hardly arguments to endear him to the military man, nor would his subsequent anti-imperialist stand win him votes. But for men like Pershing, professionally trained men who felt they had a stake in the economy, Bryan cut even deeper. Bryan was campaigning for Free Silver, for inflation. For every sixteen dollars in circulation backed by gold, Bryan wanted the government to add another dollar backed by silver. Plentiful money would free the farmer from his mortgaged land and the workman from his unending labor.

Among other things, the election of 1896 was a struggle between those who wanted money cheap and those who wanted money dear. Every election centers on how money shall be spent: this election centered on what shall constitute money, a frightening prospect to those who maintain and direct a country's credit, banking, and commercial institutions.* Whatever else a monetary change portends, it threatens class stability. And class stability compels the military mind. A reshuffling of classes always means displacement among the military hierarchy.

It was such a change that Bryan sought to bring about. By capturing the loyalty of the marginal, the disaffected, and the desperate, Bryan created a political party that would, in the coming century, invariably lure the proponents of radical change and innovation. While Democratic administrations have often reintroduced the country to economic and political stability, the fear

---

*As late as 1933, when Franklin D. Roosevelt took the United States off the gold standard, Lewis W. Douglas, Bernard Baruch, and J. P. Morgan collectively moaned that Western civilization had come to an end.

among conservatives is that one day it will go too far on behalf of the marginal and the disaffected, and wipe out all distinction between classes. The lack of distinction is intolerable to the discipline of an army. The conservative Republican Party promises that this will not happen.

There is another reason why the military mind is invariably politically conservative, a subtle psychological reason. The conservative mind, in stereotype, conceives of itself as manly. So does the military mind. Theodore Roosevelt in *The Rough Riders* characterized the gallant soldier as combining "the qualities of entire manliness with entire uprightness, and cleanliness of character." The conservative mind is in love with the words "work," "loyalty," and "independence," while the liberal mind is in love with the words "help," "equity," and "relief." Stereotypes should not govern us, but unfortunately they often do.

Perhaps the comparison between the coevals of John J. Pershing and William Jennings Bryan will highlight this stereotypical concept. No one would have described the thirty-six-year-old Pershing as anything but manly. William Jennings Bryan was called many things from "communist" to "crackpot," but no one ever called him manly, though indeed he was. He had been a superb athlete in college—he set the record in his time for the standing broad jump—and until indulgence got to him in his forties, he was a splendid figure of a man. While McKinley campaigned from his front porch, reading set speeches to hand-picked pilgrims from Bangor to Manketo, Bryan made twenty and thirty speeches a day to small crowds at every crossroads, and finished physically stronger than when he started. He had a moral courage, too, whose dictates he followed even when such obedience reduced him to foolishness, as it did during the Scopes Trial.

From Chicago, Pershing went on to New York City, to call on his friend Avery D. Andrews. Andrews had resigned from the army in 1893, after receiving a law degree from George Washington University. He had prospered immediately as a corporation counsel for a number of New York firms. Because Andrews was a West Pointer, Theodore Roosevelt had appointed him, along with

Fred Grant, Ulysses S. Grant's oldest son, to the New York City Board of Police Commissioners. One of the fortuitous events in John J. Pershing's life was his meeting with Theodore Roosevelt in Avery Andrews's box at Madison Square Garden. After watching a Buffalo Bill Wild West show the three men made an evening of it.

Pershing immediately admired Roosevelt. "Having lived in the West," he wrote, "Roosevelt knew the life well and having written *The Winning of the West*, knew the valuable part the army had played in that achievement. He spoke in high praise of the members of the police who had served in the army on the frontier."

And Roosevelt immediately and forever after admired Pershing. Roosevelt had spent a good part of his youth trying to make himself physically into a John J. Pershing. Though he probably never laid a shirker into the river with a single blow, he had boxed and chased sheep rustlers and could manage Indian dialects, too. Both men had awakened to dawns past wonder on the plains, both were horsemen, and both undoubtedly enjoyed the Buffalo Bill show.

Before concluding his leave, Pershing stopped by the Washington office of Commanding General Nelson E. Miles to pay his respects. This was a customary procedure for regulars. But Pershing had no sooner saluted than Miles informed him he was being detached from the Tenth Cavalry to serve as his aide.

Nelson E. Miles was a singularly handsome man with a bristling silver moustache and silver hair to complement his ribbons and braid. He was called a "newspaper soldier," because he loved the pomp of his office and the panoply of parades. He was also called a "political general" by West Point veterans of the Civil War, meaning he had secured his commission and advancement through influence in Washington. He was certainly foresighted in marrying the daughter of Ohio's Senator John Sherman, the brother of William Tecumseh, and the most powerful Senator of his day.

Actually, the Commanding General—and Miles was the last Commanding General of the Army—commanded nothing. The orders of the President and the Secretary of War were implemented by the various army agencies in Washington. But for General Miles the appearances were there and they satisfied him. As for

Pershing, who had recently written his brother that promotion in the army was hope deferred, Washington was the staging as well as the advance area for politicking and higher rank. Pershing's duties consisted for the most part in escorting Mrs. and Miss Miles on their gadding-about and standing behind the General when the General gadded-about. It was to prove a short tour for John J. Pershing, but during it he was able to advance his own cause importantly.

Charles E. Dawes was also in Washington, having earned a job in the incoming McKinley Administration. Pershing informed him that their mutual friend George Meiklejohn had lost his congressional seat in the election, principally because he had been the first McKinley man in Nebraska. Pershing thought Meiklejohn's distinction merited some preference. Dawes took the matter to the President, who appointed Meiklejohn Assistant Secretary of War. Every ambitious soldier needs a friend in high places. Having such a friend is sometimes due to luck and sometimes due to a soldier's making his own luck.

Pershing prevailed upon Miles for the prestigious assignment of assistant instructor in tactics at West Point. Miles gave it to him in the summer of 1897. A "tac" is the professional officer who instructs a company of cadets in drill regulations, weaponry, and the Articles of War, and supervises them in infantry, cavalry, or artillery basic training. The tac is also in charge of marching the cadets to and from the ranges and training areas. Often he is the faculty member to whom the cadets relate most perfervidly, since they see him and attend his classes continually.

It was Pershing's hope to give the cadets practice in commanding platoons and companies as well as in the conveniences of soldiering, the practices which lead to promptness in the field. In this hope he was disappointed. The Commandant opted for teaching the course as tacs had taught it fourteen years before, when Pershing himself was a cadet. Not that this attempt at innovation would have made much difference, for the cadets of Company A hated John J. Pershing.

Cadets live in a state of virtual perfection, or such perfection as the army devises for them, and Pershing tried to push the men of Company A past it. Company A was high-spirited. Ten of these cadets eventually commanded divisions, three of them armies, and one, Malin Craig, served as Chief of Staff in the 1930s. When the words "Lord, God Almighty" appeared in the text during chapel, they bellowed at the top of their voices. Pershing toned them down with punishment tours. He checked them in the morning to see if they were in proper uniform, which they expected; but he also checked at noon to see if they wore their shirt under their tunic, which they did not expect. It is the rechecking that will finally break the will of the goldbrick or the maverick and drive him to soldiering. But to the soldier-at-the-ready the rechecking is "chicken shit." Pershing's notebook, in which he listed cadet transgressions, is filled with "gloves improperly folded," "towel and washcloth reversed on bar," and "uniforms improperly stored."

As a tac, Pershing would have necessarily incurred cadet displeasure, because it is the tac who puts cadets on report for infractions and metes out punishment. What especially enraged the cadets, however, was that Pershing was on to their tricks because he had been a cadet himself. Whatever Pershing's breadth of vision, it did not encompass the memory that he, too, had once been young. He needled the cadets as only a martinet can. When he bragged about his Tenth Cavalry troopers, making invidious comparisons between their discipline and that of the cadets, trammeling on some well-established notions about the white man's supremacy, the cadets responded by nicknaming him "Nigger Jack," later softened to "Black Jack."

They made him aware of their hate. When he entered the mess hall there was a sudden silence as every cadet stopped talking simultaneously and put down his utensils quietly. The West Point "silence" can be accomplished only with the connivance of the whole corps. It is a morally devastating ploy, and the only tac to have survived it with his authority intact was John J. Pershing. As the officer of the day, he simply marched down the center aisle, in the midst of that thundering silence, called the corps to attention and dismissed them, so they could not finish their meal. It was more an object lesson for the cadets than for him. He was teaching them that in the ever-continuing drama between "life" and "system" both sides have unsuspected resources.

In this instance, however, neither side called it quits. On one of Pershing's unscheduled inspections Cadet Malin Craig whispered, "Do not go into the first sergeant's room." Pershing sent a janitor to the room, and a pail of water balanced on the partly opened door splashed down on him. This was a serious breach of discipline. Cadet Craig said he did not know who the culprit was (although he did), and Pershing placed Company A in barracks arrest. And in barracks arrest they remained, walking all-night guard duty, privileges suspended, forbidden to enter the gymnasium unless they exercised—so that the members of Company A went to the hops twirling Indian clubs. Cadet William Wooten had planned the trick and was willing to take the consequences, but his classmates to a man insisted he remain quiet.

At the cadet show traditionally staged one hundred nights before graduation, Cadet Edwin Markham, vice-president of the Academy Dialectic Society, made a curtain speech to the audience: "Owing to the fact that Mosaic Law still obtains at the Academy which requires an eye for an eye, a tooth for a tooth, and thirty days for a water bucket, I must speak for the President of the Society, who is in Company A." More punishments followed and engendered greater bitterness.

How could the same man who transformed cornhuskers into soldiers by inspiring their love and respect fail so abjectly to win the admiration and obedience of young men who had chosen to become professional soldiers? Perhaps if he had four years with the West Point cadets, instead of only ten months, they would have come to respect him. Pershing invariably won the respect, at least, of his subordinates. Then too, these were high-spirited young men. Pershing was not only older, but had not been fun-loving even as a young man. And part of the answer must be that Pershing did not want the admiration of the cadets, he wanted their obedience.

Another part of the answer is that Pershing had become what the Academy, in its Years of Iron regime, had destined him and the army to become. The army was not spiritless, but it had become a mean place for the spirit to live. Pershing's model, Wesley Merritt, a hero at Gettysburg, was now a major general, sending troops to break the heads of unemployed workmen hitching rides on freight cars to join Coxey's Army in Washington. Merritt was dispatching other troops as strike breakers against the workmen who had walked out of the Pullman Company. Since the end of the Indian campaigns, the army had been used in three hundred labor disputes. Next to the savage employer, said Samuel Gompers, the army had become the worst enemy of the working man. The glory had gone out of soldiering, and the army was policing other Americans as it had once policed Indians. The army and its commanders-in-chief had forgotten that the true purpose of soldiers is to fight the peoples of other nations and not make war against their own.

What saved the army from itself was that, in the spring of 1898, Congress declared war on Spain. To Commanding General Nelson A. Miles and Adjutant General Henry Corbin war meant terror, deprivation, hardship, and sacrifice beyond comprehension. To others, war meant national opportunity. To Pershing and the junior officers it meant promotion and, more important, relief from repressive duty. "I have existed in the service all these years for just this sort of thing," Pershing wrote to Meiklejohn, "and to tell the truth if I should accept any duty which would keep me from field service, I should never forgive myself."

Initially, however, his desire was doomed. The War Department "froze" key officers in their posts, among them the faculty members at West Point. Telling a professional soldier he is frozen behind the lines during the war is as outrageous as telling a minister the new calendar will omit Sundays.

6

The Answering Drum

The root cause of the Spanish-American War had its genesis in 1891, when President Benjamin Harrison signed a reciprocal trade agreement with Spain. The agreement exempted each country from the other's tariff duties. One of Spain's colonies was Cuba, and 95 percent of Cuba's export, $96 million, was cane sugar to the United States. In 1894 Congress nullified the trade agreement, which quickly ruined Cuba's prosperity. High duties made it impossible for Cuban cane sugar to compete with European beet sugar, and loans contracted by planters on the basis of an expanding economy became burdensome. Cubans began to agitate for independence in order to write their own treaties with their great friend and only customer. The cost of supporting the Spanish army and navy in Cuba became prohibitive as agitation turned into insurgence.

Insurgents burned and devastated Spanish establishments, and the Spaniards under General Valeriano Weyler burned and devastated the villages and plantations of the dissidents. Weyler, called "the Butcher" by the American press, was tough on the insurgents and even tougher on the noncombatants. Soon enough, insurgency became revolution, and the island drifted into economic chaos.

Guerrilla war, imprisonment, firing squads, torture, and exile were commonplace.

Europe expected the United States to intervene. German banks held $100 million of the Cuban sugar debt and pressed for payment. The lives and property of Americans and other nationals were threatened. Grover Cleveland, harassed by a Populist bloc that divided his party, didn't want war and had avoided it. McKinley promised an alternate solution to war, though just what he didn't specify. It was said of McKinley that his mind was like a bed, someone had to make it up before he could use it.

McKinley favored the American business and industrial community, which was sure war would disrupt the economy, lessen foreign trade, and endanger our coasts and commerce. Wall Street applauded when, through McKinley's efforts, Queen Maria Christina of Spain promised Cuba partial autonomy in November, 1897. To celebrate peace, Spain dispatched its warship *Vizcaya* to American ports and the United States sent the battleship *Maine* to Havana harbor.

Cuban autonomy did not quiet the hysteria engendered by the nation's press, particularly William Randolph Hearst's *New York Journal* and Joseph Pulitzer's *New York World*. Championing Cuba sold hundreds of thousands of newspapers to sympathetic readers, and in an effort to best each other's circulation, Hearst and Pulitzer sent dozens of correspondents to the island. Their stories played up both the insurgents' valor and Spanish outrages, especially outrages perpetrated against virtue. Neither publisher wanted objective reporting. William Randolph Hearst contributed an immortal phrase to the language when he replied to the artist Frederic Remington, "You furnish the pictures; I'll furnish the war."

Hearst and Pulitzer were not alone in making the Spanish-American War a popular crusade. An aroused public demanded war as a release from the frustrations and anxieties of the 1890s. The frontier had closed; the farmers wanted inflation; trusts denied the spirit of traditional enterprise; civil corruption was rampant; immigrants, crowding into the slums and ghettoes of big cities, lowered wages and changed mores. These conditions fed a restless, aggressive appetite. Americans wanted reassurance that the great deeds of the past could once again take place, that vigor and daring and courage could have a new life. Bret Harte, a fifty-two-year-old expatriate living in England, could still inspire Americans with:

"But when won the coming battle,
  What of profit springs therefrom?
What if conquest, subjugation,
  Even greater ills become?"
    But the drum
    Answered, "Come!
"You must do the sum to prove it," said the Yankee-answering
  drum.

The dynamic element that precipitated the war was furnished by a small, adventurous cabal in Washington and New York led by Under-Secretary of the Navy Theodore Roosevelt. The cabal included intellectuals and administration officials, such as John Hay, Secretary of State; Senators Henry Cabot Lodge and Albert J. Beveridge; editors Whitlaw Reid of the *New York Tribune*, Walter Hines Page of the *Atlantic Monthly*, and Albert Shaw of the *Review of Reviews*. Their military theorist was Navy Captain Alfred Mahan, who pointed out that control of the seas was the *sine qua non* of power and prosperity for nations.

This cabal felt that the United States was emergent in the world. These men understood that gaining independence for Cuba diplomatically would not get the United States a naval base at Guantanamo and another on Puerto Rico. Nor would a diplomatic victory give the United States naval and military bases in the Pacific to facilitate commercial expansion in the Orient.

And then, on February 15, 1898, at 9:40 P.M., the battleship *Maine* blew apart in Havana harbor, taking 266 officers and men to their death. A naval court of inquiry was quickly convened by McKinley to investigate the cause of the explosion. It concluded that the loss of the *Maine* was "not in any respect due to the fault or negligence on the part of the officers or men; that the ship was destroyed by a submarine mine." That the Spaniards deliberately floated the mine to sink the *Maine* is incredible; that the insurgents sank the ship is equally incredible. More likely, the *Maine* anchored over an old mine floated many years before and when it exploded it simultaneously exploded the *Maine*'s powder magazines.

McKinley, "in the name of humanity, in the name of civilization, and in behalf of endangered American interests," asked Congress for the authority to intervene in Cuba. Congress appropriated $50 million for this purpose, though it did not declare war. Through an amendment proposed by William Teller, the Senate recognized the Republic of Cuba, demanded Spain withdraw its forces and relinquish its authority, and disclaimed "any disposition or intention to exercise sovereignty, jurisdiction or control over Cuba except for its pacification."

When Spain neither withdrew its troops nor relinquished its authority, Congress voted that a state of hostilities existed between the United States and Spain. The vote, on April 25, even made this declaration of war retroactive to April 21. "Duty often dictates destiny," said William McKinley as he signed the declaration.

Pershing petitioned Secretary of War Russell A. Alger for a transfer from West Point to a regular regiment. His application was not approved. Upon receipt of this disapproval, the Academy Superintendent published it in the daily orders. Its publication may have been a lesson for other officers, but it was lost on Pershing. He sent off a spate of applications for transfer and petitions for combat service. He asked the War Department for a captaincy in one of the Immune Regiments (made up of recruits from the South, who were presumably immune from yellow fever), applied for a vacancy on the Adjutant General's staff, asked the Pershing Rifles to enlist with him as their captain, and petitioned the Governor of Nebraska to give him the command of the volunteer regiment.

Pershing was determined to exploit the army's narrow political system for a chance at field duty and promotion. He wrote to

Colonel Guy Henry of the Tenth Cavalry, and Henry requested him. Pershing asked his friend George D. Meiklejohn, Assistant Secretary of War, to approve the transfer. Meiklejohn owed Pershing a favor. On a day when Secretary of War Alger was absent from Washington, Meiklejohn paid his debt and transferred Pershing, who joined the Tenth Cavalry as a quartermaster in charge of supplies. It was not a choice assignment, but he comforted himself with the thought that Ulysses S. Grant had been a regimental quartermaster in the Mexican War. A regimental quartermaster furnishes clothing, equipment wagons, mules, horses, and housing for the troops.

On May 5, 1898, the Tenth Cavalry was in the staging area in Chickamauga Park, Georgia. Chickamauga was intended as the main training ground for the new volunteer army. The war had widespread and popular assent; when McKinley asked for volunteers he had 250,000 men before he knew what to do with them.

In the beginning, McKinley and the War Department wanted to enlarge the regular army to 61,000. A large standing army would be under federal rather than state command, and a number of politicians balked at this.

Congress and the state governors told McKinley that he, like Presidents before him, would have to rely on the volunteers and the state militias for his army. Unfortunately, the state militias always lacked support units—ordnance, supply, and medical detachments. Constitutionally, McKinley could impress the militia into federal service only to suppress insurrection, enforce federal law, or repel an invasion. If he called up the militia for an overseas war, he had to take the units on their own terms.

These units were controlled by the state governors and volunteered for service by regiments. McKinley and the War Department had to abide by explicit congressional ruling that the officers of the militia would be appointed by the President only upon recommendation of the governors. This system had proved a near disaster in the Civil War.

What the citizenry did not want was to be commanded and led by West Point martinets and regular army militarists, who, they charged, fought only for pay. The threat that command would issue from any Tom, Dick, or Harry led the Seventh New York Infantry to decline to enlist in the federal forces. Representative Oscar Underwood of Alabama, in an address from the House floor, told McKinley that Americans were proud to fight for their country as long as they were officered by their friends from home, that they would take orders as long as it was a neighbor who gave them. A quarter of a million men zealously went off to war without the expertise of a professional who could teach them how to route a train or cook in the field. In the fighting itself, the lack of trained officers who knew about sanitation, supply, and deployment was crucial. Long before peace, West Point martinets had become as valuable as they were scarce.

Mobilization was an avalanche of eager, improvident patriots. To handle the crush, the army divided the volunteers into seven corps and shunted the majority off to three secondary training areas in Virginia, Alabama, and California. The Expeditionary Army was to train at Chickamauga and sail from Tampa, Florida, the primary embarkation point. Chickamauga Battlefield Park, eleven square miles of wooded terrain, had been established by the Cleveland Administration as a military reservation for regular army and National Guard maneuvers. It had adequate water and good rail connections. Tampa was the southern port nearest Cuba and, on the west coast of Florida, the most protected.

McKinley hoped the army would not have to attack and seize Havana. In May, Admiral William Thomas Sampson of the Atlantic fleet blockaded the Spanish flotilla under Admiral Pascual Cervera in Santiago harbor on Cuba's southern coast. Perhaps the blockade would force Spain to negotiate. But Commanding General Nelson A. Miles pointed out that Spain had between 80,000 and 100,000 soldiers in Cuba. The newspapers may have described these soldiers as ill-disciplined and ill-officered, but after three years of bitter guerrilla experience they had not surrendered to Cuban insurgents, and were not likely to do so now. In addition, even if the Spanish army did surrender, the United States would still need a force to prevent arson, anarchy, and riot. Miles was sure the Spanish would surrender only to a superior force, and the only superior force he could lay hands on was roughly 25,000 officers and men of the regular army.

Originally, the War Department planned to invade Cuba in the fall. Three months was hardly enough time in which to train an army for fighting in the tropics, but it was enough time to issue uniforms, weapons, and equipment. And the three months' delay was enough to spare the army from the Cuban rainy season, when yellow fever, malaria, typhoid, and cholera were prevalent.

To satisfy the nation's enthusiasm for the war, however, General Miles agreed to send a small expeditionary force of regulars to Cuba. McKinley appointed Brigadier General William Shafter to command this force—the Fifth Corps—to make reconnaissance, transport arms and ammunition to the insurgents, and to expect relief in the fall from Miles's Sixth Corps. Shafter was chosen to lead this expedition despite the fact that he was a sick man who weighed almost three hundred pounds and reportedly couldn't walk two miles. But he was near retirement, was a Medal of Honor winner, and had absolutely no political aspirations. Just how many men Shafter was to command varied from day to day. He started with 4,000, which became 10,000, and eventually 50,000. Shafter finally determined the size of his command by the number of available transports.

When Pershing arrived at Chickamauga Park he found chaos. The army was housed in two-sided tents that stretched for acre after acre like an endless plain of isosceles triangles. The canvas for these had been purchased hurriedly. The grommets were already rusted, and hundreds of sidings flapped like sails on a windjammer. The volunteers were clothed in uniforms whose dyes were imperfect and they mustered in variegated colors. Many of the militiamen had no uniforms and no shoes. Measles was racing through the camp and typhoid was already present.

As for the Tenth Cavalry, no one had considered, let alone mastered, detail—the procurement of uniforms, weapons, ammunition, rations, bedding, medical supplies, fodder, saddles, bridles. The horse soldiers were still outfitted in their blue woolens. The mules were untrained and included constant runaways who overturned wagons. The flags and flowers that had bedecked railroad stations as the Tenth sped from Montana to Georgia diminished in number noticeably the farther south the train bore them. One of the barbershops in town posted the sign "Niggers not wanted." When a black trooper was refused a shave with an insulting remark he stepped outside, fired his automatic through the glass, killed the barber, and was hanged. Yet morale was high and rose higher when the Tenth was ordered to march from Chickamauga to Rossville, there to entrain for Florida and embarkation.

At Rossville, however, Quartermaster Pershing found there was but one chute on which to load the three hundred horses. The station platform disappeared, to be reassembled when the horses were entrained. It took the regiment two days to traverse the 675 miles, and Quartermaster Pershing spent much of the time stamping out fires set in the straw by sparks flying from the engine. At Lakeland, Florida, the horses stampeded during the unloading and thirteen of them were never corralled, a loss for which the War Department concluded it would have to hold the quartermaster monetarily responsible.

Stores, supplies, matériel, and troops rapidly transported from northern points jammed Florida. Troop trains waited for clear tracks as far north as Gainesville and Cross City, 100 miles north of Tampa. From Tampa itself, troops and supplies had to move along a single-track railroad to Port Tampa, where there was only one long pier to accommodate the loading of the Fifth Corps. Freight cars arrived without bills of lading, so that Pershing and other quartermasters had to scavenge for equipment from car to car, breaking open crates to see if they contained needed supplies. Projectiles arrived without fuses. Fuses were shipped with the leggings and canvas belts. Harnesses for the artillery caissons were shipped with naval stores.

The War Department failed to provision adequately and dispatch the troops efficiently because it never expected to raise such a large army or ship a corps so quickly. Though the President was commissioning dozens of volunteer generals, he did not commission any for the desperately needed staff work. Shafter was commanding a corps that had no plan and schedule for embarkation and none for resupply. "We had a perfectly good organization going on very smoothly," complained a War Department general, "until we had this God-damned war which busted it."

On May 30, Secretary of War Alger changed Shafter's orders. His was no longer a reconnaissance mission, but an attack force, and he was to board his command on transports. "Proceed under the convoy of the Navy to Santiago," he was told, "and there land the expedition east or west of that point as judgment dictates to capture or destroy the garrison and with the aid of the navy capture or destroy the Spanish fleet. When will you sail?"

Shafter's immediate problem was how to load 25,000 men on transports that could hold barely half that number. The problem was insoluble, and Shafter did not attempt its solution. He ordered the colonels to board their regiments on any available transport within the next three days, trusting to their enterprise.

The loading was completed on June 9, and the Fifth Corps was ready to steam out of Port Tampa with 819 officers, 15,058 enlisted men, 30 civilian clerks, 272 teamsters and packers, 114 six-mule army wagons, 81 escort wagons, and 7 ambulances. The ships held 2,259 horses and mules, and artillery consisting of four 7-inch howitzers, four 5-inch siege guns, one Hotchkiss revolving cannon, one pneumatic dynamite gun, eight 3.6-inch field mortars, and four Gatling machine guns. As the convoy got up steam orders came to stop engines: the navy reported the presence of a Spanish cruiser and torpedo boat escort in the San Nicolas Channel west of Havana. The *Leona*, which carried Pershing, hove to. Twelve hundred men, crowded between decks in three tiers of canvas hammocks under a six-foot ceiling, sweltered in their woolens. There were two men to each bunk, two ventilating shafts for below deck, and twelve sinkholes for the entire regiment, a scene Aeschylean in its tedium.

The navy was wrong about the cruiser and torpedo boat. Finally, on June 14, thirty-two transports, one of them towing a barge and another a water schooner, steamed from Tampa Bay in three long lines that soon spread over fifty miles of ocean. The regimental bands had long since sought refuge from the sun and pretty ladies with parasols no longer fluttered lace hankies at the heroes. Only some sweaty stevedores waved goodbye to the expeditionary force. On the *Leona* the soldiers were massed along the rails with their rifles at the ready, ordered by their brigadier to fire at any Spanish craft they sighted.

Calm weather and smooth seas made it possible for the soldiers to stay on the upper decks in the fresh air. Had they been confined below, surely hundreds would have fallen prey to illness and death. The expeditionary force took eight days to sail from Tampa around the eastern tip of Cuba and along the southern shore to the encircling blockade at Santiago. Admiral Sampson suggested that Shafter storm ashore to seize both Morro Castle, the fort that overlooked the harbor, and its neighboring battery, Socapa. Then Sampson would move into the harbor to engage the Spanish ships.

Shafter studied Morro Castle, which was perched atop a 230-foot cliff. Mounting the precipitous approaches were the lines of the well-garrisoned trenches. Without heavy artillery, Shafter judged, the mission would be suicidal. He decided to disembark his troops farther east, at Daiquiri, even though his transports would have to anchor where heavy winds raised a surf every afternoon. He would move the Fifth Corps against Santiago, attacking from the east and the north.

Shafter knew that his Fifth Corps was not an integrated army capable of quick and decisive movement, but really a collection of small though efficient units. He knew his officers would have to be educated in battle and he wanted the initial battles to be as inexpensive as possible.

On Wednesday, June 22, troops began dropping one by one through the freight portholes into steam launches fifteen feet below. Each man carried his rifle, 100 rounds of ammunition, blanket roll, shelter tent, poncho, and three days' rations. To miss the launch was to drown. Remarkably only two men missed. As soon as the steam launches were loaded, they puffed toward the old pier of the Spanish-American Ore Company which extended fifty yards into the water. The horses and the mules were unloaded by throwing them overboard. Many swam to the open sea and drowned.

There was no opposition. "One thousand determined men," wrote Pershing, "could have made this disembarkation difficult if not impossible. . . . Speaking not of the details of the fighting on land and sea but of the whole war, it would seem that Spain, realizing the ultimate outcome, waged it much as an inferior swordsman who had been challenged by a master of the art; she accepted the engagement and let the adversary shed a certain amount of her blood. In other words she saved her honor."

Pershing did not go ashore with the Tenth Cavalry on the day of the landing. Instead, he and Lieutenant W. C. Rivers, the quartermaster for the First Cavalry, sailed aboard the *Leona* to Aserrados, to the west of Santiago, to bring back the army of Cuban insurgents led by General Calixto García. Pershing found this army more in need of provisioning than of transport. What was supposed to be a force of 3,000 fierce revolutionaries was instead a ragged, hungry lot of 1,500 poorly armed illiterates. All he and Rivers could dig out of the hold was hard bread and some sacks of sugar, which the insurgents ate ravenously. This ragged little army was to spend more of its energies in begging and pilfering from the Americans than in fighting.

Old Confederate General Joe Wheeler's cavalry division, which consisted of the First, the Tenth, and the Rough Riders, landed and pushed west over a narrow road to the now-deserted port of Siboney. Wheeler occupied the town on the morning of the twenty-third. With its calmer waters and wider expanse of beach, Siboney was to become Shafter's main base for the trek through the jungle to Santiago.

Though the infantry divisions under General H. W. Lawton were on the beach the next morning, Shafter himself was not. As the senior major general, Wheeler took it upon himself to move the cavalry inland, along two matted jungle paths, toward a gap in the hills near a little graveyard called Las Guasimas. Beyond this gap was an open plain that would serve as a staging area for the artillery and supply depots. The Spaniards had taken a position at Las Guasimas behind a stone breastwork. They met the two prongs of Wheeler's attack with heavy rifle fire.

Wheeler took heavy casualties and sent for Lawton's help. At the sight of the infantry column, the Spanish directly to Wheeler's front withdrew. The Tenth Cavalry charged to the breastworks and moved on the Spanish flank, which had pinned down the Rough Riders. The Rough Riders were accompanied by correspondent Richard Harding Davis in a pith helmet and white suit. It was Davis who pointed out the Spanish line to Leonard Wood and Teddy Roosevelt, the Rough Riders' leaders. And it was Davis who described the hour-long battle with such florid and heroic detail that McKinley soon made Wood a brigadier general and wanted to give Roosevelt command of the regiment.

Shafter congratulated Wheeler on his initiative, but General Lawton warned him: "This is no political campaign, but a military one; and I have been given command of the advance and propose to keep it if I have to post a guard to keep your troops where they belong."

Though the skirmish was a minor one, Pershing believed the war was won at Las Guasimas:

> The Spanish position was naturally very strong and the ease with which it was taken surprised our command. Without prejudice to later operations, Linares, the general commanding the Santiago district, could have brought to Las Guasimas as reinforcements not only the sailors of Cervera's fleet but other troops from the west of the city. The road to Santiago was the only one available to the Americans and by holding the favorable position at Las Guasimas the Spaniards could have delayed our forces there till disease drove us off.*

Shafter knew he was in a race with time. He had to accomplish

*These remarks by Pershing were reprinted by Hershell Cashin in *Under Fire With the 10th Cavalry*, published immediately after the war. They came from a speech delivered by Pershing in November, 1899, at a patriotic Thanksgiving service at Hyde Park Methodist Episcopal Church in Chicago.

his mission before fever took its toll. Disease had beaten two British invasions of Cuba in 1741 and 1762. Shafter had to flush the Spanish flotilla before General Ramón Blanco, at Havana, could reinforce Santiago with some of the 80,000 troops garrisoned in the north. Lastly, it was hurricane season, and a hurricane would not only cut Shafter off from his supplies, but disperse the blockade. He faced almost insuperable difficulties. Food and ammunition ran short, and mule trains made their way very slowly through the jungles. The men lived on hardtack and salt pork, with little coffee and less sugar. The ravaged island offered no provisions, and it was little comfort that the Spaniards were no better off. There was a shortage of packers, and the mule wagons often overturned on the rutted roads and paths, snarling all traffic to the rear. Shafter could not move up his siege cannon for fear they would bog down and make the road impassable.

Though few were killed in these minor skirmishes, many were wounded, and others were beginning to succumb to the tropical fevers and the heat. Shafter himself was a victim, and had to be transported from place to place on a barn door carried by four men.

In addition, American weaponry still employed black powder. A few rounds of artillery blinded the cannoneers with their own smoke. The smoke quickly marked the position for Spanish riflemen. Only the Rough Riders were armed with the new Krag-Jorgensen rifles; the others used old, black-powder, single-shot Springfields. The blue-clad Spanish infantry was armed with the smokeless Mauser rifle, which was not only more accurate, but had a low, flat trajectory and could raise as much havoc among the rear as the forward ranks. It was coming up against this rifle fire in the open field that convinced Pershing no weapon was as effective and terrifying as a rifle in the hands of an infantry marksman.

The Fifth Corps was out of the jungle by July 1, on the rim of the landward defenses. Pershing and his troops glimpsed a tranquil scene of rolling, quiet hills. Before them was a basin a mile and a half in length from which a white mist rose every morning. Pershing compared his experience at viewing this vista with the wonder of a pilgrim viewing the Holy Land. At the end of the basin loomed

San Juan Hill, ringed with trenches and ditches often two and three lines deep. These trenches ran from Santiago Bay around the entire western perimeter of the city to a stone fort in the north, El Caney, whose presence doomed a flanking movement. Wrote Pershing:

> We had come from out the jungle to the ridge of a hill and could now see the dark lines of the masked intrenchments and the mysterious blockhouses of the heights of San Juan. To the left of the first hill, holding a horse, stood a lone Spanish soldier; further to the west were plainly visible the successive lines of defenses, while behind stood the spires and towers of the seemingly lifeless city of Santiago.

As the dismounted troopers of the Tenth Cavalry Regiment deployed for the charge up the steep hill, their brigadier, S. M. Young, realized that the third squadron was not yet across the Aguadores River. Pershing volunteered to make his way back through the jungle and lead the troopers across the ford. Waist-deep in the water, Pershing saw Major General Joe Wheeler riding downstream with his aides to direct the attack of the cavalry division. Pershing halted and saluted. A shell fragment plowed the water between him and Wheeler, splashing both. Turning back to his mission, Pershing saw a surgeon on the far bank grappling with two wounded troopers to save them from drowning.

Shafter sent one infantry division under Lawton to attack El Caney. Another infantry division, under General J. F. Kent, and the cavalry division were to attack the heights. As the Fifth Corps tried to deploy from the jungle into the clearing, galling fire from the hills kept the men in the forest. They were also obstructed by roll upon roll of barbed wire lashed to trees. The progress of the Tenth Cavalry and the Seventy-first New York was attended by an observation balloon sailing over the tops of trees, pulled by troopers manning guy wires. The observers, Lieutenant Colonel George M. Derby and Major John Maxfield, pointed out paths to the clearing. But the balloon made a prominent target for the Spaniards. They zeroed in below it with rifle and artillery fire.

"You're drawing fire," noticed one of the observers.

"Goddamn it, we know it," yelled Pershing. "Get down. Get down."

So accurate and heavy was the fire that the Seventy-first panicked and the men ran from the road to hide in defilades. The Tenth moved by them, warned by a colonel to pay no attention to this irregular conduct.

To have retreated along the narrow paths jammed for miles with mules and wagons and wounded men was impossible. To stay where they were meant decimation. To survive, the men would have to go forward through the barbed wire and up the hill against equally resolute soldiers.

Pershing began guiding the Second Squadron through the barbed wire thicket, for which he would win the Silver Star. Out of the jungle they came, the Tenth and First Cavalry heading for San Juan Hill, the Rough Riders for Kettle Hill, slightly to the west and lower. The Americans had to march across six hundred yards of open field before they could begin their scrambling ascent. Men pitched forward and disappeared into the tall grass, but those behind kept up their steady, heavy-footed advance, rifles across their breasts. A long line of blue and khaki began to shave the hill.

Over one thousand men died in the charge. The Tenth lost 20 percent of its men and 50 percent of its officers. But by dusk they had the hill. "It was glorious," wrote Pershing. "For the moment every thought was forgotten but victory. We officers of the 10th Cavalry could have taken our black heroes in our arms."

But it was a depleted force, one which had taken too many casualties to go forward. There were no reserves to take their place. Worse, there was a diminishing store of supplies. That night Lawton brought his equally depleted force over from El Caney to strengthen weaker parts of the line. Picks and shovels came up and some men began entrenching while others guarded the digging parties. Behind them, they could hear the groans of the wounded who lay undiscovered in the grass. Under the flickering lights of field lanterns, surgeons worked at top speed. At dawn, the men could see the barbed wire, the entrenchments, and the heavy gun positions that guarded Santiago. Only another frontal assault could take it and force the Spanish flotilla to sea. Shafter didn't have the muscle for this last push, although he was sure his men had the nerve.

The Fifth Corps was in a precarious position, a fact made plain by Teddy Roosevelt's letter to Senator Lodge:

> Tell the President for Heaven's sake to send us every regiment and above all every battery possible. We have won so far at a heavy cost. . . . We are within measurable distance of a terrible military disaster: we must have help—thousands of men, batteries, and food and ammunition.

If Shafter had written as much, General Miles would have replaced him on the instant. But not only was Roosevelt commended for his prescience, many thought he was taking charge. Roosevelt was consumed by a desire to end the war quickly. He was aware that, though the constituency had opted for this war, they had by no means opted for a long one.

Shafter asked the navy to force an entrance to the harbor to avoid further losses to the Fifth Corps which were impermissibly heavy. (Aside from the casualties, yellow fever, malaria, and typhoid were eventually to hospitalize 75 percent of the corps.) Sampson replied that capital ships were too expensive to risk in a fight, that he would not dare attempt clearing the harbor of mines until the army had captured Morro Castle and Socapa. The refusal left Shafter with one acceptable option: he sent word that he was ready to accept the surrender of the Santiago defenders. If they did not surrender, Shafter threatened to reduce Santiago to rubble with artillery.

Shafter had no more chance of reducing Santiago with his cannon than he had of reducing it with the bare hands of his troops. But the Spanish didn't know that, and committed themselves to negotiation. In so doing, they gave the Americans breathing space. The more the Spaniards thought things over, the more menacing the Americans on the hill became. Then, on July 3, the Spanish government in Madrid ordered Admiral Cervera to move his fleet from Santiago. Admiral Cervera pointed out that some of his ships dated from 1784 and were no match for the American fleet. The Spanish government refused to modify its orders.

Cervera led six ships out of Santiago Bay. His flagship, the *Maria Theresa*, headed for the battleship *Brooklyn* in order to let the others escape. By dusk all of the Spanish ships were burning hulks. The sortie had ended in complete disaster.* In Washington, it was a Fourth of July to rival that of thirty-five years before, when the news of Vicksburg and Gettysburg reached the capital.

With the destruction of the Spanish fleet there was no reason for the continued investment of Santiago by the Fifth Corps. But the siege continued because the idea of packing up and simply leaving the Cubans to settle their differences with the Spanish military did not commend itself to any American military commander.

General José Toral reinforced Santiago with three thousand troops under Colonel Frederico Escario. Peace talks were broken off. The navy cursorily shelled Santiago. Some of the populace fled, an exodus of the old, the very young, the forlorn, and the helpless. Pershing saw them passing through the lines: a boy pushing a weak old woman in a wheelbarrow, women in white dresses made muddy from crossing swamps, hungry children trailing at their mothers' skirts.

In the morning Shafter halted the bombardment and offered to

---

*Unfortunately, the battle of Santiago provoked one of the most acrimonious scandals ever to afflict the navy. On the morning of July 3, Admiral Sampson had sailed off to the east, aboard his flagship *New York*, to confer with Shafter. The admiral was in the process of buckling on his spurs for the horseback ride up-country when, nine miles behind him, he saw the *Maria Theresa* steaming out. By the time Sampson caught up, Commodore Winfield Scott Schley had effectively concluded the action. To determine who was responsible for the victory, the navy convened a board of inquiry. It discovered that the Americans had drawn abreast of the flotilla only because the bottoms of the Spanish ships were so fouled that their flight was impeded. Shelling had had zero effectiveness. The Spanish lost the flotilla because Cervera's ships had wooden decks which had caught fire. In fact, the American fleet had fired 9,433 shells, of which only 122 had hit. On top of everything, the War Department published the telegrams and messages that passed between Shafter and Sampson, which clearly indicated that the navy had consistently refused to lend the army critical support.

exchange wounded prisoners. Toral accepted. As this truce began to expire, Toral offered Shafter all of Santiago on the condition that Spanish troops and matériel could safely evacuate the city. While Theodore Roosevelt complained of the general's "incompetency and timidity," Shafter played his trump. He offered to ship the Santiago garrison back to Spain free of charge. Toral asked for time to get in touch with his government.

On July 15, Toral said his government would authorize the surrender if his entire command could be repatriated. When Shafter asked how many men that included, Toral replied it included every soldier in Santiago and another twelve thousand in the bush. The thunderstruck Shafter, who had no way of attacking the twelve thousand, leaped at the offer. At noon on July 17, after surrender ceremonies in the field, the cavalry raised the colors atop Santiago Palace while bands played "Hail Columbia." General Miles, who had arrived with reinforcements to relieve Shafter, quickly transferred his command to Puerto Rico and easily took San Juan a few weeks later.

The strain of battle, the tropic heat, and torrential rains did to the Fifth Corps what the Spaniards could not. The presence of yellow fever not only felled soldiers, but began to inspire fear, and fear became as epidemic as any fever. Pershing shivered with the rest. But he had enough strength to expropriate a mule wagon, drive it to Siboney, load it with provisions, and drive back. Commissary Colonel John Weston asked no questions about requisitions, but told each quartermaster to take the most of what he needed. On the way back, Pershing passed Colonel Roosevelt on a road that was a streak of mud. Roosevelt's wagon was mired and the Rough Rider was swearing a blue streak at the mules, who had heard blue streaks before. Pershing hitched his mules to Roosevelt's and extricated him.

Shafter notified Washington that he would have to move the Fifth Corps at once. Secretary Alger suggested taking the army to the hills beyond Santiago. Shafter replied there was no rolling stock for the hospitals, and the men were incapable of marching. He was losing men at such a rate—fifteen a day—that he forbade burial parties to fire the salute lest so many salutes further de-moralize his sick corps. Alger instructed Shafter to move his men at once with whatever ships were available, to Montauk Point, Long Island, where a quarantine camp had been established. Montauk was chosen as the Fifth Corps's debarkation point prin-cipally because it was remote and isolated. The role of the mosquito in carrying and spreading yellow fever was as yet un-known. Some navy commanders, in fact, flatly disobeyed orders and steamed home, rather than board army personnel.

Alger dispatched any ship he could hire, and the soldiers began streaming into Montauk in August, where they found the camp only half completed and ill prepared to receive them. The sick troopers had to pitch in to construct tents and barracks, dig slit trenches for latrines, and move the litters of the fully incapacitated into unequipped hospitals. On August 14, three months after leav-ing Chickamauga Park, the Tenth Cavalry arrived back in the United States.

Wrote Pershing:

> Mr. McKinley visited Montauk Point at this time and those who had political aspirations McKinley interested. I recall hearing Theodore Roosevelt remark that he expected to test the "old man's" attitude toward his candidacy for governor of New York. Without disparage-ment of Mr. Roosevelt's brief few weeks of military experience, it must be said that it was the extensive publicity it received rather than the actual service that brought him such exceptional political preferment.

Theodore Roosevelt was a peculiar hero to have emerged from a war. Other American wars produced heroes who were invariably soldiers and who became, after victory, their own or their party's political creation. But when he joined the Rough Riders, Teddy Roosevelt was already his own political creation, hungry for per-sonal acclaim and yet possessed of a singular political vision for the United States.

Pershing himself had no more combat experience than Roosevelt and he, too, gained certain preferences from the war. He was promoted to major of volunteers, which meant that in the event of another war he would command a volunteer battalion; and he was made a brevet captain, which meant that among the regulars he had the rank but not the pay.

It distressed Americans to think of wounded boys lying untended and without help in the Cuban jungles; it dismayed them to think of a whole corps so afflicted by fever on San Juan Hill as to be near utter collapse; but it outraged Americans to see the grisly spectacle of boys dying by the hundreds in army camps in neighboring states. These soldiers, who also lacked shoes, uniforms, bedding, weapons, and medical supplies, revealed to the public a complete breakdown of the army organization. The newspapers made of this breakdown a national scandal.

What had occasioned the breakdown was that neither the army nor the War Department nor the Congress had ever formulated a policy for the nation's military organization. It had been nobody's business to find out if there were adequate terminal facilities for handling supply trains at Tampa; it had been nobody's business to find out if the Ordnance Department had supplied the artillery with effective cannon and shells; it had been nobody's business to insure that there was a plentiful stockpile of medical supplies; it had been nobody's business to locate posts and military reservations advantageously so that the army could act as a cohesive whole in wartime.

Instead of commanding military units, such as a division or a corps or an army, generals presided over geographic departments, each of which was made up of small garrisons and smaller arsenals. The army was fragmented, and lacked communication between the parts. This fragmented army was administered by ten bureaus, all located in Washington, D.C., operating under chiefs who, once appointed, held their posts until retirement. They had established their own autonomy, and were not responsible to the Commanding General; nor did they seek counsel from officers in the line or work in concert. The offices of the Commanding General, the Adjutant General, the Inspector General, the Judge Advocate General, the

Quartermaster, the Corps of Engineers, the Medical Department, and the Subsistence, the Pay, and the Signal departments each tried to encroach upon the duties and authority of the others. By 1898 they had become politically secure, self-sustained spheres, and had robbed the generals in the field of responsibility and authority. Every decision on the line had first to go through Washington. And now the war had overwhelmed them.

There were bureaucrats enough, in and out of the army, to blame for the mess, but the public chose Secretary of War Russell A. Alger. A sixty-two-year-old self-made lumber millionaire who had commanded the Fifth Michigan Regiment in the brigade led by General George Custer, Alger had left the army a brevet major general. He built an impressive mansion in Detroit, bought a private railroad car, became national commander of the GAR, was elected governor, and, in 1896, delivered Michigan's delegates at the convention to William McKinley. Alger was popular with the older veterans, was humane and practical, but also vain, optimistic, untrained in managing a large military organization, and loyal.

Loyalty did him in. The weak and vacillating McKinley, determined to prosecute the war himself, had imposed his will upon the army through Alger. But, when the tactical and administrative inefficiency of McKinley's prosecution became apparent, he failed to acknowledge his responsibility and let Alger shoulder the blame for the total mismanagement. Under pressure, Alger asked for a presidential commission to investigate the army's administration of the war. McKinley appointed Grenville M. Dodge of Iowa, a Civil War veteran and a staunch Republican, to head this commission, along with eight other members all adept in the arts of the whitewash.

The Dodge Commission held hearings from September, 1898, into January, 1899. The members heard hundreds of witnesses, collected reams of records, checked over tons of correspondence, and toured army camps and navy yards. The commission reported that, though there had been mismanagement and inefficiency, it was due to the public's failure to maintain a well-equipped peacetime military force. The report helped quell the public furor.

Meanwhile, the shooting war in Cuba had ended, and the army had pulled itself together, mostly on the initiative of officers in the field.

The last witness the Dodge Commission heard was Commanding General Nelson E. Miles. For reasons unfathomable to himself, Miles had not emerged as the hero of the war. When he took the oath before the Dodge Commission he became a bomb with a short fuse. He charged that Secretary of War Alger and Adjutant General Henry C. Corbin had conspired to prevent him from winning the war quickly and cheaply. He charged the War Department with widespread malfeasance, citing as a specific example the venality that had led the Commissary Department, under General Charles P. Eagen, to supply the army with beef to which poisonous embalming fluids had been added as a preservative.*

Miles's charges were true in none of their particulars. The Commissary Department had supplied stateside troops with refrigerated beef, which met with unanimous gustatory approval, and the troops in Cuba and Puerto Rico with canned roast beef, which was bland, stringy, tasteless, disagreeable in appearance, and quick to spoil. The department had intended this canned beef to serve as a base for stew. It sent four million rations of vegetables to Cuba but none found their way to the field. Food sent to the expeditionary force was packed first and unloaded last. By the time it came from the steaming holds it was rotting. For weeks on end the soldiers in Cuba ate only beef directly from the can. It nauseated them. They found scraps, gristle, pieces of rope, and even maggots in their tins; and no doubt meat packers, in their greed, foisted off all they could on the Commissary Department.

---

*Alger and Corbin kept their heads while scorn heaped upon them as a result of this allegation. Eagen lost his. He challenged Miles to a duel. He had worked himself to exhaustion during the war and was one of the few competent professionals who had gotten something done. He charged before the Dodge Commission in white-hot anger "to force the lie back into Miles's throat covered with the contents of a camp latrine." He said Miles was a liar "with as black a heart as the man who blew up the *Maine*." Promptly the army court-martialed him for insubordination and sentenced him to dismissal from the service. McKinley commuted this to suspension from rank and duty for six years with full pay.

Unscrupulous packers had also foisted off bad beef on the army in the Civil War, but no one in the army or the War Department had lent himself to such practices knowingly. The public understandably confused the beef Miles was talking about, the refrigerated beef, with this tinned beef. Though a subsequent congressional investigating committee found Miles could not substantiate his charges, the ordinary citizen found the Spanish-American War permeated with the odor of embalmed beef.

Now Secretary of War Alger became expendable. When he began to campaign for the Michigan Senate seat held by a McKinley supporter, the President asked for his resignation.* To take his place, McKinley asked Elihu Root to join the cabinet.

Root was a New Yorker, a big-city corporation lawyer, and a close friend of Theodore Roosevelt, with whom he saw eye to eye on the future of America. Where McKinley was pious and rhetorical, and Roosevelt passionate and impulsive, Root was patient and steady. He refused the appointment at first, arguing that he knew nothing about military affairs. McKinley said the administration needed a corporation lawyer in the War Department to formulate the legal grounds for governing America's newly acquired colonial possessions. What distinguished Root's tenure as Secretary of War, however, was his quick apprehension that, if the United States was to govern colonial possessions effectively, the War Department had to transform the army into a responsive fighting force.

Almost immediately Root set out to reorganize the army, which in itself was nothing new. Pershing once stated that every young lieutenant carried an army reorganization plan in his blouse pocket. These plans, depending upon the lieutenant, would cost Congress between $4 million and $40 million a year. They always provided for the lieutenant's captaincy.

Root's reforms took four years and were accomplished by con-

---

*Alger lost this round, but he did win the seat in 1902 and served in the Senate until his death in 1907. He also wrote a book about his tenure in the War Department which should be required reading for any modern Secretary of Defense.

gressional passage of a variety of bills. His principal measures were to increase the size of the army; to abolish the permanent administrative departments; to establish a system of military education, with the Army War College at the apex; to create a General Staff; and to bring the militia system of the country under the same organization, discipline, armament, supply, accounting methods, and instructions as the regular army.

Root told Congress, in his first report, that the real object of having an army is to provide for war; and that the regular army of the United States will probably never be the whole machine with which any war would be fought. To prepare for war, the army had to prepare, in peacetime, systematic plans for action in all possible contingencies. It had to make provision for the modern matériel of war, and the men who made these decisions had to have the authority to implement their decisions. The army had to introduce a practicable merit system for promotion and abolish the flat rule of promotion through regimental seniority. Last, the army had to conduct field maneuvers with large bodies of troops.

Reorganization was hampered by the friction generated by dual control of the army. Constitutionally, the army was under the command of the President, a civilian commander-in-chief, and under the direct orders of his civilian appointee, the Secretary of War, who controlled all fiscal matters pertaining to the army. The Secretary had as an aide, but rarely as a colleague, the Commanding General. This constitutional provision was ingrained in the American democratic process, a clear insistence by the people that the civilian arm of government control and direct the military. The way to unite military with civilian authority was for the Congress to abolish the post of Commanding General and create instead the post of Chief of Staff. It would be the duty of the Chief of Staff to advise, inform, and assist his superior officers, the President and the Secretary, and to represent them in carrying out administration policies and securing the execution of their commands. Root also insisted that the Chief of Staff succeed to his post by virtue of his compatability with the President, rather than his seniority in command. The Chief of Staff would exercise direct command over the General Staff, which was neither an executive nor administrative body, but a planning group with authority to implement its plans.

The General Staff was to gather in advance the essential supplies and equipment for war; establish and protect depots; draw up the orders and the routes for assembling and moving the army; prepare combat orders; direct reconnaissance; coordinate movement and tactical dispositions of the troops; and establish and organize lines of communications and operations. It was also to maintain archives in which to store historical, statistical, economic, topographical, geographic, and strategic information. The General Staff was to work in close harmony with the Army War College, a school for line and field grade officers that concentrated on the study of war. Along with teaching such subjects as military history, emerging tactics and weapons, the War College undertook to specify the organization and equipment necessary for American armies of 25,000, 50,000, 150,000, and 250,000 men. It developed plans for improving the army's reserve; and it established uniform specifications for matériel in terms of cost and availability. It also provided the curricula for the line schools of infantry, cavalry, artillery, ordnance, and transportation.

Root's reorganization brought the line and the staff together. Under the old detail system, officers were taken from the line and posted to permanent staff jobs in Washington. Staff men had become insulated in Washington offices, often ignorant of and indifferent to the needs of the line. Root's reforms established the short detail system, whereby officers came from the line to the staff for a limited term and then returned to the line troops.* Root did away with the rule that promoted an officer upon transfer to the staff. This helped eliminate the desire and political pressure for such appointments.

---

*Some years later the army found the short detail system not universally compatible with its interests. It made little sense to train a supply or transportation expert and then ship him back to the line, where his expertise was lost. The army altered Root's ideas as it grew to realize the crucial role of the technological expert in making war.

He tried also to resolve the duality of the federal-state control of the militia. In this he was less successful, but at least he broadened the powers of the President to defend the country in war. Congress passed a law empowering the President to call up the organized militia, now legally constituted as the National Guard, for any war duty, as long as the President specified its length of service and as long as the President respected and honored the individual guardsman's term of enlistment.

Root was able to enlarge the regular army, a task made easier than expected because of the exigencies of the Philippine insurrection. He made provision for officering this growing army with men other than West Point graduates. One of these was a recent VMI graduate, George C. Marshall, and another a lieutenant from the ranks, James G. Harbord, later Pershing's Chief of Staff with the AEF. The idea of a Chief of Staff and a General Staff was not original with Root. He depended in part on the writings of Spenser Wilkinson, a British military scholar, and in part upon Emory Upton's *The Armies of Asia and Europe* and *The Military Policy of the United States*.

Root's success in reorganizing the army, where so many before had failed, was due to his clear perception of the changing role of the United States as a world power. Much of his success was due to common sense and his general humanity. He wanted soldiers to be able to buy beer at the post canteens, a fight he lost only because of growing prohibitionist sentiment in the country, and particularly among the generals. When the Governor of Colorado implored Root for several battalions to police a copper strike, Root answered:

> The true purpose of an army is to fight with the peoples of other nations, and the less our own people are subjected to military control and coercion, the better. If our citizens are unwilling to behave themselves in any direction it is much better that they should be compelled to do so by civil police officers than by soldiers.

He had a ready wit and humor—which he needed. When President Roosevelt, in annoyance, once barked, "Oh, go to the devil,

Root," the Secretary answered, "I come, sire, I come." When subordinates criticized the irascible Senator Redfield Proctor of Vermont, a staunch War Department supporter, Root replied, "The only trouble with Proctor is that he wants everything built of Vermont marble." To Congressmen who complained that too many regular officers were bull-headed know-it-alls, Root said politicians had to respect fundamental fictions: officers are supposed to know it all.

His signal contribution to the American democratic process remains the creation of the Chief of Staff and the General Staff. Malin Craig, himself a Chief of Staff, said the General Staff owed its existence and efficiency to three men: to Elihu Root, without whose perseverance and great influence the important reform would have been long delayed; to General William Carter, Root's adjutant, whose exhaustive research and painstaking logic produced the actual bills for congressional approval; and to John J. Pershing, whose sound judgment and unsuspected genius for organization made the General Staff organization in France the principal means by which the war was won in 1918.

PROCONSUL

It was fascinating work. It was the work of applying to some ten millions of people of Cuba and Puerto Rico and the Philippines the principles of American liberty. . . . Those principles were alien to their thoughts and conceptions, to their habits of life, to their ideas of the relations between men and between men and their governments. In the first instance they had to be applied at the hand of military officers who had their own code and methods of procedure.

Elihu Root
Military and Colonial Policy of the United States:
Addresses and Reports

7

Pershing in the Sunshine

When the Tenth Cavalry reached Montauk Point, Pershing, wracked with malarial chills, was furloughed for several months to regain his health. For the next decade he suffered chills intermittently, and in time he would be invalided, but not for years. Doctors knew as early as the mid-eighteenth century that malaria could be cured with quinine, an extract from the bark of the cinchona tree. Administered steadily, it will eventually overcome malaria, which is not usually lethal. Pershing suffered from quartan malaria, which produced a paroxysm every fourth day. A strong-willed, stubborn man, he stopped taking quinine when his malaria symptoms lessened perceptibly. He was cured only when he was ordered to a hospital where a doctor supervised the daily administration of quinine for several months.

Pershing reported for duty in Washington in December, 1898. At the War Department George Meiklejohn assigned him as the chief of the newly created Division of Customs and Insular Affairs. The War Department was charged with the administration and government of Cuba, Puerto Rico, and the soon-to-be-annexed possessions in the Pacific.

The military occupation of these places occasioned problems and introduced questions the War Department had never considered.

91

The only precedents were rulings handed down fifty years before, during the military occupation of California and Mexico. The War Department was by no means equipped to meet such an emergency, and it went about preparing for it by creating *ad hoc* bureaus. These bureaus were eventually incorporated into the Divison of Customs and Insular Affairs. Pershing was chosen as its chief administrator because he was a lawyer.

He quickly found he was settling many questions temporarily and relying often on the Attorney General's office which, in turn, was awaiting determination of its decisions by the United States Supreme Court. Pershing recommended that the division obtain special legal counsel, and he and Meiklejohn agreed on the selection of Charles Magoon, whose subsequent career in government flourished. With Magoon installed, however, Pershing wanted relief from desk work. He wanted duty in the Philippines, where 100,000 American soldiers were trying to put down an insurrection, an action which had become a full-scale war.

One of his West Point classmates wrote, "Don't come out here—you will be sick if you do. All Cuban malarial cases do poorly here." Pershing said, "All my life I've been in command of troops and now when there is a chance to get in a real campaign, I am put behind a desk." He finally had his way. In August, 1899, Elihu Root detailed Pershing to the Philippines. He went by way of London, Paris, and Cairo.

Europe, as it had for countless other Americans, awakened Pershing's realization of culture's possibilities. With some amazement, he wrote that he spent more time in the art galleries during these six weeks than he spent anywhere else. The quietude of London amid the Boer War surprised him. He visited Hampton Court, "the sumptuous estate," he wrote, "that Cardinal Woolsey created for himself while serving Henry VIII more loyally than he served his God." At the Mansion House he watched the Lord Mayor ride forth in a fairy-tale gold coach (in which he himself was to ride one day). He saw the docks of Liverpool, then equipped with every modern facility, and little dreamed that one day he would want to know to the ounce the tonnage these docks could accommodate.

He was not particularly impressed with Napoleon's tomb in Paris but he was impressed with his ability to pick up French. At West Point he had often skipped mess to assimilate the intricacies of the pluperfect. After leaving Messina for Cairo, his ship ran into a Mediterranean storm and Pershing was as seasick as the Italian sailors. Like Mark Twain, he climbed the Great Pyramid in Egypt and ran down holding tightly to two dragomen on either side. He noticed the great wealth and the wretched poverty, the underfed donkeys and the stately camels. He reached Manila on December 1, 1899, reported to Major Elwell Otis for assignment, and was detailed to the Island Department of Mindanao–Jolo.

In December, 1897, Theodore Roosevelt wanted a man in command of the Asiatic squadron "who could act without referring things back home." Commodore George Dewey, an intellectual and a vigorous innovator, cordially hated by his superiors, took command of the Pacific fleet at Hong Kong, the most advantageously positioned port from which to sail to the attack. On his own responsibility, Roosevelt ordered Dewey to keep his ships full of coal and, in the event of war, to move to offensive operations against the Spanish fleet in the Philippines.

After midnight on May 1, 1898, Dewey sailed quietly into Manila Harbor and at dawn engaged the Spaniards. The assumption was that the Spanish fleet might cross the Pacific and bombard our west coast cities, a questionable assumption for old, decrepit Spanish ships of the line. Dewey destroyed the Spanish fleet with the loss of only one man, which many Americans saw as proof positive that in this war God had obviously taken sides.

In Hong Kong, Dewey had made an alliance with Emilio Aguinaldo, the leader of the Philippine revolutionary junta. The native islanders had been in revolt and insurrection for a decade. After the battle the U.S. dispatch boat McColloch landed Aguinaldo on Luzon, where he seized the arsenal at Cavite, while Dewey blockaded the Spanish garrison from the sea.

In June, five German cruisers arrived at Manila escorting a troopship. The German fleet was joined by three British men-of-war. French and Japanese destroyers soon sailed in. It was obvious that one of these nations would move on Luzon as soon as Dewey departed. Dewey asked McKinley for five thousand troops to occupy Manila. McKinley sent eleven thousand, under General Wesley Merritt, whose orders were to move into the city and avoid any joint occupation with the insurrectionists.

As American troops prepared to disembark on August 13, the German fleet threatened Dewey. But British Admiral Chichester brought his line between the German and American ships, and the landing force proceeded without incident. Aguinaldo watched in dismay. The Filipinos saw the handwriting on the wall. The United States had freed them from the Spaniards, but now they would have to fight to be freed from the United States.

When McKinley learned of Dewey's victory he had to spin the globe to find the Philippines. But in the ensuing weeks McKinley was to learn a great deal about the Philippine Archipelago, which had been a Spanish fief since 1542. Its strategic value was made plain to him when Japan suggested that it and the United States establish a co-protectorate there; when the British offered to buy the islands forthwith; and when the Germans had tried to force their way in.

The Philippines and Hawaii (which had been annexed at the outbreak of the war) represented a dream the American navy had indulged since 1812—bases in the far Pacific. What made the Philippines central to American navy men was that Russia, England, France, Germany, and Japan had begun to partition China. Each of these nations had seized or leased a port on the mainland in preparation for an immense colonizing effort. In dividing up China, these powers had no intention of leaving a piece for the United States, an omission the navy had been trying to impress on an indifferent Congress for ten years.

When the Spanish queen asked for an armistice, Spain agreed to relinquish all claims to Cuba and to cede Puerto Rico to the United States, along with the island of Guam in the West Pacific. The status of the Philippines was left to the peace conference. The American Constitution, however, provided no machinery for the annexation and governing of dependencies. Acquiring the Philippines marked a turning point in our history. By acquisition, the United States extended itself into extrahemispheric colonies, controlling by force millions of Asians. It meant assuming vast liabilities where American interests, though profitable, were not vital.

"We must keep all we get," wrote Lieutenant Colonel Roosevelt to Senator Lodge, "and when the war is over we must keep what we want." McKinley was so impressed with the sentiment, he copied it out himself. Roosevelt was giving voice to a division that has always existed in American foreign policy. Americans, "isolationists" as far as Europe was concerned, have never been isolationists regarding Asia.

Other considerations urged the country toward acquisition. General Wesley Merritt said it was easier to defend all of the Philippines than just a part, and to retire might well precipitate a war in the Far East. There was also growing sentiment among the electorate that to leave the Filipinos to their own devices was to leave them to anarchy. In addition to saving the Filipinos from themselves, Americans also wanted to save them for Christ. The Protestant clergy saw a beckoning missionary task in the archipelago. Church council, synod, Bible society, and choir importuned McKinley to guarantee salvation for our little brown brothers. It was, in the long run, the telling argument. McKinley explained that the decision to take the Philippines came to him after he prayed to God for guidance. God answered his prayer, he said, and he determined to take the islands "and educate Filipinos, and uplift and civilize and Christianize them, and by God's grace do the very best we could by them, our fellow men, for whom Christ also died."

Historian Woodrow Wilson of Princeton University stamped the imprimatur of the intellectuals on this policy when he wrote in the *Atlantic Monthly*:

It is our peculiar duty, as it is also England's . . . to impart to the people thus driven out upon the road of change, so far as we have the opportunity, or can make it, our own principles of self help;

teach them order and self control in the midst of change; impart to them, if it be possible, by contact and sympathy, and example, the drill and habit of law and obedience which we long ago got out of the strenuous processes of English history.

This was not rhetoric designed to disguise greed. The American establishment labored under the myth and illusion that Asia's toiling millions were groping toward a Christian democracy patterned upon the Republic of the United States. It was therefore a categorical imperative that good Americans aid them. Then too, some Americans and Europeans believed that when the millions of toiling Orientals succeeded, their demand for industrial and consumer goods would promptly make Occidentals rich. It is a central thesis of the American society that because Christianity and democracy work for the United States, Christianity and democracy will work for everyone.

The President instructed his peace commissioners in Paris to demand from Spain all of the Philippines in exchange for $20 million. In explaining this policy to Europe, McKinley said the United States sought no advantage in the Orient not available to all. "Asking only the open door for ourselves," he promised, "we are ready to accord the open door to others." Annexation was destined and Americans have always believed in destiny. "Manifest Destiny" decreed they would populate the continent from ocean to ocean. Another destiny beckoned them to the Pacific and Asia.

The Senate ratified the peace treaty in February, 1899, and accepted the Philippines as a responsibility thrust upon the nation by the exigencies of war. Hawaii became a Pacific halfway house and the Philippines became the equivalent of a Yankee Hong Kong. Rudyard Kipling wrote "The White Man's Burden" to celebrate American annexation.

What Americans, and for that matter Europeans, did not then realize was that colonialism was already dying. It cost more to occupy and pacify colonies than could ever be realized from profits the colonies yielded. The Philippines never absorbed more than

1 percent of American industrial production, and the Far East no more than 2 percent. The Spanish-American War cost $250 million and 2,910 lives. Putting down the Philippine insurrections cost another $600 million and 4,000 dead and 2,000 wounded in 3,000 skirmishes. Sixteen thousand Filipinos died in battle, and Philippine partisans claimed that 100,000 noncombatants perished. Yet, over a period of forty years, the occupation showed profits only for Filipinos and losses for Americans. In one year in the 1920s America purchased $64 million of Philippine hemp but sold only $1 million of American goods. American investment never went into the Philippines; it went into new projects like the automobile, or into Hawaii, Puerto Rico, and Cuba, which promised more lucrative returns.

More important, while the Philippines became a monument to American good works and goodwill, they also became a military and diplomatic liability. They were the Achilles' heel of the American defense system, a hostage to Japan for American foreign policy in the Far East. Theodore Roosevelt was the first, but by no means the last, American President to make concessions to Japanese aggression in Asia in return for implicit or explicit disavowal of Japanese intentions toward the Philippines. Before he left office, Roosevelt advised that the United States make the Philippines independent as soon as possible and get out. By the time Roosevelt left office, however, the Philippines were as integral a part of the military and naval apparatus as West Point or Annapolis.

The vanguard of General Wesley Merritt's army of occupation, 2,500 men, reached Manila Bay on June 30, 1898. They found Manila in an ever-tightening vise. Dewey's fleet was training its guns on the city of 300,000 and its Spanish garrison of 13,000 soldiers. Meanwhile, Aguinaldo's nationalist army of 12,000 was ringing the city in siege. The job was to get American troops into the city while keeping Filipinos out. Because Aguinaldo was already suspicious of American intentions, the military problem was delicate. But Brigadier General Thomas M. Anderson managed to disembark his command south of the city, where he established

Camp Dewey, destined to become the main American base for the campaign.

Some 3,500 additional troops under Brigadier General Francis V. Greene arrived the first week in July, and on the twenty-fifth General Merritt reached the bay along with 4,800 troops commanded by Brigadier General Arthur MacArthur. These soldiers constituted the Eighth Corps. When the monsoons ended in early August, Merritt was ready to move on the city. He persuaded a reluctant Aguinaldo to shift his line of insurgents to the right, to make room for troops from Camp Dewey.

Through the Belgian counsel, Merritt and Dewey negotiated secretly with General Fermin Jaudenes, the Spanish commander. They pointed out the hopelessness of his situation and that it would be better for Spanish soldiers if Manila fell to the Americans rather than the insurgents. Jaudenes agreed that capitulation was inevitable. He wanted, however, to preserve his and his country's honor. If the Americans promised not to shell the city, he would order his soldiers to fight only for the outer trenches and block-houses. When they fell, he would surrender.

Wesley Merritt did not inform Aguinaldo of this arrangement. When the Americans began their charade on August 14, the Filipinos took the fighting seriously. Though the Americans won the Old City, the Filipinos captured some of the southern suburbs and, in fact, flanked the Americans on the east. Having captured the citadel, the Americans found they were in one line of trenches, with their backs to the bay, facing their little brown brothers in another, their backs to the jungle.

The praise heaped upon Dewey and Merritt for their stunning capture was somewhat muted when the public learned of the sham battle in which five Americans had lost their lives. As for El General Jaudenes, who lost forty-six men, the queen of Spain threw him in prison for the rest of his natural life.

Without quite finishing one war, American troops were willy-nilly committed to another. Aguinaldo had set up a government, constituting himself its dictator until free elections could be held. He and his countrymen argued that they were better off governing themselves, no matter how badly, than they were being governed by an intruder. The Americans argued that the Philippines had legally belonged to Spain and that Spain had legally ceded them. Meanwhile, short-sighted policy and arrogant behavior on the part of the Americans, and retaliatory actions by the Filipinos, lit an already short fuse.

The United States Senate was scheduled to ratify the peace treaty with Spain in February, 1899, after bitter debate and an uneasy compromise. But on February 4, before the Senate voted, a force of Filipinos tried to infiltrate the United States lines. Two American sentries fired. The entire line opened up. The war was on, a war known as the Philippine Insurrection. It would last for more than two years. The Filipinos were able to carry on the war because of a healthy war chest, accumulated by past extortions from the Spaniards. They fought also to bring home to the American people and the world their desire for independence.

The Senate ratified the peace treaty just days after the insurrection broke out. Aguinaldo kept his army in the field in the hopes that the many vocal opponents to annexation in the United States would have a divisive effect on the American body politic and lead it eventually to tire of the war and withdraw. The *insurrectos* counted heavily on Bryan's election in 1900.

The Filipinos faced serious disadvantages, some of their own making. Few insurgent soldiers understood the purpose of the rear sight on the rifle. Most of them removed it as an inconvenience and sighted along the barrel. Invariably they fired high. Nor did they master the trigger squeeze, which accentuated their error. They did not defend their cities. A "scorched earth" policy would have seriously impeded American military progress by depriving Americans of forward bases. In addition, the Filipino elite, the business and professional men, relatively well educated, were against a break with the United States. Lastly, Filipinos faced an enemy tactically more skilled, who commanded heavier firepower, and who fought with equal courage and savagery.

The Americans faced difficulties, too. Never before had an American army campaigned near the equator and never before had it attempted to put down an inspired insurrection of a people fighting for their independence. Never before had an American officer been given supreme dictatorial authority over 120,000 square miles of American-owned territory.

The American army suffered twice as many killed as wounded. The majority of soldiers died in ambush from firing at close range. Many soldiers were hacked to death by a bolo knife wielded by a Filipino running amuck, "gone *juramentado*" (the word, derived from the Spanish, means "one who has sworn an oath"). Americans had to fight determined groups of men who tilled the fields by day and stalked outposts at night. And in stealth, as John J. Pershing noted, the Filipino was the superior of the American Indian.

There are more than 7,000 islands in the Philippine Archipelago, 4,000 of which are uninhabited, many of them awash at high tide. The islands extend north and south for 1,152 miles. There is a large island in the north, Luzon, the size of Illinois, and another large island in the south, Mindanao, the size of Indiana, with the smaller islands in between. The northernmost city of Luzon is Aparri, where the Japanese would fight a rearguard action in 1945, and the southernmost city of Mindanao is Zamboanga, where the monkeys have no tails. The population was then eight million, half of whom lived on Luzon. They were for the most part Malaysian, with some Negritos living in the mountains, and some Chinese and Japanese in the cities. The Moros in the south, however, were the descendants of Arabs.

By the fall of 1899, the army had secured and enlarged the perimeter around Manila. It had also secured footholds on some of the islands. In October, one column under General Henry Lawton moved northeast out of Manila along the Rio Grande River; another under General Arthur MacArthur proceeded northwest along the island's one railroad. A third force under General Lloyd V. Wheaton proceeded north by transports to a landing at Dagupan in the Lingayen Gulf. In conventional fighting, close and ferocious enough to cost Lawton his life, the United States dispersed the Philippine insurgents and drove them into the hills. Aguinaldo, who realized the futility of fighting with regular forces, reorganized and redistributed his men for guerrilla warfare. With experience gained in the insurgency against Spain, the guerrillas extended the war. The Americans were faced with the task of convincing the Filipinos that this strategy would not achieve the goal of independence either.

The Philippine pacification became an unending process of supplying isolated outposts and maintaining difficult communication. In addition, the morale of the troops, who were for the most part volunteers, often collapsed under the stress of fatigue, fear, and disease. And the moral question of Philippine annexation, which was debated furiously in the United States, contributed to the soldier's sense of meaningless purpose. Anti-imperialists argued that the Filipinos were only battling for their rights. The superpatriots blamed the Philippine insurgency on Bryan, and charged him and his followers with treason. Those in the middle, the moderates, grew tired of the war, its casualty lists and high taxes, and wanted it concluded as quickly as possible. They blamed the President for not attempting conciliation, for inept prosecution of the war, and for suppressing the news from the Philippines. They blamed the army for arrogance, inefficiency, and dangerous optimism.

McKinley applied pressure on the army to end the war in such a way that the anti-imperialists could not make capital of it. Volunteer regiments were sent home to be replaced by regulars, who were more tenacious and resolute. The fight became a struggle to win the minds and the hearts of the villagers, who supplied the guerrilla bands and offered them bases and sanctuaries.

Two events persuaded the villagers that the insurgents could not win. The first was the reelection of William McKinley in November, 1900; the second was the capture of Aguinaldo in March, 1901, by an adventurous band of soldiers who tracked him to his northern lair. From captivity Aguinaldo informed his generals that the game was up. Two thousand insurgents had already surrendered their arms to the Americans the week after McKinley's election.

These two events were not in themselves momentous enough to

end the insurgency. The Filipinos could have continued their harassment indefinitely. But the United States became more judicious in its use of force and politics. To realize the prospects offered by annexation, the United States needed universal and eternal pacification of the Philippines. To secure that at the expense of a terrorized and decimated population would be to defeat the purpose. Pacification had to proceed by transferring native allegiance from the guerrilla force to the invading force.

One of the ways the invading force won this allegiance was by setting an example, by proving that life would be better and more acceptable under American than under insurgent hegemony. The army made sure that those villages which did pledge allegiance suffered no reprisals from the insurgents. As soon as a village was pacified, the army reestablished locally accepted government, and cultivated the urban middle class, who preferred order and stability to independence. In rural areas the army cultivated the village leaders, who wanted to work their fields in safety.

The military dealt severely with the insurgents by invoking General Order 100 of the Articles of War, which authorized the summary execution of murderers, spies, highway robbers, saboteurs, conspirators, and guerrillas. The torture of captured insurgents was commonplace. Many were hanged as an example. Often the army tried to soften this repressive policy by paying a reward in gold coin for any rifle turned in to the quartermaster. However, General Order 100 instructed the noncombatants that war is a grim business, and that in this grim business the United States had the upper hand.

In every instance when the army stormed and destroyed a village, it promptly rebuilt it, reopened its market, hacked out new roads, and set up a school. It was an effective military policy. "Benevolent pacification" and "beneficent administration" were key words in McKinley's vocabulary, and the emphasis of the army was always on reform rather than on control.

The two signal contributions the army made to the Filipinos to win their allegiance were in public health and education. Sanitary conditions in Manila were execrable when the army arrived; conditions in the countryside were worse. Americans are nothing if not sanitary and their cleanup campaign was revolutionary. Within weeks after the Spanish surrender, Manila was a storybook wonderland. Garbage collection, though novel, was soon routine and efficient. Residents were fined for disposing of slops from their windows and for littering. The army burned contaminated buildings and clothes, and destroyed contaminated food and livestock. In rural areas doctors examined everyone for communicable or contagious diseases and established quarantine procedures. They vaccinated whole villages, under duress if necessary, and treated the sick. The immediate result was a sudden decrease in infant mortality—and no gift to a people is more precious than the life of its infants, or prompts a more impulsive and long-lasting gratitude. Sanitary procedures and army-supplied medicine lengthened the life of the adult population. It was true that the army was making the Filipinos cleaner than they wanted to be, but Americans are imbued with the idea of controlling an environment to make it salubrious, which has been extended to the contemporary world mission of abolishing body odor.

Wherever the army went, it established schools, often before it reinstituted municipal government. Ordinary soldiers became teachers; ponchos became blackboards; lumps of starch became chalk; churches became classrooms, and if there were no churches, the army mess accommodated students. The children learned the English alphabet from Campbell soup cans. A hardened top sergeant confessed that his detail as a teacher was the best six months of his life.

On July 4, 1901, William Howard Taft took the oath of office as the first Governor-General of the Philippines, and control of the islands passed from the military arm of government. Not all the problems had been solved. Philippine society remained ill suited to the concept of representative democratic government, primarily because it is not one culture but several. The Filipinos in the northern islands were Tagalog Christians, those in the south were Moros (the word means "Mohammedan") who had long resisted Tagalog encroachment. A tribal people, they were fiercely jealous

of their semi-savage freedom. Wisely, the Spaniards had left them
to their own devices; but the Americans wanted to clean up and
educate everybody.

So the army established a garrison at Balangiga, on Samar, in
the south, where Magellan had sighted the Philippines and where
he was to die at the hands of natives. On September 1, 1901, the
natives from the surrounding hills of Balangiga fell on the American garrison, and in devastating surprise littered the street with
the heads, brains, blood, and intestines of the soldiery. Within
months after the United States had returned Aguinaldo from his
exile on Guam to his home in Manila (where he would live long
enough to see Philippine independence) another war was loosed.
This was the beginning of a religious war with the Moros, one that
took longer to settle than the war against Aguinaldo's political
insurrectos. It was the Philippine war John J. Pershing fought.

Much of Pershing's first tour was spent in a small war of patrols
and company-sized expeditions sent out to persuade Moros to accept American sovereignty, or else to subjugate them.* This endless perseverance resulted in the pacification of Mindanao, with the
loss of but twenty American soldiers and fewer than two hundred
Moro warriors.

Pershing spent 1900, his first year in the Philippines, in Zamboanga as the adjutant general of the Department of Mindanao-
Jolo (Jolo is one of three small islands dropping off Mindanao into
the Sulu Sea). His commanding general was William Kobbé, an
Austrian-born regular who affected only a cane for a weapon.
Pershing's duties included supplying, transporting, and quartering
several regiments.

During this tour, Pershing was made a regular army captain.
"Fifteen years to go from lieutenant to captain," he complained in
a letter, "and this during a time of war." Promotion sent him to the
Fifteenth Cavalry, which was due to arrive from San Francisco.
When these troops arrived in Zamboanga in 1901, he wrote, they

*See Appendix for a chronology of Pershing's first tour.

came with one hundred horses who had never seen a soldier, one hundred soldiers who had never seen a horse, and officers who had never seen either.

By no means a soft or idealistic man, Pershing blanched at local politics. An election in Zamboanga was decided by which Filipino shot the other candidates first. As Pershing defined the intrinsic characteristics of the Moros, they were neither uncivilized nor primitive, they were simply barbaric. They had tried fair play and found it wanting and time-consuming.

Pershing's administrative duties afforded him the time to master Spanish and study the Moros and some of their dialects. He reported clearly on what he observed:

> The Moro is of a peculiar make-up as to character, though the reason is plain when it is considered, first, that he is a savage; second that he is a Malay; and third, that he is a Mohammedan. The almost infinite combination of superstitions, prejudices, and suspicions blended into his character make him a difficult person to handle until fully understood. In order to control him other than by brute force, one must first win his implicit confidence, nor is this as difficult as it would seem; but once accomplished one can accordingly by patient and continuous effort, largely guide and direct his thoughts and actions. He is jealous of his religion, but he knows very little about its teachings. The observance of a few rites and rituals is about all that is required to satisfy him that he is a good Mohammedan. As long as he is undisturbed in the possession of his women and children, and his slaves, who are really but serfs or vassals, as members of his family; but any interference with what he thinks his right regarding them had best be made gradually by the natural process of development, which must logically come by contact with and under the wise supervision of a civilized people.

The army had no trouble clearing the Mindanao shoreline of *insurrectos*, who retreated inland, where the Moros killed those who were not Mohammedans and enslaved those who were. But the Moros had no liking for the presence of Americans—infidels and Christians—as the army soon discovered. In the folds of his *sarong* every Moro carried a dagger—a *kris*, if he was a man of caste. For battle, the Moro armed himself with a *campilan*, a two-handed, broad-bladed sword with a razor edge. Both the *kris* and the *campilan* were made in Germany. Moros also took after unsuspecting or inattentive soldiers with a *bolo* knife, a native Philippine product that resembled a machete. These Moros had "gone *juramentado*," sworn an oath to assassinate Christians, to gain admission to the Mohammedan Seventh Heaven. The assassins wrapped their bodies tightly in cloth so that, if wounded, they would not bleed to death before hacking away at their enemies. Sometimes it took a fusilade to stop one. Pershing countered with the promise to bury Moros with the body of a pig, which denied a Mohammedan admission to any of his heavens. The threat did not deter the Moros, although it got Pershing in hot water with the stateside Society for the Prevention of Cruelty to Animals.

Moros were also armed with Mausers, Remingtons, and old Spanish blunderbusses. In their villages they set up rudimentary artillery employing a *lanteca*, a cannon that hurled slugs, one blast of which could clear away the vegetation faster and more efficiently than a battalion of machetes. These warlike Moros lived in concentrated clusters around Lake Lanao in north-central Mindanao, 80,000 of them in more than 400 villages. Lake Lanao is shaped like an equilateral triangle, each leg measuring roughly one hundred miles. Around its rim Moro sultans and *dattos* ruled a people devoted to brigandage and raiding, one tribe victimizing another.

The shore town of Iligan offered the one accessible point to the lake area, which the Moros called the "Forbidden Kingdom." It was by no means an easy inland journey to this area from Iligan, but the army was determined to reach the Moros. Zamboanga's brigadiers began to lean heavily on Pershing's knowledge. In November, 1901, General George Davis detached Pershing from Zamboanga and sent him to the small garrison at Iligan. "I'll give you two troops of your regiment and three companies of infantry," said Davis. "Do everything possible to get in touch with the Moros of central Mindanao and make friends with them."

At Iligan Pershing found that the men lacked discipline and purpose. The company street was overgrown with weeds and soldiers lackadaisically went about meaningless tasks. Pershing saw rust in the bores of the rifles, unshined shoes, missing buttons, and unshaved faces. He informed the men in no uncertain terms that "Sir" was the only way to address an officer. He went through the Iligan mess with white gloves, rubbing them along the bottom of each pot. He flipped each offending utensil backhanded so that it skittered along the floor and came to a stop with a bump in the corner. When he finished, his gloves looked like those of an oil wildcatter and the corner of the mess as though men had been bowling with pots and pans for duckpins.

Soon the company street was as bald as a desert. Shoes looked like patent leather pumps. A man could blind himself from the gleam of the rifle bores. Privates sweated silently while they performed their details. The mess was as clean as a hospital. Every sentence began with "Sir." At inspection the men were sometimes rewarded with a grim, almost imperceptible smile.

Iligan was Pershing's first separate field command, and in the army in those days a separate field command of fifty men was better than second in command of five hundred. His orders were to make friends, which ruled out any bold strike into the interior.

Pershing patrolled the Iligan marketplace, talking through an interpreter to as many Moros as came down from the hills. He admired their produce, bought some of their artifacts, asked about their leaders, and distributed American flags to all who would take one. He entertained the son of a powerful Moro sultan who eventually persuaded his father to visit Iligan. Wearing a jeweled turban, the sultan, Manibilang, arrived in Iligan astride a black stallion. Beside him trotted his slaves, carrying white and red umbrellas. One slave bore a jeweled silver box containing betel nut, which sent the mind in flight while turning the mouth a brilliant red. Another slave carried the American flag.

Pershing and Manibilang made palaver for three days. The sultan wanted to know if the Americans intended to stay, if they intended to depose the sultans and *dattos*, if they would impose new laws on the Moro people, and if they would try to make Christians of them.

Pershing assured Manibilang that the United States exchanged ambassadors with many Moslem countries. There was a minister at Constantinople, then the capital of the Moslem world. Americans did not desecrate other religions. Yes, they would stay, but they would stay to make the Moros rich. Americans built roads wherever they went and always paid fair prices. The *dattos* and sultans could rule forever, as long as they and their people obeyed the law which prohibited killing and stealing. Pershing did not choose to discuss polygamy and slavery and the sultan did not press him. Manibilang allowed as how he could live with the Americans —he was particularly interested in getting rich.

The visit had practical results. Other Moro *dattos* and sultans came to Iligan and Pershing welcomed them all. He began to exchange letters, written in Arabic, with the Moros of Lake Lanao. Manibilang invited Pershing to his *rancheria,* the name the Moros gave to the sultan's district. Pershing decided to go alone, despite numerous warnings of treachery. White men had tried to visit the Forbidden Kingdom before only to stay there forever, pushing up bamboo. Pershing said that if it came to that, he was sure he could grow good bamboo. To win the trust of the Moros, Pershing would have to show his own trust. He left Iligan with three native interpreters.

Under a thatched roof, Pershing ate delicious steamed chicken, played chess, and declined the virgin offered him for the night. Manibilang told him the Moros had rarely raised anything beyond their immediate needs for fear the Spaniards would confiscate it. It was hard for them to understand why the Americans would voluntarily build a road. Pershing was aware that he was talking to a man who understood only one-man government, that he had a poor concept of dealing with different men who represented the same power. But he swore that his country would build the road. Manibilang believed him and got a road for his trust. Pershing became indispensable. He was the voice of the American government.

As a result of Pershing's efforts, engineers began connecting the villages on the north side of Lake Lanao with a network of roads. On the south side of the lake unrest and ambushes only increased. General Davis mounted an expedition from Zamboanga to invade the southern reaches of the Forbidden Kingdom. Twelve hundred troopers met the Moros at their *cotta* in Pandapatan. A *cotta* was a Moro fort, a breastwork about twelve feet high and twelve feet thick, made of rock or piled dirt laced with bamboo trees covered by thorns. Wide moats, sometimes thirty feet deep, ringed the *cotta* in concentric circles. The *lanteca* cannons guarding the breastwork were mounted on parapets and aimed through embrasures.

The army breached the *cotta* at Pandapatan with a loss of sixty men killed and many more wounded. The force withdrew and established a post on the outskirts of the Forbidden Kingdom, called Camp Vicars, in honor of Lieutenant Thomas Vicars, the first man to fall in the attack. General Adna Chaffee, the new military commander in the Philippines, thought that Colonel Frank Baldwin, who had field command of the expedition, was impulsive. Pandapatan had damn near whipped a regiment; while a single captain had united the villages on the north shore and secured their allegiance without firing a shot.

Chaffee ordered Pershing to Camp Vicars with precise orders: Colonel Baldwin was in charge of the camp, Captain Pershing was in charge of Moro affairs. When Baldwin wanted to move on one of the sturdiest *cottas* on Lake Lanao, Pershing refused. "To move in strength against enemies will force the hands of friends," Pershing warned. Baldwin insisted. Chaffee transferred the colonel and left Pershing in complete command. Pershing undertook the interminable task of palavering with *dattos* and sultans, interminable because each strong man had to be persuaded and cajoled individually.

When finally Pershing determined on a move against the Moros in Maciu, to show other Moros that the United States could take effective action if goaded, his force of six hundred men ran into an ambush. Pershing pulled back, uncovered artillery pieces, and began banging away. American firepower was vastly superior and Pershing knew that, once engaged, the Moros had no chance against a disciplined, well-armed force. Rather than charge, he settled his troops for the night and thus gave the Moro defenders time to slip away. In the morning Pershing again began pursuit.

The Maciu *cotta* he was after was located on a small peninsula protected by impassable jungle. When Pershing reached the area, he asked the sultan for a parlay. "We are waiting for you," answered the sultan. Pershing returned a week later with a detachment of engineers who felled trees and built a corduroy road to the *cotta*. As the American force came closer, Moro warriors jumped up and down on the parapet, waving *campilans* and rifles, pointing to their red flags, vowing to fight to the death. Priests beat metallic war drums, and the *lantecas* discharged their slugs. The artillery banged away, out of range of Moro arms. The *cotta* was twenty feet high and its moat was almost as wide. Again Pershing did not attack, but waited through the dark. In the morning the flags were gone from the *cotta* and its defenders had vanished. Pershing held his troops in place for an hour. Then from the moat six Moros gone *juramentado* suddenly leaped up and charged with fanatic whoops. Steady firing killed them. Soldiers burned the *cotta* afterward.

Again Pershing sent a round of friendship letters to *dattos* and sultans, many of whom now saw the wisdom of cooperation. Some recalcitrants remained at Bacoclod on the west coast of the lake, at Gata and Taraca on the east, and at Bayan on the south, a *rancheria* not far from Vicars. Sajiduciamen, ruler of Bayan, told his followers that the Americans would make the warriors wear hats and the women wear skirts, and would make pork a mandatory staple. Pershing asked for friendship, and Sajiduciamen proposed that he pay a visit. Prudently, Pershing took along his artillery.

The expedition was joined by streams of Moros. Chanting and singing, twirling their umbrellas, hundreds accompanied Pershing and his men to the Bayan *cotta*, which commanded a high bluff on the lake. Sajiduciamen came out. Pershing drew up the troops to present arms and fired an impressive five-gun salute over the water. Sajiduciamen and his *dattos* and Pershing squatted on their heels by the shore.

The soldiers saw Pershing kneel forward on a mat placed in the center of the sultans and *dattos* in their brilliant silks. A slave produced a Koran, on which Pershing placed his hand, while another slave moved to cover the captain with a red umbrella. The *dattos* crowded near now to put their hands atop Pershing's. Sajiduciamen gestured for the men to rise and said, "Commandante Per-shering, you have been made a *datto*." The *dattos* walked solemnly to the wall, past the rank and file of soldiers, and raised the American flag. All chewed betel nuts in honor of the occasion.

But from Bacoclod came the message, "What we want is war. If you come to Bacoclod, our priests will circumcise you and your soldiers." Pershing delayed a punitive expedition when a cholera epidemic broke out around the lake, claiming the lives of 1,500 villagers. Pershing enforced a quarantine and dispatched medical supplies and letters to the *rancherias* with instructions on how to control the disease. But in March, 1903, he resolved to move on Bacoclod, so that the pacified *rancherias* would not construe the waiting game as American weakness.

The expedition left Vicars with six hundred men, each man carrying a hundred rounds of ammunition, a haversack, and two canteens. Pershing's orders were to drink no water unless it was boiled first. Two soldiers satisfied their thirst from a mountain stream and went back to Vicars on mules covered with a shroud. "Damn them," said Captain Pershing. "They disobeyed orders." Five more men died of cholera and several barely survived.

Bacoclod was a fort one hundred feet square protected by a *cotta* twelve feet high and fifteen feet thick. The site was roofed, which made it hard to determine the number of defending forces. Pershing estimated that two hundred Moro warriors guarded the parapet. The surrounding moat was thirty feet wide by forty feet deep with a trench that ran to Lake Lanao, so that the Moros could supply themselves with water.

In a torrential downpour, Pershing's men scaled a mountain to flank the *cotta* from the rear. They began dropping mortar shells on the roof. Then Pershing deployed his force in a cordon that surrounded the *cotta,* leaving here and there an obviously undefended space so that those who chose to could escape. Several of the Moro warriors took advantage of this opportunity and spirited away the women and children.

When the rain subsided, Pershing, under a flag of truce, asked for a surrender. The sultan complained, "If the Americans want to fight us, let them fight. But tell them to fight like men. While my fort is besieged, I see American soldiers down by the water eating up my coconuts. This is infamous and is not war."

Pershing set the troops to felling brush and small trees, which they used to fill up two sections of the moat. An assault party crept forward with bamboo bridges. The infantry kept up a rapid fire on the parapet, to keep the Moros down while the assault party crawled over the bridges and began clambering up the *cotta*. Moros streamed to the parapet to meet them. The Moros swung *campilans*, amputating arms at a blow, while the Americans bashed skulls with rifle butts. It was savage but quick. One hundred and twenty Moros died on the wall. Nine Americans fell wounded. All survived, but several were amputees. The Moros surrendered and the soldiers went inside and burned the cholera-infected *cotta*.

On the march back, Pershing and his soldiers saw more American flags waving than they realized there were in the whole of the archipelago. Moros from other *rancherias* joined the parade as though they had participated in the capture of Bacoclod. The flushed pride of the expeditionary force was subdued by its arrival at Vicars. The garrison didn't want them to come inside the camp because they had been exposed to cholera. Pershing mulled this over and ordered the expeditionary force inside the camp and the garrison outside.

In May, Pershing left Camp Vicars with a force of 500 men and 340 animals on an expedition that would completely encircle Lake Lanao. *Cotta* after *cotta* flew the Stars and Stripes. When the troops passed still-smoking Bacoclod they saw the new Moro cemetery, large mounds of earth supported by small rock walls, with white umbrellas for gravestones.

Pershing's March Around the Lake captured the fancy of the American public. He had by no means concluded the war in the Philippines, but he had certainly ended a part of it. And the March Around the Lake captured the fancy of the Moros, too. It became for them the beginning of the American era. Some years later, when Pershing returned as the Commanding General of the Moro Province, he visited the Forbidden Kingdom. "I stopped at a school on the east side of Lake Lanao," he wrote. "Among the forty Moro children in the little wooden building was a particularly bright boy who attracted my attention and I asked him his age. 'I don't know exactly, sir, but I was about so high (holding his hand at the height of seven) when you marched around the Lake.'"

Back in Washington, Charles Magoon wrote to his friend Pershing, asking when the captain would come home, perhaps to a promotion, certainly to easier tasks. Pershing wrote he was coming stateside as soon as possible, that he had already served three and one-half years in the Philippines. "Another way of saying that a man has done too much service in the tropics," Pershing concluded, "is to say that he has had too much sunshine."

Military historians have often seen in the Philippines the playing fields of Eton, and have argued that it was in the cogon grass of Mindanao and the rain forests of Luzon that World War I was won. The roster of the high command in 1917–1918 was the roster of lieutenants and captains who served in the Philippines between 1899 and 1912. It was there, it is argued, that these future division, corps, and army commanders gained their practical military experience.

Historians see the past as a process of becoming. But there is no logical necessity for predicating the future upon the past. Americans at the turn of the century regarded the Philippine adventure as pure being and those who participated in it at its higher levels enjoyed an apostolic vision.

McKinley, in a message to Congress, proclaimed: "Without any original thought of complete or even partial annexation, the presence and success of our arms at Manila imposes upon us obligations which we cannot disregard. The march of events rules and overrules human action." William Howard Taft, the first Governor-General of the Philippines, hoped all his political life to become a Supreme Court Justice. Yet when Roosevelt tendered this nomination in 1903, Taft refused it because his work in the Philippines was more important.*

In a letter to Avery D. Andrews Pershing put succinctly the apostolic creed to which he himself subscribed:

> It has been urged by some people at home that the Filipinos should be given their independence. Such a thing would result in anarchy. To whom would we turn over the government? Tagalog, Viscayan, Igorrote, Macabebe or Moro? No one can answer that any of these tribes represents the people in any sense, any more than the Sioux represents all the Indians in America. There is no national spirit, and except for the few agitators, these people do not want to try independence. They will have to be educated up to it and to self government as we understand it, and their education will take time and patience. It is a grand work cut out for us from which there should be no shirking.

It was a creed hammered out of expediency rather than one hurled down from the heights. For the truth about the Philippines was that its destiny as the great American warehouse for the Orient trade was doomed. An astute horse soldier like John J. Pershing was able to see that Manila was two days' sail out of the way from the routes to Shanghai, Hong Kong, or Tokyo. And two days was enough to diminish and discourage profits. The Americans stayed on, Pershing said, because "the American people being

---

*Taft's work in the Philippines was attended by a grave health risk. He weighed 340 pounds and the unaccustomed tropical heat was hard on him. However, he was able to wire his friend Elihu Root that he had ridden thirty-five miles on horseback to a point 5,000 feet above sea level and was feeling fine. To which Root replied, "How is the horse?"

obsessed with the idea of maintaining their new position as a world power insisted on keeping the flag flying over territory once it was in our possession."

The creed proved persuasive for almost everyone except the soldiers who fought the wars, the snakes, the jungle rot, and the boredom. The most repeated of the barracks ballads was the one the regulars sang to the tune of "Tramp, Tramp, Tramp":

> Damn, damn, damn the Filipino
> Pock-marked Kodiac ladrone [bandit];
> Underneath the starry flag
> Civilize him with a Krag
> And return us to our old Kentucky home.

As for Christianizing and uplifting the Filipinos, another ballad concluded:

> He may be a brother to big Bill Taft
> But he ain't no brother to me.

8

German Maps,
American Hearts

Pershing came back to Washington, D.C., a war hero and a celebrity. But in the core of his being, the good professional soldier is antiheroic. Moreover, Pershing understood intuitively that modest stillness and humility was what was wanted, not the action of a tiger. He disdained the heroic role—going so far as to refuse the Congressional Medal of Honor—and sought the trappings and distinction of rank, the true preferment for the soldier.

His duties were on the newly commissioned General Staff, and the appointment marked him and the other line grade officers for better things. (Major George Goethals, with whom Pershing shared an office in 1903, would go on to build the Panama Canal.) The General Staff in 1903 numbered three general officers, four colonels, six lieutenant colonels, twelve majors, and twenty captains. Congress charged them with the study of military problems and the preparation of plans for national defense.

Among its first subjects, the General Staff studied "The Organization, Use and Equipment of Machine Guns," "The Function of Field Artillery," "The Genesis and Progress of Riots in Large Cities With the Means to Protect the Public Utilities from Violence," "The Ways and Means of Supplying the Embarkation and Withdrawal to Cuba of 3,600 Men," and "The Cost of Telephone Installation on Army Bases." For his part, Pershing had to submit a cost estimate for the maneuvers to be held that summer at Manassas. Among other expenses, he determined to pay the State of Virginia and farmers 35 cents a day for every acre used for campsites and 20 cents for every acre used for maneuvers.

He also became one of the charter "mailing list" officers who requested all problems formulated by the War College be mailed them for practice. The first of these was: "Presume War With Britain: Problem: Secure Buffalo from Canadian Attack." The respondent had to estimate the number of troops needed to secure the roads and bridges in the area, the amount of rolling stock needed to supply the command, and the administration of the area. Pershing was a devoted student of war problems and undertook the solution to as many as the War College sent him.

Though the army had been enlarged, it still operated on an austerity budget. The War College found it difficult to furnish its students and respondents with good maps, which were expensive to reproduce. So it purchased quire upon quire of the cheapest maps it could find and related the specific military problem to the terrain, population and singularities of the geography described. The maps came from Germany. Pershing, among others, once complained that congressional parsimony resulted in the absurdity of dozens of American military men repeatedly studying the Franco-German frontier and knowing the Moselle country more intimately than their own seacoasts.

Pershing completed his first year on the General Staff in the Southwestern Department at Oklahoma City, where he formulated the plans for supplying the 1,357 members of the area's organized militia. It was, of course, done with thoroughness and dispatch, but not typical Pershing thoroughness and dispatch. John J. Pershing had other things on his mind; he had fallen in love.

The girl was Helen Frances Warren, a twenty-three-year-old debutante, a recent Wellesley graduate, and the daughter of Senator Francis E. Warren, chairman of the Military Affairs Committee. The Senator was a widower, and his daughter presided in Washington in her mother's place. Pershing met her at a dinner given by Senator Joseph H. Millard of Nebraska, once a member of the University of Nebraska faculty. She was thrilled to meet the hero of the March Around the Lake, and he couldn't keep his eyes off her. She had generous features and a trim figure, was a brunette, and had a sprightly sense of humor, as well as the ability to make conversation. He changed his plans for the evening at the dinner table and followed her to a dance at Fort Myers.

At two in the morning he woke up his friend Charles Magoon to tell him about the girl and ask his opinion on whether younger women should marry older men. "Jack," said Magoon, "if you're in love, I'm not. I want to get some sleep. If you're still in love tomorrow, come around and tell me about it." That same morning, Helen Frances Warren artlessly asked the wife of General John R. Brooke if she knew Captain Pershing. Astutely divining the situation, Mrs. Brooke said, "If you think you could stand the life, you couldn't do better than John Pershing."

There was a twenty-one-year difference in their ages, but both were hardy people and devoted to good health and physical well-being. Helen was an excellent horsewoman and liked camping, hiking, and outdoor activity. She loved church, sobriety, traditional virtues, and community activity. She also knew her own mind. She was of that generation of American women who made universal suffrage an actuality, Prohibition the law, and transformed female employment into careers. She also had the good manners of a wealthy girl.

Helen worried not at all about the difference in their ages. The real obstacle to their marriage was money. Pershing had lent his brother, Jim, $6,000, a loan that failed to save Jim's business. The captain was also contributing to the support of his sisters, one of whom was ill, while the other was caring for their ailing father. Pershing was living on far less than his captain's pay, and when he discussed the problem with Helen she said she had $10,000 in her own name he might have. Sometimes he thought he'd take it, but always drew back.

Courtship at the turn of the century was still the proverbial pursuit of the precious object. Though Helen Frances Warren met John J. Pershing on December 9, 1903, and confided in her diary on December 11, *"Have lost my heart,"* they did not kiss until she had formally accepted his proposal nine months later. While he was in Oklahoma, they continued their courtship by letter. He always addressed her as "Dear Miss Warren" and signed even his most ardent letters "John J. Pershing." She addressed him as "Captain Pershing" and signed herself "Frances." It is perhaps cruel to judge any man by what he writes to a good woman. Pershing suffers more than most: "Don't think me in the least conceited when I say that I know and *knew* that you liked me," and "Did it ever occur to you that a soldier's profession is a jealous mistress?"

She was the more genuine romantic when she replied, "I want you to love me so much that you will ask me to marry you in spite of anything in the world. I am trembling as I let this letter go from me." Later, he called her "Frankie" and she called him "Jack." If their correspondence proves their love and respect for each other, it also proves they were not another Heloise and Abelard.

Pershing spent his furlough at the Warren ranch in Wyoming, unaware that her father was wondering aloud why she didn't marry this Pershing fellow, who seemed a good sort. On Christmas Day, 1904, they announced their engagement. On December 27, the army ordered Pershing to Tokyo as military attaché. He would be detached to serve as a military observer to the Russo-Japanese War. It was a choice assignment and, though Pershing merited it, he was chosen principally because Lloyd Griscom, the American Ambassador, had specified he wanted a bachelor who could play bridge.

Senator Warren sent Pershing over to see William Howard Taft, now Secretary of War (Root had become Secretary of State). Pershing told the genial Taft that he wanted the assignment, but that the General Staff wanted to assign only single men as military attachés. Taft said that was the general sentiment. Pershing said, "Mr. Secretary, I am engaged to marry Miss Warren."

Taft asked, "But you are a bachelor now?"

"Yes," said Pershing.

"And you do have the appointment?"

"Yes."

"And the Army Regs do not prohibit marriage?"

"That is right," said Pershing.

"Then accept the appointment," laughed Taft, "then get married and then go to Tokyo. No Army court or board will revoke an appointment because a man gets married."

Instead of a June wedding, John Pershing and Helen Frances Warren were married in January, during a cold wave so severe the ships were frozen to their anchorages in the Potomac. On Wednesday, January 25, 1905, at the Epiphany Episcopal Church, the Reverend Randolph McKim reading, John J. and Helen Frances took their vows. Charles Magoon served as best man and the ushers were Generals William Crozier and William Lassiter, Major Charles McCawley, Captain Archibald Butts (who went down on the *Titanic*), Lieutenant Commander Henry Gibbon, Captain Sidney Cloman, and Lieutenant Fulmer Bristol, all of whom, like the groom, wore full dress blues.

The church rose when President Theodore and Mrs. Roosevelt, accompanied by his daughter, Alice, entered and were ushered to a front pew. Thirty Senators and their wives attended the ceremony as well as the cabinet and the Supreme Court Justices.

For the church nearly five thousand invitations went out, and six hundred for the wedding breakfast, which was held at the Hotel Willard, where the Senator and his daughter had made their home for the past two years.

The Pershings spent their honeymoon traveling across the continent. In Chicago, Pershing saw his father for the last time. John Fletcher succumbed to a heart attack in the spring. The couple also stopped in Lincoln, Nebraska. By March 5, 1905, Captain and Mrs. Pershing were "At Home" in Tokyo.

9

"Banzai, Jack"

As the United States moved toward a colonial enterprise in Asia in the 1890s, so too did Japan. Forty-one million Japanese lived on a string of mountainous islands only 15 percent of which was arable land. For geographic expansion as well as markets and raw materials, Japan looked to Korea, the "Hermit Kingdom," no farther away than Cuba is from the United States. Korea's influential neighbor and protector was China. When China moved troops into Korea, Japan struck. With the loss of only eighteen men, the Japanese army seized the Liaotung Peninsula in 1894; and the Japanese navy, in two efficient engagements, sent the Chinese fleet to the bottom of the Yellow Sea. Under the Treaty of Shimonoseki, China agreed to recognize the independence of Korea, which betokened eventual Japanese annexation; to pay a $25 million war indemnity; and to cede the entire Liaotung Peninsula, at whose tip was the prize of Port Arthur. France, Germany, and Russia protested strongly against Japanese occupation of the city. Realistically, Japan saw that she could not afford the enmity of this powerful coalition and, in the words of the emperor, "yielded to the dictates of humanity" by a prompt evacuation.

Korea is a peninsula; on its eastern coast is the Sea of Japan; on its western coast is the Yellow Sea. Two hundred miles to the

west, across Korea Bay, is the Liaotung Peninsula. At its tip is Port
Arthur, named after one of Queen Victoria's sons. Russia needed
this peninsula to compete with the other European powers who
had established protectorates in China. Though the czar had completed the Trans-Siberian Railway, which stretched from St.
Petersburg on the Baltic Sea to Vladivostok on the Sea of Japan,
Vladivostok was icebound three months of the year. Port Arthur
was the one warm-water port to the south to which this railroad
could link up.

To get it, Russia agreed to pay China's indemnity to Japan,
receiving in return a twenty-five-year lease on Port Arthur and its
sister port of Darien, a few miles to the north. The lease, which
was renewable into perpetuity, allowed Russia to fortify the city.
In 1900, when the European powers sent armed forces into Peking
to put down the Boxer Rebellion, Russia sent troops from Port
Arthur east along the Yalu River to set up military outposts. With
the Trans-Siberian railroad now stretching south from Vladivostok
to Mukden, it was clearly only a matter of time before Korea
disappeared into the Russian maw, and with it the bulk of Japan's
foreign trade. Japan protested. This time the Japanese had a powerful ally—England. In the event of a Japanese war with another
power, England promised neutrality. In the event of a war with
two powers, England promised intervention. Theodore Roosevelt,
who also feared Russian aims in the Far East, thought the alliance
a display of uncommonly good sense.

Japan asked Russia to withdraw her troops from Korea and
Manchuria. The czar agreed, but the negotiations became pro-
tracted, for Russia had begun a sizable timbering operation in
Korea. It was a multi-million-dollar investment, and to protect it
Russia strengthened its fleet at Port Arthur and its military garri-
sons along the Yalu.

On the night of February 8, 1904, a Japanese fleet under the
command of Admiral Heihachiro Togo surprised the Russian Asiatic squadron in the Port Arthur basin. While Togo did not sink the
Russian squadron, he bottled it up and thereby gave Japan undis-
puted command of the sea-lanes. General Baron Kuroki landed an

army corps at Inchon, the Korean port that services Seoul. The Japanese army marched north to the Yalu, where Kuroki defeated the Russians, who lost three thousand men in the battle. The magnitude of the event shocked Europe. It was the first victory by an Asian over a European army in more than a thousand years.

As the Russians fell back into Manchuria, the Japanese landed another army on the Liaotung Peninsula at Houtushihi, sixty miles north of Port Arthur. Japanese generals were skillfully waging a complicated war with two theaters of operations: in one theater an army pushed north toward Mukden, the depot for Russian reinforcements; and in the other the Japanese were pushing south against a heavily fortified port. This strategy taxed Japanese manpower to its utmost. To win the war, Japan had to win it fast, for Russia could eventually send an army of three and a half million men against her. But the Russians faced the almost insuperable task of transporting troops thousands of miles across Russia and Siberia to Vladivostok, then hundreds of miles south to Mukden. Had the Russians pulled back to Harbin, two hundred miles north of Mukden, they would have forced the Japanese to extend their lines of communication and supply too far. But political dissidence at home and incompetent and ill-informed advice from his military counselors led the czar to compel his army to fight where it stood.

Port Arthur proved a tough nut to crack, but its capture was crucial to Japanese strategy. Once General Maresuke Nogi took the heights outside the city, his howitzers could sink the Russian fleet; and with the surrender of the strong Russian garrison, his army could move north and join Kuroki's in the advance on Mukden. Russian General Alexei Kuropatkin, commanding the Manchurian army, saw the Japanese strategy clearly. Twice he tried to stem the advance of Kuroki and break through to relieve Port Arthur. Twice he was defeated, in battles that literally consumed Japanese and Russian divisions. On both occasions, however, Kuropatkin saved his army by withdrawing. He was trading space for time. The Russians had launched the Great Baltic Fleet, which would sail from Kronstadt, on the Atlantic, around Africa, across the Indian Ocean, to the Sea of Japan, where it would engage and then defeat Togo's fleet. It would thus trap the Japanese on the mainland, depriving them of supplies, ammunition, and reinforcements.

Before Christmas, Nogi's army captured the heights outside Port Arthur and rapidly demolished the Russian Asiatic Squadron with cannon. In January, 1905, the Russians surrendered the port itself. Nogi marched north to take a place in the assault against Mukden. In a battle that lasted for almost three weeks, 207,000 Japanese faced 276,000 Russians. Despite subzero weather, day after day the Japanese hurled themselves against the Russian lines. Pitilessly the snow covered thousands upon thousands of mutilated Japanese and Russian dead. Nogi's army was the decisive element. In early March, Kuropatkin ordered a retreat and gave up Mukden. Again he had saved his army from decimation, though not from humiliation.

After sailing 21,000 miles, the Great Baltic Fleet tried to steam through the Straits of Korea for Vladivostok. But Admiral Togo found it on the morning of May 27 near the small island of Tsushima and inflicted a catastrophic and annihilating defeat. Only three small Russian destroyers escaped. The rest of the fleet, including eight battleships, lay at the bottom or were interned at Sasebo after a mid-sea surrender.

When Theodore Roosevelt offered his services as a peace mediator, both the Japanese and Russians quickly accepted. The Russians, their dream of a Far Eastern empire shattered, would after all only have to surrender what was not theirs to begin with; and the Japanese, their armies exhausted, recognized that a continuation of the war would lead to bankruptcy. At Portsmouth, New Hampshire—because Washington, D.C., was too hot in August—the Japanese and Russians concluded a peace in which Russia accepted the paramount political, military, and economic interests of Japan in Korea, ceded the lease on the Liaotung, and gave away the southern half of the Sakhalin Islands opposite Vladivostok.

Military men in the West hoped the war would provide some demonstration of the effect of technology upon the battlefield.

While strategic thinking and planning had progressed arithmetically, weaponry had developed geometrically. What effect new weapons would have in actual war was a lesson every major power wanted to learn at someone else's expense.

The Russo-Japanese War was the last major conflict between 1870 and 1914 that gave military and naval observers a chance to test theories confined so far to textbooks and service journals.* Such lessons as were offered were learned by a unique personality, the military observer, the more knowledgeable brother of the military attaché. His role in war was made possible by diplomacy and by the military man's belief that soldiers everywhere belong to the same brotherhood. The duties of the military observer were to attend military and naval campaigns and maneuvers and to extract from them lessons for the instruction of his own country. Newspaper correspondents had often done as much, but they lacked the technical expertise to report on such subjects as gun-barrel erosion, sanitation, and military justice, which Pershing dealt with in his reports. The military observer was expected to endure the same hardships and deprivation, including capture and death, as the unit to which he was attached.

The Russo-Japanese War drew more military observers than any other war. The American contingent alone numbered seventeen, although they all did not serve jointly, but rotated, one group relieving another. Several of these observers rose to prominence: Captain Peyton C. March was to become General of the Artillery in the AEF and serve as Chief of Staff from 1918 to 1921; Colonel Enoch Crowder was to become Judge Advocate General of the Army and direct Selective Service during World War I; Lieutenant Douglas MacArthur, who served as an aide-de-camp for his father, was to command the Forty-second Division; Major Joseph E. Kuhn was to become president of the War College.

They had been handpicked by Theodore Roosevelt and Elihu

---

*For much of the following I am indebted to *The American Military Observers of the Russo-Japanese War, 1904–1905* by J. Greenwood, unpublished doctorate, Kansas State University, Manhattan, Kansas (1971).

Root, as a nucleus for the emerging American General Staff. They were intellectually alert and not bound by any single school of military thought, as the French were bound by a Jesuitical belief in the attack, the Germans by the *blitzkrieg*, and the English by a reliance on the premier navy in the world. Both their European colleagues and their Japanese hosts noted the Americans' remarkable professionalism, remarkable because they served in a small army perpetually starved for funds, whose chief experience consisted of fighting Indians (Pershing was the only observer who had served in Cuba and the Philippines).

Among the other observers were British Major General Ian Hamilton, who was to command at Gallipoli, and General Sir William Nicholsen, Chief of the British Imperial Staff until 1914. Major Enrico Caviglia, who sang arias as he shaved, was a corps commander in World War I and later a marshal of Italy. Charles Covisart of France and Baron von Etzel of Germany faced each other as generals at Verdun. Captain Max Hoffman, who quarreled constantly with his superior von Etzel, was to become the one authentic military genius of World War I, Ludendorff's *éminence gris*.

The Japanese had wanted none of them, but it was hard to refuse a diplomatic courtesy to Britain, the ally that made her war possible, and to the United States, through whose offices the Japanese expected to make peace. Having extended the courtesy to one, the Japanese had to extend it to all. But they exercised an iron control on the observers. The ever-imperturbable and polite General Fujii delivered daily lectures from which the observers learned nothing. Pershing was aware once that General Fujii was detouring the contingent several miles out of the way. On the pretext of going back to his quarters, he made his way forward alone and saw Chinese coolies carrying back scores of Japanese wounded. When he protested the deception, General Fujii explained that Japanese soldiers were not dying in order to furnish information to military observers.

Japanese censorship and secrecy proved formidable obstacles. This impenetrable wall so frustrated the correspondent Jack London that he came back to the United States warning Americans of the "Yellow Peril." When London's critics pointed out that his sympathies were misplaced, that he ought to champion the Japanese cause since the Russians had suppressed a revolution, London replied, "What the hell! I am first of all a white man and only then a Socialist."

There were deep-rooted reasons for Japanese secrecy. The rest of the world, including the Russians, thought after the first battles that the Japanese soldier was invincible, which the Japanese knew was far from the truth. They did not want the observers to learn how hard the fighting bore on their troops. They could have spared themselves the trouble. Pershing prefaced one of his reports with the comment that the Japanese soldier grew just as discouraged in the wet and the cold as any other soldier. He added:

Conscription is far from popular in Japan. Japanese men forwarded many excuses from ill-health to aged relatives to escape it. It is a common thing for those about to be conscripted to leave the province in which they were born and set up in a neighboring province to escape service.

The Japanese had also capitalized on a spy network and come to realize the importance of intelligence. They took no chances with one of the observers betraying his diplomatic status to make revelations to the Russians. In addition, the Japanese were about to embark on a competitive economic race against Europe. They wanted to hide from their allies the contempt most Japanese had for white men. Japanese orderlies always preceded Peyton March and Pershing to warn the troops that the approaching white men were Americans, not Russians. Even so, they were vilified, which annoyed the Americans, although the British seemed to expect it.

Nothing about the British surprised Pershing. He had climbed a hill littered with Russian dead—for the most part bearded, middle-aged reservists. The dead men carried Bibles which had been donated by the British Bible Society. Pershing thought the British never missed a trick. "They sold guns to one side," he said, "and furnished the Good Book to the other."

Although Pershing was always to claim the experience was invaluable, it was unpleasant and arduous duty. He arrived in captured Darien aboard a Japanese troopship, debarking with the soldiers. Moreover, he had been obliged to leave his wife in the middle of their honeymoon—she called out, "Banzai, Jack," as his train left the station. Despite his age, Pershing was the junior officer among the observers and consequently ate at the foot of the table. The correspondents and observers provided their own food, and the Americans laid the best table, principally because they hired a Japanese cook who was facile with the simple American cuisine.

Quarters were in a Chinese village. The houses admitted the wet and cold and the street was always muddy. According to Frederick Palmer, a newspaperman who later served under Pershing and still later became his biographer, life was harder on Black Jack than on the others. Pershing was compulsively neat, devoted to personal cleanliness and physical fitness. He liked riding and hiking and vigorous exercise, all of which Palmer also enjoyed. The two of them often slogged through the muck for an hour's exercise, convincing themselves afterward they were the better for it.

Palmer owned a tent of light, strong canvas, especially made to his order, as a correspondent's privilege in providing for himself. Pershing wanted to purchase it to take on a camping expedition with his wife when his assignment ended. The transfer of the tent began a close and lasting friendship. Palmer felt that what others termed Pershing's bluntness was really a simplicity of approach. He was privileged to listen to daily disquisitions about strategy, and more than thirty years later remembered what Pershing told him. "Grand strategy," said Pershing, "depended upon a nation's political objective, the mission of the army, the terrain, the gaining of the objective sought, the numbers, the supplies, the arms, the roads and the distances to be marched against the enemy's power, positions and matériel."

The observers saw all the basic conditions that would conspire to make World War I a killing stalemate, though not the submarine, the airplane, poison gas, and the tank. All planned for a short war, even though they saw that first shocks did not make armies retreat. They saw massed artillery dominate battles and machine guns become "concentrated infantry." They saw trench warfare make a cavalry attack absolutely useless.

The short-legged Japanese cavalry recruits amused Pershing. They perched on a high saddle, feet barely in the stirrups, a rein held separately in each hand. At the beginning of World War I every warring power mounted division after division of cavalrymen, and they remained until Verdun bled them all so white they moved the horsemen into the trenches.

The invisibility of the Japanese soldier as he deployed for attack was due to his practical use of cover, his training, and his new khaki uniform (which shortly became army issue in the Philippines). Yet the French mounted their early attacks with soldiers wearing red pantaloons. Despite the superiority of German firepower, Lord Kitchener, as late as 1916, was of the opinion that the machine gun was overrated, although he conceded four per battalion might be an advantage. And the Russians, who always outnumbered the Japanese in position, were never able to deploy this superiority all at once. Yet Russia entered World War I confident that its massive supply of men would defeat the Germans. Defeated Russian soldiers complained they were fighting for Korean timber; victorious Japanese soldiers said they were fighting for national survival.

This is not to insist that the observers learned nothing. Pershing saw quickly that direct artillery fire from exposed positions was the quickest way to denude a battery of gun crews. But indirect artillery, its fire guided by sophisticated spotting techniques, including the telephone, decimated assaulting and defending troops. Russian redoubts and trenches were invariably well built and well sited, but lacked overhead cover. The Japanese rarely carried these positions by assault. Instead, artillery and machine gun fire made the Russians crouch down, and while they did the Japanese infantry moved up. Russian officers then pulled their men back. Pershing believed that these positions could have been held if the Russian soldier had been trained to hold them.

Russian discipline and organization were totally incompetent and ineffective. Commanders withdrew troops not knowing that ammunition trains had arrived to replenish their short supplies. At Port Arthur vodka cases got in the way of foodstuffs. On the other hand, the discipline of the Japanese soldier was crucial to victory, not superiority in weapons or position. Straggling, Pershing noted, was unknown in the Japanese army. It was a disgrace for a soldier to be absent from his unit if it was at all possible to be present.

Japanese soldiers fared simply. "Coolies prepare the food," wrote Pershing, "and each squad is served by a man who goes to the galley when the food is cooked and gets the allowance for his squad. The food consists of rice and tea. The tea is cooked in large cauldrons. The rice is cooked in steam and is then placed in large buckets."

It was obvious to the American observers that the Japanese were incapable at critical moments of the quick movement that would insure a decisive result in battle. The Japanese did not move fast because their particular organization and communication precluded bold, quick tactics. To the professional soldier, the victory that surprised the rest of the world came as a result of safe and cautious maneuver.

Far from being able to destroy Kuropatkin's Russians, the Japanese were fought out. They had taken nothing that would force the Russians to make peace. And the Russian army, Pershing thought, was the poorest army in Europe. The Japanese were incapable of waging fierce war any longer. Captain Pershing told Washington that the decisive battle of the war did not occur in Manchuria, but in New Hampshire, around the council table. In 1905 Japan was the one check on colossal Russia's encroachment on the open door policy.

Along with Crowder, March, and MacArthur, Pershing was convinced that the conditions of modern war prohibited quick victories by brilliant movements like Napoleon's at Austerlitz. Battles were of long duration—it took more than two weeks of fierce and grueling battle for the Japanese to take Mukden. Beyond strict discipline, battles required superb stamina. Gone too was the role of the battlefield brigadier and major general who could lead the courageous charge or personally direct the deployment of men. The masses of soldiers maneuvering for battle required administrative skills of rare order to move men and supplies forward.

Firepower placed an inordinate strain on ammunition supply. The Japanese were unable to hide the fact that their huge expenditure of ammunition resulted in low Russian casualties. Pershing, as a brigadier and later as a major general, was to insist on continual training in marksmanship and target procedures. "The bayonet," Pershing wrote, "has become a moral and not a physical weapon." He meant that success in battle no longer depended solely upon closing with the enemy, breast to the line. What counted more was the proper training, the efficient tactical use of arms, and the precise administration of supply and transport. War had become organization.

10

The Brigadier
as Colonialist

When Pershing returned to Japan as a military attaché, he and his wife rented a bungalow on the Hayama seashore outside Tokyo. In the morning, they could see Fujiyama, its cone crusted with snow. In the evening, a light breeze always tinkled the temple bells as it rustled through the pines. On September 20, 1906, when they had returned to Tokyo, Pershing received a wire from the adjutant general: President Roosevelt had promoted him from captain to brigadier general, jumping him over 257 captains, 364 majors, 131 lieutenant colonels, and 110 colonels—862 officers senior to him. Pershing was now one of fourteen brigadier generals in the United States Army and, at forty-six, the youngest save for Leonard Wood, who was only a few months younger.

The promotion was unusual but by no means unique. Among the regular army captains jumped to brigadier were Leonard Wood of the Medical Corps (who had, however, been a colonel of volunteers); J. Franklin Bell of the Cavalry, who had jumped over 1,041 senior officers; William Crozier of Ordnance; A. L. Mills of the Cavalry; and Tasker Bliss, who had jumped from commissary major to the General Staff. Pershing's promotion was special in that this particular captain-jumped-to-brigadier had a father-in-law who was a Senator, the chairman of the Military Affairs

Committee. Every newspaper that noted Pershing's promotion noted also Senator Warren's position, and speculated on that gentleman's probable influence. Senator Warren denied these imputations, and Theodore Roosevelt said, "To promote a man because he married a senator's daughter would be an infamy; and to refuse him promotion for the same reason would be an equal infamy."

But the newspapers continued to misconstrue Roosevelt's motives and accused Senator Warren of manipulation. Roosevelt was never one for tolerating misconstruction. He wrote a letter to Senator Warren that was made public:

> ... Your son-in-law was promoted so strictly on his own merits that I had absolutely forgotten that he was your son-in-law until I received your letter. Even now I cannot remember whether he was married to your daughter or engaged to her at the time he won the victory for which I promoted him (the *March around the Lake*). My impression is that he was not yet married to her. In any event, the promotion was made purely on merits, and unless I am mistaken you never spoke to me on the subject until I had announced that he would be promoted. The article that you enclosed from the *Washington Herald* is a tissue of malicious falsehoods. It is a case of a man being guilty of malicious and willful untruth.

Pershing and his wife missed the byplay. She remained in Tokyo while he was en route to San Francisco, ordered to report to the Commandant of the Department of the West. Many years later, however, Pershing remarked of his promotion that having a Senator for a father-in-law didn't hurt. On presenting himself at the Presidio, Pershing was forthwith ordered to the Philippines. He had to ask permission to return to Manila by way of Tokyo to claim wife, child, and property.

The *Manila News*, in a story widely circulated by the American press, charged that Pershing had been wantonly promiscuous in Mindanao, so wantonly promiscuous that he had fathered two children. The story emanated from officers in the Philippines who were senior to Pershing and were jealous of his promotion. It has been remarked that regular army officers were as busy with their gossip as any number of maiden aunts in a New England quilting bee. Pershing's supposed transgressions inspired dismayed sermons from preachers on sexual morality and disparaging comments from politicians on the honor of our soldiery.

The censorious scolding prompted a backlash. Friends of Pershing, fellow officers, and Philippine missionaries rebutted the charges. They pointed out that it was common for one *datto* to adopt the children of another as a mark of respect, and that in this manner Pershing had "fathered" dozens of Philippine children. It was also common for an unwed mother to fix the paternity of her child on "William Howard Taft," or "General Arsur MacArsur" or "Captain Per-shering."

Frances Warren Pershing wrote to her father that the charges and innuendos were false and base. Pershing himself denied the charges publicly and, in his private correspondence to friends, said he had been libeled. On arriving in the Philippines he secured affidavits of his innocence from the woman named as his paramour, and from her husband, and forwarded them to the War Department, along with an endorsement of his probity by Leonard Wood. Later, the scandal cost him the post of Superintendent of the Military Academy, when the *New York World* exhumed it in 1912. Pershing sued for libel on this occasion and won a retraction.

More to the point is Theodore Roosevelt's rationale in promoting Pershing. Roosevelt enunciated it in his State of the Union Message to the Congress, delivered on December 7, 1903.* He asked Congress to enact legislation that would permit the President to promote officers below the rank of brigadier:

> The only people that are contented with a system of promotion by seniority are those who are contented with the triumph of mediocrity over excellence. On the other hand, a system which encouraged the exercise of social or political favoritism in promotions would be even worse. But it would surely be easy to devise a method of promotion from grade to grade in which the opinion of higher offi-

---

*Pershing was the first junior officer ever mentioned in a State of the Union address.

cers... upon the candidate should be decisive upon the standing and promotion of the latter. Just such a system now obtains at West Point.... Ability, energy, fidelity and all other similar qualities determine the rank of a man year after year in West Point and his standing in the army when he graduates... but from that time on, all effort to find which man is best or worst, and reward or punish him accordingly, is abandoned.... Until this system is changed we cannot hope that our officers will be of as high a grade as we have a right to expect.... Moreover, when a man renders such services as Captain Pershing rendered last spring in the Moro campaign, it ought to be possible to reward him without at once jumping him to the grade of brigadier general.

Promoting a captain to brigadier was something Theodore Roosevelt had to do. He was not only the first twentieth-century President but the first, consciously and deliberately, without a crisis motivation, to set about enlarging the offices and the power of the presidency. One of these offices he wanted to enlarge was the President's role as commander-in-chief of the armed forces. He accomplished this by Root's reforms of the army organization and by the dispatch of the Great White Fleet around the world.

It is by now a truism that far-reaching and innovative military reforms transpire under civilian presidents. Neither Ulysses S. Grant nor the generals who followed him into the White House nor Dwight D. Eisenhower ever dreamed of accomplishing the military reforms of the two Roosevelts and Harry Truman.

Pershing's new post took him to Luzon, to the command of Fort McKinley, a trolley ride from Manila. He replaced Colonel Henry Kingsbury, who had been a captain in the Sixth Cavalry at Fort Bayard when Pershing joined the regiment in 1886. Though appreciably older, Kingsbury was now Pershing's junior officer and was bound by protocol to be the first member of the post to pay his respects to its new commander. Kingsbury told George MacAdam that he never got the chance. His phone rang on the day of Pershing's arrival and when he picked it up, he heard, "How are you, Colonel?"

"I'm all right, General," he said, recognizing Pershing's voice.

"How are you?"

"You don't like my coming here, perhaps?"

"Why, General, I'm glad you came to the post."

"May I come over and see you?" Pershing asked.

"I'd be highly honored if you did," said Kingsbury. Kingsbury thought the simple gesture by Pershing was inspired by the memory of the slights and minor humiliations that befall captains overage in grade. A captain who had raised a family in a post residence had to surrender the house on the instant if an incoming major desired it, and a captain's wife would have to surrender without murmur her office in a ladies' organization if the major's wife wanted it. On a military conveyance, all junior officers and their wives had to disembark when senior officers boarded.

These, however, were not the forms Pershing wanted. He wanted discipline and unswerving loyalty. For several years after his promotion, contemporaries saw that he was socially uncomfortable and ill at ease among majors and colonels who normally would have outranked him. But he was never ill at ease in giving orders.

Pershing's situation as a brigadier sprung fully grown from Zeus's head was replicated by his senior officer, Major General Leonard Wood, commanding the Division of the Philippines. "The Army," wrote Pershing in his memoirs, as though his own experience could be subtracted, "had never become reconciled to the promotion of a captain in the medical corps with little military training to the rank of brigadier general of the line. But while General Wood was not a trained soldier, he had the good sense to select trained soldiers on his staff and also to permit those of the line who were trained to perform their duties to do so without interference."

Wood was not without reservations about Pershing. When Pershing sought to stage large-scale maneuvers, Wood worried whether detaching other units for Pershing's command was "tieing a tail to the Pershing kite." Though the relationship between the two was never more than professional, still this relationship was to have symbolic and prophetic overtones during World War I. Pershing and Wood had much in common. Wood was brainy and affected a dog-eared riding crop. Pershing was stern and insisted on the Sam Browne belt, for which there was no use at all. Each was wholeheartedly intent on his own orbit. Friendship was an indifferent matter to both.

Pershing wasn't long at Fort McKinley when Taft, now the Secretary of War and the likely Republican-designate to succeed Roosevelt, came to Manila to inaugurate the islands' first Assembly. Before the state dinner in his honor, Taft discovered he had forgotten his waistcoat. Pershing volunteered to find him another, no easy task for a man of Taft's amazing girth. But Pershing succeeded. He borrowed a waistcoat from Frank Helms, chief of the Island Transportation Department, who was also no lightweight. Still, Helms's waistcoat squeezed Taft, so Pershing tore it in half and pinned the two sides to Taft's shirt.

It was at this dinner that Taft, who believed the Philippine Assembly the instrument by which the islands would secure independence, announced that its Speaker would take rank immediately after the American Governor-General, a ruling that did little to endear Taft to the military or business communities. "That even the Vice-Governor and the Major General commanding the American forces," Pershing wrote, "to say nothing of all the commissioners should in the future follow the Filipino speaker and his wife in public functions was thought to make natives haughty and difficult." Americans were already aware that the Filipinos were securing by legalisms what they had not secured by insurrection. Taft's decision also disregarded American racial prejudice, which was by no means covert.

But Taft's action struck a responsive chord in Pershing. He was at the moment dealing with an impassioned correspondence from a captain and his wife over a lieutenant who had married a Filipina. The captain wanted the lieutenant transferred because "he had become a squaw man, hurting the service in general and us here in particular." When Pershing took no action, the captain's wife wrote, begging Pershing to transfer the scandalous pair to another command "where the lieutenant would be given a chance to atone by hard work and faithful service." The social distress and clamor

left Pershing unmoved. He was eventually to promote the lieutenant to captain, by which time the new captain and the old had gone
native together, at least to the extent of drinking beer in each
other's company.

Pershing reflected on the men he served with:

The commander of the Department of Luzon was General John F.
Weston, who had been promoted from the subsistence department
for exceptional services in Cuba. He had seen line service before
going to staff but often spoke of himself as a grocer. He had a
delightful sense of humor and it was a pleasure to be in his company. Sometimes he indulged in jests at the expense of his superiors
and others. For instance, in speaking of Major General Adolphus
W. Greely, the distinguished Arctic explorer who, it will be remembered, ran out of rations, obliging the party to live on human
flesh, Weston said, "Now there's Greely; why he never had but one
small command and he ate that." And of Major General Hugh L.
Scott, who had mastered the Indian sign language, Weston would
say, "Yes, but he learned it after all the Indians had forgotten it."
He always referred to General Wood as "Old Doc Wood." Once
when I applied for the return of an artillery officer who was assigned temporarily, General Wood disapproved and General Weston
in returning the application could not refrain from making a joke of
it. He added this facetious interrogation to the official reply he sent
me: "If a doctor (Wood) can command a division, and a grocer (me)
can command a department, and a cavalry captain (Pershing) can
command an infantry brigade, why can't a lieutenant of engineers
command a battery of artillery?"

In the eighteen months he commanded the McKinley garrison,
Pershing pioneered in brigade maneuvers. He encountered many
commissioned and noncommissioned officers who understood little
of their field duties, a failing that would make them inefficient in
time of war. He directed the men of his command to learn how to
take long marches, read maps, reconnoiter, and attack simulated
enemy positions.

The finished soldier [Pershing said] must have special training in
such work—brigade training—to develop initiative; he must know

how to estimate distances quickly and accurately; he has to be good at scouting and trailing; he should know the best way to attack positions over unknown ground and how to construct hasty entrenchments and field fortifications. He cannot learn these on the parade ground.

On one of these maneuvers a young lieutenant reported that he could not get a rope across a surging river. Pershing said, "You must find a way to execute your orders. Now follow me." Fastening the rope to his pommel, Pershing swam his horse across the raging water and returned to find a chastened lieutenant. He explained to the lieutenant that he did not give orders he thought men incapable of achieving.

He set up schools for officers and enlisted men in scouting, rifle fire, mule packing, baking, and carpentry. These schools were not separate details, but part of the daily command.

In July, 1908, Pershing was reassigned. He and his family left the Philippines by way of Vladivostok, where customs inspectors uncovered Pershing's revolver and suspected immediately that he was an anarchist. His train traversed north Asia, a land vast enough to impress a cavalryman of the American West with its depths, mountain ranges, and somber forests, the trees shaking off continents of heavy snow. "Imagine travelling in a modern train," he wrote, "from Alaska to Panama in the early days when the settlements in Canada, the United States, and Mexico were only begun, and you will get an idea of what the journey was."

In Moscow, typically, he shopped with Mrs. Pershing for ikons, and when she found a perfect samovar, he wrestled with it through the capitals of Europe. The family abandoned St. Petersburg when the bellboys began dropping dead of cholera, and Warsaw when the hotel ran out of prunes for the children. In Berlin, "where clicking heels were almost as frequent as the ticking of the clock," he saw the "most complete military machine that had ever been organized." From Brussels he went to see Waterloo. In Paris he received orders to hold, because a European war seemed imminent. If it came, Pershing was to serve as a military observer.

There were two causes for alarm in 1908. In the spring, Alfred von Tirpitz had announced Germany would build dreadnoughts in number to equal those of Britain. The dreadnought was a battleship, armed only with big guns, all of the same caliber, which naval experts thought would make all other ships of the line obsolete. Admiral Tirpitz's announcement was a direct challenge to Britain's naval superiority. Britain promised to build two dreadnoughts for every one Germany launched, a race that was a financial impossibility for both governments, but which insured Britain's hostility in the event of a European war.

The second alarm was given by Emperor Franz-Joseph, who annexed Bosnia and Herzegovina into the Austro-Hungarian empire that summer. This was a challenge to Russian ambitions. Kaiser Wilhelm of Germany issued an ultimatum that, unless the czar recognized the annexation unequivocally and without delay, Berlin would not restrain Austria-Hungary from an attack to secure the two provinces. Russia, drained economically by the Russo-Japanese War and politically wracked by dissension at home, swallowed the humiliation.

Pershing, in describing these events from the vantage point of the 1930s, interrupted his narrative to urge American "preparedness" for what seemed the likely prospect of World War II. Military men define preparedness as the nation's ability to maintain economic strength, national unity, a spirit of self-sacrifice and, above all, confidence in the armed forces. But it is more than that. Preparedness is a political concept that began to make sense to some Americans after 1898 and became an imperative for even more Americans after 1918. Military preparedness discourages war, which is to say military preparedness is a way of keeping what you have without the necessity of fighting for it. Preparedness has always proved a hard concept for Americans to assimilate, because they believe that what they have (or what is now called their "spheres of influence") has willingly gravitated toward them. They often resent paying hard money to preserve what is morally theirs—while preparedness does not cost as much as war, it still commands a heavy cost.

While the Pershings waited for war that fall of 1908 they studied French, and Pershing took the time to go over the battlefield of Metz, where an entire French army had surrendered to the Germans in 1870. As a ten-year-old in Laclede, he had followed the course of the war in the newspapers and listened to neighbors in front of his father's store compare the campaign to those waged by Ulysses S. Grant and Robert E. Lee. The battle of Metz was then considered the perfect maneuver of modern war, but soldiers soon learned it was the anomalous battle. Modern war was typified by the decimation of the cavalry across the south African veldt, the loosening grip of sick soldiers on San Juan Hill, and the thousands of shivering men lined in trenches in Manchuria.

When Pershing arrived in Washington in February, 1909, William Howard Taft, about to be inaugurated President on March 4, chose him as a member of the inaugural ball committee. Pershing was to manage the festivities. The inaugural ball was held in the Pension Building. Politicians and their wives came from every state in the Union—"one of the gratifications of the pilgrimage being that their names," wrote Pershing, "were telegraphed back home as 'among the notables present.'" One of the adornments of the ball was the presence of ninety-two of the handsomest men in America, two from each state—but for some reason, Pershing noted, none of them Democrats. When the consort made its appearance at the Pension Building, where the ball was in progress, no one knew what to do with them. "These stars," wrote Pershing, "who were expected to form a galaxy of satellites about the new President were about to go into eclipse when they made an appeal to me to save them from this humiliation." Pershing placed these men around the fountain, an antic staging later copied by Florenz Ziegfeld, who substituted shapely women for a softer yet livelier effect.

Though he wanted to return to the Philippines, Pershing entered the Army and Navy Hospital at Hot Springs, Arkansas. Here he was finally cured of malaria and many of its after-effects, including heart palpitations. He had been a cigar smoker, wreathing himself constantly in a poisonous aura. The doctors suggested that he abandon the habit. He said later that giving up cigars wasn't hard at all, what was hard was making up his mind. He turned to chewing tobacco which, if it improved his health, doomed to a quick withering the potted plants he kept in his office instead of cuspidors.

The hospital stay aroused his interest in soldiers' health. He exchanged a lengthy and profitable correspondence with his doctor, Colonel George Deshon, about physical fitness. Deshon pointed out that asking a soldier to cover a mile in five or six minutes was foolhardy when it was more likely that a soldier would be asked to cover twenty miles in a day. The ability to perform the first precluded a man's accomplishing the second. Deshon also pointed out that since much of an officer's work was sedentary it was wasteful and futile to insist he be as hard as a farmboy. The extraordinary time it took to keep muscles hard could be devoted to other pursuits. Muscles, said Deshon, should be only as hard as the task that needs doing. Pershing became one of the first commanders to insist on daily calisthenic exercises rather than muscular ordeals as a way of keeping men fit.

The brightest prize of the army administration was military command of the Moro Province in the Philippines. It made a brigadier both commander of a large, if widespread, garrison as well as civil governor. Pershing succeeded to this post in November, 1909, appointed by William Howard Taft. The appointment was strongly seconded by the Philippines' Governor-General, James Forbes Smith. Pershing would command 5,500 officers and men, 2,500 of them Filipinos organized into a constabulary.

The Moro Province consisted of Mindanao, Basilan, Jolo, and the comet tail of islands that stretched across the Sulu Sea to Borneo. These were then potentially (and are now) the richest, though the most sparsely settled, islands of the Philippines. The Moro Province had more than 500,000 inhabitants in 1909: 325,000 of them Moros, 85,000 Filipinos, and 105,000 headhunters and wildmen. The province was so far from pacification and civilization (outside of the Lake Lanao district) that the United States had considered separating the Moro Archipelago from the rest of the Philippines. It put aside the notion only when it aroused the cupidity of European powers.

The Spaniards had made only minimal gains around the shoreline of Mindanao, and had established one garrison on the islands of the Sulu Archipelago, on Jolo. Under Generals J. Franklin Bell, Leonard Wood, and Tasker Bliss, the United States Army had secured permanent military establishments on Mindanao, Basilan, and Jolo. But the army had not brought law or the opportunities for profitable industry to the accommodating Moros on these islands. When the United States Army ended Moro piracy, the warlike Moro tribes simply turned upon their more peaceful land-locked neighbors.

Pershing decided that hunting Moro bandits was the full-time duty of his garrison. He stationed small detachments of soldiers throughout the interior, to guarantee the peaceful existence of those tribes that wanted to raise hemp, produce timber, or farm. It was a scattershot method of bringing peace, and dissipated the large garrison into minuscule detachments. Pershing admitted that his method did not promote military efficiency, but he argued, "No influence can ever reach these people except the influence that comes by direct contact."

The plan produced results. Soldiers drove off marauders and tracked down bandits, aided often by the Moro villagers. Once Pershing was presented with a burlap bag that contained the head of a notorious bandit. The body had been too heavy to carry through the backcountry. "It looks like the right head," he said, shuddering.

White planters exploited native labor by paying low wages and charging excessive prices in the company store. Pershing instituted a minimum wage and, despite the tears and complaints of the entrepreneurs, established price controls. He promulgated a labor law that simplified employer-employee relationships: employers could no longer sue employees who did not appear for work and an employer without work could not be brought to litigation.

Officers brutally punished Moro misdemeanors and winked at

military atrocities. When Pershing told his provost marshal he wanted discipline, he meant he did not want sermons, pep talks, or coaxing; he wanted post stockades for military personnel who broke the law. For Moro miscreants he established a provincial prison at San Ramón, a 2,500-acre farm northwest of Zamboanga that served as an experimental work camp. The prisoners cleared the land, built the barracks, and planted coconuts in a climate so conducive and in soil so fertile that the profits from the grove were eventually to maintain the entire Philippine prison system.

Pershing published newspapers in the Moro dialects; they always included one of his jovial but paternal letters. He set up an island fair to which twenty thousand Moros trekked to sell their produce and their crafts. The Moros from Jolo sold their entire brass collection and went home enthusiastically rich; and the Bagabos, who designed costumes of multicolored shells, also went home similarly rich but naked. Pershing traveled to each of the five districts of Mindanao, assuring the Moro *dattos* and sultans that the United States wanted the Moros to live according to the teaching of the Koran. He promised that his government would pay them fairly for their produce and for their labor in building roads, schools, and hospitals.

Good intentions and good deeds, however, do not make a stable government. In 1909 a stable government was, in the words of General Leonard Wood, "A government under which capital seeks investment at normal rates of interest." The main island of Luzon was ripe for investment. The Visayan Islands below it—Negros, Cebu, Panay, Samar, and Leyte—showed promise, though their populace still raised only corn, abaca, copra, and rice, the mainstays of a subsistence economy. But Mindanao and the other islands of the Sulu Archipelago, potentially the richest of the Philippines, contained a population with a violent, piratical past, some of whom were anxious to rend the land with religious fanaticism.

In the process of ordinary trade, when one Moro disagreed with another, he resolved their differences by shooting him. Moros, who had a low birth rate, replenished their tribes by capturing women from the northern islands. Every so often, American soldiers had to beat off these raiding parties, or small units had to plunge into the jungles to rescue kidnapped maidens. With alarming regularity warriors either ran amuck, boloing to pieces anyone who crossed their path, or went *juramentado,* in which case they boloed only white Christians, regardless of rank or sex. Religious fanaticism in one area fanned it in another as lawlessness in one area fanned it in another.

What was called for, Pershing decided, was to disarm the entire Moro Province, to confiscate or buy every rifle, pistol, *campilan,* *bolo,* and *krise* on the islands. It was not an original idea. The army had disarmed insurgents on Luzon some years before and other generals had suggested the same program for the Moro Province. Every attempt at disarmament, however, had brought province-wide mutiny. General Leonard Wood, who left the Philippines in 1910 to become Chief of Staff, advised Pershing:

> You cannot disarm the people. It means they will bury their best arms and turn in a few poor ones, especially some who want to make a show of obedience. It is an extremely ill-timed move. It will bring on an embarrassing situation at an unfortunate time. [Wood meant the oncoming presidential election of 1912.] Moreover it is highly uncalled for. It seems to be rather ill-judged and ill-timed although apparently well-meant.

However, General Wood was now in Washington and Pershing was in Zamboanga. Pershing would go on with his program to disarm the Moros until ordered to desist, an order he cannily presumed would never come. He cut roads into the disaffected areas and held conferences with every Moro leader whose sympathy was genuine. He promised the Governor-General to show force only where necessary and only in rare instances, but he concluded, "Disarmament must come and I desire to have it accomplished under the present insular and provincial administration." The force he would use, he explained, was only to place the weak, law-abiding Moros on an equal footing with the strong.

On September 8, 1911, Pershing promulgated Executive Order

24, which made it a crime to carry a rifle, gun, or cutting blade. He made barely perceptible progress in Mindanao and no progress at all in Jolo. Disarming a civilian population is basically police work and is best accomplished through precincts. The American army was operating with a police mentality but without precincts. To disarm a people, a general must know how many weapons they have; otherwise he will never know when he has the last one. Without a registry of weapons and a customs manifest of weapons imported, a soldier might better prepare to defend his garrison.

Pershing's program in Jolo, a hot spot of disaffection, mutiny, and religious fervor, could only prompt a pitched battle. Jolo, one hundred miles west of Zamboanga, with the island of Basilan between it and Mindanao, seemed advantageous to the Moros. The United States could spare only a small detachment for its garrison, and the Moros could easily spot any reinforcements. Whenever the island garrison was reinforced, the Moros laid low until the soldiers withdrew to quell urgent troubles elsewhere. Then the Moros charged out again, and the only safety for the soldiers and American personnel was within the wooden walls of Jolo City. When the Moros rushed an American camp at Lake Seit, near the city, Pershing decided force would have to settle the matter of disarmament.

He reinforced the Jolo City garrison and moved the command out of the city to the east, near Mount Dajo. Here the men entrenched and cleared a wide perimeter which was strung with barbed wire. The entrenchments blocked the Taglibi Moros, who lived on the mountain, from all access to the fields and the sea. In late November, the Moros tried to breach these defenses, and were repulsed. Pershing now would have to move against them in their mountain lair, a decision he determined upon with some reluctance. He well knew the repercussions of a bloody victory in "unfortunate times."

Five years before, General Leonard Wood had engaged these same Moros in the Bud Dajo *cotta* sanctuary atop the mountain, losing a hundred men while killing the six hundred defenders, among whom were many women and children. The victory sparked

outrage in America. Wood nearly lost his command and would
have if Theodore Roosevelt and William Howard Taft had not
backed his action. Even Pershing had remarked to Frances, "I
would not have Bud Dajo on my conscience for the fame of Napoleon." But Wood was innocent of one charge: wanton killing.
Moros subscribed to the belief that the families of warriors should
not survive them. They took women and children into the *cottas*
well aware of, even courting, the danger. The women dressed like
men, wielded weapons with them, often holding infants and young
children as shields before the fighting warriors.

Pershing did not want another such victory. The purpose of his
show of force was to convince all Moros on Jolo that the United
States meant business but not slaughter. Consequently, he
marched the thousand-man force from its defensive positions in
two columns up the mountain with firm orders: "Set up no outposts nearer than 300 yards of the summit. Avoid contact if possible. Do not return fire, but keep hidden."

With the soldiers now near the summit, Pershing dispatched
friendly Moros to the *cotta* with the offer that all who would
surrender their guns could go home. Twenty Moros defected. As
the force waited through the week, another two hundred surrendered. On December 23, Pershing sent his last message: no more
surrender terms save unconditional surrender. The next morning
the *cotta* was deserted. Its defenders had slipped from it down the
mountainside, but remained cut off by the outposts. Some of the
Moro diehards tried to breach the American lines and failed.
Forty-six surrendered and were imprisoned. Pershing demanded a
number of guns from the islanders in return for each prisoner.
The remaining Moros were flushed by a skirmish line that moved
around the mountain like a cook's finger around the outside of a
bowl. In all, twelve Moros were killed and several more were
wounded. Pershing had conducted a campaign that was successful
without being newsworthy. It revealed to his superiors his resolution and restraint, a notable accomplishment in a pacification program that had often spilled barrels of blood.

The victory at Bud Dajo, however, did not end fanaticism on

Jolo. It quelled the eastern part of the island, but in the west Moros under Sultan Amil began killing Americans as soon as Pershing's reinforcements returned to Zamboanga. Moros who had surrendered their arms were victimized by those who had not. Fanatics fired into Jolo City itself, and the wives and children of military personnel had to be evacuated. Governor-General Forbes offered to dispatch any number of troops Pershing needed. Pershing replied that while force subdued a Moro, a *show* of force never did. "You cannot bluff him," Pershing told Forbes. "If he takes a notion to fight, he will fight." And if it came to a fight, Pershing said he had enough men at hand.

United States soldiers came out of Jolo City and in two quick skirmishes chased five thousand Moros to another mountain crater, Bad Bagsak. Enough Moros were ensconced in their *cotta* so that the economy of the island was threatened. If these Moros did not till their fields now, other Moros would starve later. Pershing conducted protracted negotiations, promising that, if the Moros would come down from the mountain to their fields, he would pull the troops back into the city. He determined that the first priority was getting the crop in, the harvest of guns would have to come later.

The Moros embarked on even bolder attacks after taking care of their fields. They terrorized Jolo. Further palavering was fruitless. Pershing had retreated once; to retreat again was simply to make more enemies. He faced a dilemma: by moving in force against Amil, he would stampede an entire provincial area to the *cotta* atop Bad Bagsak. How many women and children would perish? Too many, he thought. So he planned to take Amil and his warriors by surprise, in the hopes that he could separate the noncombatants from the warring force.

He canceled field operations, ordered all United States troops into Jolo City, and sent several detachments from Zamboanga into the back hills of Mindanao. Then he boarded the transport *Wright*, which was bound for northwest Mindanao, even farther from Jolo. Once out of Zamboanga, the *Wright* changed course and took on Captain George C. Charlton and his company of Philippine Scouts at Basilan. At noon the next day, off the coast of Jolo at Siasi, it took on Captain Taylor A. Nichols and another company. These troops disembarked at Jolo City at midnight, where the *Wright* berthed with its lights out. The two detachments of scouts headed for Bad Bagsak to the south. Pershing ordered all the troops into the field by daybreak. So well had the secret been kept that, when Pershing's aide delivered the orders to the Jolo commandant, all the officers were in dress whites at a post summer dance. Fifty men of the Eighth Cavalry marched out with two field guns. Six infantry companies boarded four transports that had slipped in beside the *Wright* and sailed around the island to disembark on the beaches and invest Bad Bagsak from the south. The surprise was virtually complete. Thousands of Moros in the field now had no way of joining the fierce contingent on the mountaintop. It remained for Pershing to blast Amil from the crest or coax him down.

Bad Bagsak was an extinct volcano. It was 220 feet higher than Bud Dajo, with a horseshoe-shaped crater 1,000 yards in the curve, its prongs 800 yards apart. This gap was the most accessible entryway, but it was guarded by Moro trenches. *Cottas* grew like excrescences along the curve, the most heavily fortified of them at the heel. The mountain itself rose precipitously from the valley, sheer vertical rock ascending the last 300 feet.

The battle for this fort, which lasted for five days, began on June 10, 1913. It took a day for the troops to work their way up to level ground from which to start banging away with the field guns. Another column of infantry scrambled near enough to knock out one of the *cottas* on the prong. But this brought fire upon them from the remaining forts and the soldiers had to dig in with their mess kits since they had no entrenching tools. It was a black night and the infantrymen slept by turn.

While these men pinned down the Moros in the morning, the cavalrymen disassembled their mountain guns and began transporting the pieces by hoist up the cliffs; some of the men climbing hand-over-hand by the sinuous vines. By nightfall the guns were up, though still disassembled. It was obvious that, in the morning, these guns could bring some of the *cottas* under direct fire. In the *cotta* nearest the guns, the Moros dressed in battle finery on which they had sewn gold coins. At daybreak they charged. The crews worked the guns, blunting and turning back the attack. On the other prong, the infantry swept into two more *cottas* before coming up against a narrow ridge that Moro fire effectively defended.

Pershing then sent the mountain guns even higher against the heavily defended *cotta*, Bunga, that guarded the last *cotta*, Bagsak. The cavalry took the place, then found they could not elevate the guns to fire upon Bagsak. Pershing ordered them to break off the fight, move the guns back in disassembly, assemble them again, and begin firing. This took twelve hours. The soldiers were also busy burying the dead, because the intense tropic heat, continual rain, and flies and insects made the corpses loathesome.

The next morning Pershing brought up Philippine Scouts to a position in front of the Moro trenches which, once taken, would expose Bagsak to attack on three sides. The battle for these trenches lasted nine hours. The Scouts had no room to maneuver. Scouts rolled down with spears quivering in their chests or tumbled from bullets that smashed their heads. The attack faltered. At that moment, Pershing came to the front line and, waving his .45, directed the American officers to rise, go to the fore, and lead the Filipinos in a charge. The effect was electric. Pershing's aide, James L. Collins, remembered that "a wave of energy seemed to sweep over the attackers and they pushed the assault. Disregarding the flying barongs, they began to tear down bamboo fences on the right. Soon they flanked the trench defenders who dashed out to throw themselves against the troops. But it was over."

The mountain guns came up and blasted away at Bagsak and soon there was no more enemy left. Atop a mountain littered with expended cartridge shells, webbing, tools, stakes, iron fragments, spears, clothing, and bones, were the bodies of fifteen dead and twenty-five wounded Americans and five hundred Moros, of whom fifty were women and children.

The United States had joined a battle it could not lose, though if Pershing had two hundred men on the mountaintop, he had a lot.

Perhaps that was one of the reasons Pershing wrote the War Department that he would not accept the Congressional Medal of Honor, for which he had been recommended by his junior officers. "I went to that part of the line," he explained, "because my presence there was needed."* Pershing was always a puritan about promotions and decorations, yet there was something undeniably splendid in his action.

Bad Bagsak frightened the dissident Moros and the mountain victory helped bring a peace to the province. Because of peace, Pershing claimed—and his superiors supported his claims—that he had disarmed the Moros. Probably he knew better. It is as hard to disarm a people as it is to make them give up a religious belief. In 1917, in fact, the Moros staged another uprising on Mindanao, this time with repeating rifles.

When Francis Burton Harrison became Woodrow Wilson's appointee as Governor-General in late 1913, he found the Moro Province completely quiescent. Two hundred miles of telephone wire had been strung, a thousand miles of roads built, and the new banana and grain plantations were thriving. In addition, the district governors and secretaries who administered the Moro Province were all civilians. The last military man holding civil office in Mindanao was Pershing himself. Pershing refused to stay on, pointing out that four years in the island was usually enough to start undermining a man's health, and his was failing. He also pointed out that it was time he was replaced by a civilian if the work of establishing a free, stable, and representative Filipino government was to continue.

Thus ended Pershing's experience in the Philippines, an experience that had advanced his career, but, as he saw clearly, was all the Philippines had ever done for anyone. When still a captain, Pershing realized that the United States had not needed to occupy Cuba because it was easy to send an American expeditionary force to the Caribbean. Indeed, the United States has sent an armed

*Franklin D. Roosevelt awarded Pershing the Distinguished Service Cross for the action at Bagsak on Pershing's eightieth birthday.

expedition to Cuba on four different occasions. But the United States occupied the Philippines because it was hard to send an army to the Pacific. The Philippines was the first American outpost in Asia, a continent to which the United States considered its future was somehow wedded. In the long run, the only advantage the United States or the Philippines realized from the occupation was the military mission.

The archipelago was never destined to become a great way station to exploit trade with the Orient. And while Merritt, MacArthur, Otis, Wood, Bell, and Pershing eventually made it a safe place for investment, they could not make it an honest one. America and the world economy were finding uses for Philippine products, especially hemp, sugar, timber, and minerals. But as the world discovered these products, the Filipinos were discovering corruption.

Woodrow Wilson's Administration persuaded the Congress to pass the Jones Bill in 1916, which augmented Philippine self-government and, among other benefits, allowed the Filipinos to charter the Philippine National Bank. Capitalized by Wall Street, the bank's purpose was to facilitate the rapid development of the archipelago's economy. By 1920 Wall Street learned that the directors of the bank had dealt out so many unsecured loans that $24 million had simply evaporated. The bank's reserves, which should have been retained in New York, had also vanished in alarming fashion.

Similarly, American rail industries had capitalized the Manila Railroad Company, which piled up astronomical losses in only eight years. By 1921 the Islands were insolvent. United States economists and investment experts set to straightening up the mess. In doing so they discovered that land reform had totally failed. The Philippine legislature had abolished the American-inspired Court of Land Registration some time before. The only sector of the Philippine economy with plentiful monetary resources was that of the aristocratic landowning class created by the Spaniards. They dominated the legislature and, instead of redistributing lands, had grabbed off the estates themselves at cheap rates.

Democracy and equal opportunity have always been problematic for the people of this archipelago. William Howard Taft warned the American electorate in 1912 that only 3 percent of the Filipinos voted and only 5 percent read the public press; to confer democracy on such a society was to subject the great mass to the dominance of an oligarchical and exploiting minority. "The idea that public office is a public trust," Taft said, "has not been planted in the Filipino mind by experience and the conception that an officer who fails in his duty by embezzlement and otherwise is violating an obligation is difficult to grasp."

Still, the only Asians to side with the Western powers in World War II were the Filipinos (although there were indeed collaborators, among them Aguinaldo). Of the 50,000 defenders of Bataan, 47,000 were Filipinos and of the eleven division commanders, five were natives.

During World War I the Japanese cast their lot with the Allies, but instead of fighting, concentrated on expropriating Germany's leased territory in the Shantung Province of China and in occupying the German protectorates in the Marshall, Marianas, and Caroline islands in the Pacific, cutting across America's line of communication. Between 1918 and 1939 the Japanese population in the Philippines increased by 17,000 immigrants, and Japanese owned considerable amounts of agricultural land by the mid-1930s. In Manila, Davao, and Iloilo strong Japanese enclaves flourished to become a well-organized fifth column. Pershing himself deported two Japanese consular employees who were arrested for spying in 1912. That year the army discovered that someone had stolen the plans for the defense of Corregidor. Neither Pershing nor any other general officer doubted it was the Japanese.

Before he left the Philippines Pershing presided over a staff-engendered plan against Japanese invasion. The plan called for a defense of the Bataan Peninsula rather than the northern passes of Luzon or Manila. It was a workable plan, although staff officers

were skeptical even then about a successful defense. Douglas
MacArthur adopted this plan because he was sure that the addition of thirty-five B-17 bombers could effectively disrupt the
Japanese supply line. But in 1941 the Japanese caught these bombers on the ground. At that, the defense of Bataan was less a
military defeat than a failure in organization. Food supplies failed,
medical aid and drugs were unobtainable; twenty thousand civilian
refugees utterly confused military movement. Yet the defenders
held the Japanese at bay for three months, long enough for a fleet,
if there had been one, to have engaged in a decisive battle.

A more successful plan that Pershing left behind was to turn
mountainous Mindanao into a guerrilla bastion. During the war,
Colonel Wendell Fertig not only built up an army of thirty-four
thousand Filipinos, but formed a civil government with law courts,
currency, post offices, and hospitals. In both Mindanao and the
Visayan Islands, the Japanese could occupy only coastal towns and
the constant guerrilla warfare prevented them from using the
Philippines either as a granary or as a secure base for a wider
Pacific campaign against the Hawaiian Islands.

EAGLE BEARER

The soldier who carries the eagle is the first centurion in the first rank of the first legion.

Julius Caesar
Commentaries

11

The Maw

Zamboanga is only seven degrees above the equator, but it is on the Sulu Sea and the prevailing winds clear it of humidity and blow away the insects. In Pershing's time Zamboanga had crooked, narrow cobblestone streets, great rain trees, and a sweep of curving beach. The homes built by the Spaniards had delicately wrought iron window grilles and the shanties and the shacks of the populace were made graceful by the profusion of flowers, frangipani, hibiscus, poinsettia, and bougainvillea, which blossomed without tending. Mrs. Pershing loved this city and her husband remembered this tour of duty as the happiest of his life.

The governor's residence in which they lived was an old Spanish barracks, a spacious two-story building in which translucent seashells served for windows. It was finished in Philippine mahogany, a wood so hard it often will not float, and whose texture and grain are as colorful as a tapestry. On three sides of the residence were broad verandas, and the dining room could seat sixty. Coconut trees lined the entryway like sentinels.

The house overlooked the Basilan Strait of unimaginable blue. The Pershings swam every morning, diving from the pier when the tide was in, wading over clean sea sands to deep water when it was out. Frances was an excellent swimmer and could strike out for a

157

half-mile in the water. Pershing had the stroke of most Midwest-
erners, which is only strong enough to save them from drowning
in a flood. He splashed along in his depth, guarding the children,
waving at her to come in. They rode every afternoon, Pershing
with the welded seat of the cavalryman, Frances sidesaddle, an
accomplished equestrienne from Wyoming. They were served in
this palace by a Filipino houseboy, a Japanese amah, and Ah-
Ching, a Chinese cook. There were two soldiers who also waited
upon them: a black private named Johnson, who was their
coachman, and a corporal named Frank Lanckton, Pershing's orderly. Both soldiers drank. Johnson was once so drunk he fell
asleep in his box and Pershing, annoyed, climbed up, took the
reins, and made the woozy soldier walk home. It took the general
longer to detect Lanckton's drinking. Whenever Pershing suspected him, Lanckton, who held his liquor well, swore on his
mother's grave that he never touched a drop. Both soldiers were
loyal and faithful, their deportment good, so Pershing only complained. He took both wherever he went, Lanckton serving with
him through World War I.

Twice during these years Pershing was sent on diplomatic missions, once to Hong Kong, once to Japan. In 1911, he went to Hong
Kong as America's representative to that colony's celebration of the
coronation of George V. Things went off as swimmingly as a proper
Englishman could want, except on the night of the coronation
when soldiers on the mountainside set off a fireworks display that
spelled out "Go save the King." Everybody noticed the misspelling
but no one said anything.

Pershing went to Japan as the special representative of the President to the emperor's funeral in 1912. Here he was with Philan-
der Knox, Taft's Secretary of State, when they spied the American
ambassador drunk. Unlike Englishmen, both Pershing and Knox
warned the ambassador to straighten up. Pershing confessed awe
when General Nogi, the victor of the Russo-Japanese War, committed hara-kari in grief at the emperor's passing and his wife
followed him with her own suicide.

The Pershing's first child, Helen Elizabeth, had been born in Tokyo in September, 1906. Anne, their second, was born at Baguio in the Philippines in March, 1908. Their only son, Warren, named after his grandfather, was born at Cheyenne in June, 1909. Mary Margaret was born at Zamboanga in May, 1912. Pershing doted on all of them, teaching them to ride, reciting nursery rhymes, administering castor oil—his sovereign remedy for childhood illnesses. He was particularly drawn to the boy and intuitively, like most good fathers, understood how to get along with a young child: young children want to be played with, not talked to. The general was often found playing on hands and knees, or holding Warren atop a short-legged Philippine pony, or returning the little boy's smart salute, a gesture Corporal Lanckton had taught Warren (which explains why Lanckton was able to serve Pershing for so long while still indulging now and then a good man's weakness).

When Pershing brought his family home in 1914, Senator Warren was so anxious to see them that he met the transport on a tug and nimbly climbed the rope ladder. The newsroom of the *San Francisco Bulletin* made up a composite photograph of the Pershing family; the general in mufti, Frances in a fur-collared coat and fur-trimmed hat, and the four children in cameo orbiting around the two parents. It was widely reproduced, the last photograph for which the four of them posed.

Pershing's new assignment was command of the Eighth Brigade, stationed at the Presidio, the military garrison just outside San Francisco which took its name from the Spanish penal colony established before the turn of the eighteenth century. Frances Pershing had the unfortunate distinction of becoming the garrison's first traffic victim when a runaway auto banged into her carriage and she suffered a broken arm.

She had to contend with settling the family alone. Pershing no sooner took command of the fort than he received orders, in late April, 1914, to entrain with 3,500 men for El Paso. The orders read in part, "ENTERTAIN NO DELAY." Minor eruptions were expected along the Texas-Mexican border, because Woodrow Wilson had sent the Marines to occupy Vera Cruz in the early part of the month.

"General Pushing Has Been Ordered to El Paso to Counteract General Shoving From the Other Side" read the headline in the *Bulletin*. Pershing wrote Colonel George Deshon that he presumed he was to go right through Mexico without further discussion. "We fully expected to be in Mexico City before we again drew rein." Upon arrival in El Paso, however, Pershing found more panic than cause for it. Mexican *Federales* and *rurales* often redrew their lines from north and south to east and west to avoid shooting into or over American territory. El Pasenos rode out to watch these combat maneuvers much as Washington society once rode out to observe the battle of Bull Run. They clambered to the roofs of freight cars with field glasses and chartered trains that skirted the battleground. These Mexican armies and armed bands had no intention of raiding El Paso or Brownsville or Douglas. The raids across the American border were by bandits after horses, money, arms, and occasionally mayhem.

Entrusted with the defense of the American border from Columbus, New Mexico, to Sierra Blanco, Texas, Pershing commanded the troops stationed in El Paso and at Fort Bliss. This was enough to keep him busy. He began training the large command in fire control, fire discipline, and fire direction, with special drills in street fighting and the military government of an occupied town. The duty, which seemed temporary at first, lengthened. Eventually, he realized that he and the Eighth Brigade would not be returning to the Presidio.

The time consumed in visiting his family was four days in travel alone. He decided to move Frances and the children to El Paso in the fall of 1915. Had he decided this sooner, he would have spared himself the surpassing grievous moment of his life, a grief that pursued him for the rest of his days.

The general's quarters at the Presidio, in which Frances and the children lived, was a far cry from the home they occupied in Zamboanga. It was an old, ramshackle, two-story, frame bungalow

that sat directly behind the parade ground. It looked more impos-
ing than it was by virtue of a huge pillared porch that encircled it.
It was a gerrybuilt structure that had persevered for several decades because most generals assigned to the quarters did not deign
to live there. Being a general's wife made life easier for Frances,
but it was by no means an easy life for a wealthy Senator's daughter. She put the bungalow in the best shape she could, though she
was never sure when they would abandon it. She was an atten-
tive, loving mother. She was interested in women's suffrage and
planned to attend the Republican National Convention.

On the night of August 26, 1915, Frances Pershing had as
overnight guests Ann Orr Boswell, a college classmate, and her
two boys. Ann Orr had also married a West Pointer, James Boswell
of Pershing's Philippine staff. Mrs. Boswell was awaiting her husband's arrival from Mindanao and she and Frances talked until
midnight, then went upstairs to bed.

While the two women and six children slept, live coals rolled
from the fireplace grate onto the newly finished dining room floor,
which John J. Pershing himself had burnished on his last visit.
Quickly the fire ate away and spread across the room to the stair-
case, which served as a flue, speeding the flames upward to the
second floor. Smoke billowed in suffocating clouds into the bedrooms, all the doors of which were open save that of the Boswell
family. The flames began to roar like a speeding train as they
snapped up the oxygen and the noise awoke Mrs. Boswell. The
hall was an inferno. She got her sons, Philip and James, to the
window, opened it, and saw running soldiers. She crawled out on
the roof and dropped her children into waiting arms below. Then
she jumped, landing in the hedges, suffering a badly sprained
back. Soldiers quickly helped her and the boys to the Officers
Club.

Lieutenant Eugene Santschel and Private C. J. Hazlitt on guard
duty were among the first rescuers to reach the blazing bungalow.
They were ready to storm up the front porch to force their way in
when they heard the cry that the family was out. They retreated to
the ring of excited onlookers, amazed by the fury of the fire, who

managed to form a corridor for the fire-fighting equipment. The windows of the first story gleamed like diamonds.

Johnson, Pershing's coachman who now served as the family's majordomo, burst upon them. He couldn't find the family. Mrs. Boswell was at the Officers Club, not Mrs. Pershing. Santschel, Hazlitt, and another soldier ran to the back of the bungalow, climbed up to one of the bedroom windows, broke in, and, coughing, stumbled through the poisonous smoke. One of them tripped over the body of Warren Pershing. They passed the unconscious boy back, tried to move into the hall, could not, then saved themselves. Other soldiers had climbed by ladder to the front bedrooms, where they found Frances Pershing and the three girls in their beds, the four of them still. The men swept up the Pershings, came down fast from the roof and brought the women to the parade ground. Blue had begun to tint their lips. The post doctor could bring only Warren around. The girls and Mrs. Pershing were dead of smoke inhalation.

General S. L. A. Marshall, the war historian, was a young reporter covering the border imbroglio for a Midwestern paper. He was in the newsroom of the *El Paso Herald* on the morning of the twenty-seventh. Later, in two widely separated articles and in an interview with Donald Smyth, Marshall recalled that when the news of the Presidio fire came over the wire, the AP correspondent, Norman Walker, called Fort Bliss to inquire of the general's aide Pershing's reaction. Walker intended to read to Lieutenant James L. Collins some of the details of the fire that the general might not have learned. But it was Pershing who picked up the telephone without introducing himself and then asked Walker, "Fire? What fire?"

Frightened at what he had to relate, Walker slowly and hesitatingly read the story.

"Oh, my God! Read it again. Can it be true? Can it be true?"

"I'm sorry to have had to break the news this way," said Walker.

"Who is this?" Pershing asked. Then, "Thank you, Walker. It was considerate of you to phone."

When Lieutenant Collins returned from his ride, Pershing

rushed to him. "My God, Collins. Something terrible has happened. There's been a fire at the house." He did not tell Collins about the deaths, probably because he was denying them to himself.

He left Friday noon for San Francisco and spent two days on the train. At night, sleepless, he walked the length of the cars. He was a coil of apprehension and alone until the train reached Bakersfield, where his friend, Frank Helms, who had sacrificed his waistcoat to William Howard Taft, joined him. By then he had admitted the loss to himself. He was no stoic. Helm rode the last three hundred miles, Pershing's arms around his neck, the general sobbing against his chest. At Oakland, Major General Arthur Murray, Major Henry Whitney, and Frederick Warren, Frances's brother, met them. By ferry, the party crossed the bay to San Francisco. More composed now but gray, Pershing met his father-in-law at the dock. The six men proceeded to the undertaking parlor at Geary and Divisadero streets. It was the last time Pershing would see his wife and children: their funeral was scheduled for Sunday afternoon. Alone, Pershing knelt before each of the coffins. He believed in a Divine Plan partly because he was a military man; he said without a Divine Plan everything was in disorder. But he did not mention heaven on this occasion.

At Letterman Hospital he rushed to his son's embrace. Friends left them alone. When he came out, his head was bowed and the friends could hear the little boy's suppressed sobbing. Pershing stopped by Mrs. Boswell's room. Then he insisted on going to the Presidio before the funeral. Helm tried to dissuade him. Pershing said he wanted to see for himself, wanted to satisfy himself that everything that could have been done to save his family had been done.

Glumly Pershing stared at the bungalow, the center of the roof burned through, now in half collapse. Witnesses convinced him that Mrs. Pershing and the children could have not suffered from the fire. Frances's arm had dangled from the bed. The girls' positions portrayed no restlessness.

The caskets were in white casing borne by twenty-four enlisted men. In morning coat, Pershing bore himself with composure and dignity and read the card on each of the floral tributes. "The death of your dear wife and children has crushed me," wrote Myron B. Marshall, who read the Episcopal service. "I baptized her. I can see you both before the bishop for confirmation and the tears in her eyes. Many kindnesses make her memory blessed to me. My tears are mingled with yours." The railroad station, where the coffins were put aboard the train that would carry them to Cheyenne, was also filled with flowers.

Taking Warren by car to the Hotel Stewart, Pershing was wracked with sobs when the boy mentioned his mother. Frank Helms had to hold Warren the rest of the way.

Pershing received hundreds of letters of condolence, which he saved. In the next few months he talked incessantly about the fire, so incessantly that friends grew bored hearing about it. He cried again when he opened a trunk of Frances's personal possessions. He confided in Bishop Charles H. Brent, "I have been able to get so little consolation out of life since that time. About the only respite I have known is by keeping every minute occupied."

Soldiers razed the bungalow in September. A little later, when Congress reconvened, it appropriated $2,245,000 for modern structures to replace the officers' shacks on army posts.

Pershing returned to El Paso with his sister May, whom he adored, to care for Warren. Outwardly, he remained the hard-boiled brigadier. But to old classmate Avery Andrews he confided he had no idea how he lived through the loss. He said that time did not make the slightest difference. It was always that dreadful morning with a strange voice on the telephone informing him of the disaster.

The tragedy changed him. It did not make him less soldierly, probably it made him more, but it did make him sympathetic, and this is not true of every man who survives the whirlwind. The loss made Pershing sympathetic at a time when he knew he was the instrument that condemned other fathers to the same grief.

In November of that year Pershing staged a picnic for Texas school children at Fort Bliss. Four military bands played and marched in formation. Six battalions of mule- and motorized-artillery circled the parade ground. A military tournament between two cavalry troops simulated real battle, then horse-drawn ambulances bounced across the field to revive "wounded" soldiers. The cooks fried thousands of doughnuts and KP's struggled under trays laden with pitchers of milk. An old photograph reveals a tall Pershing in campaign hat in the center of a mass of children, at least one thousand of them.

To a member of his staff who lost a son in World War I, Pershing said, "I know how you must feel. All one can do is get on with life. One must get over sorrow or it will break you. What happens is God's will."

"Neither of us was saying anything," wrote Charles G. Dawes of a day with Pershing in late 1917, "but I was thinking of my lost boy and of John's loss and looking out of the window, and he was doing the same thing on the other side of the automobile. We both turned at the same time and each was in tears. All John said was, 'Even this war can't keep it out of my mind.'"

On July 17, 1918, Pershing cabled Theodore Roosevelt:

> Regret very much that your son Lieutenant Quentin Roosevelt is reported missing. On July fourteenth with a patrol of twelve planes he left on a mission of protecting photographic section. Seven enemy planes were sighted and attacked. After which enemy planes retreated and our planes broke off combat, returning to their base. Lieutenant Roosevelt did not return. A member of the squadron reports seeing one of our planes fall out of combat and into the clouds and the French report an American plane was seen descending. I hope he may have landed safely. Will advise you immediately upon receipt of further information.

Ten days later Pershing sent another message:

> Since my cablegram of July 17th, I have delayed writing you in the hope that we might still learn that, through some good fortune, your son Quentin had managed to land safely inside the German lines. Now the telegram from the International Red Cross at Berne, stating that the German Red Cross confirms the newspaper reports of

his death, has taken even this hope away. Quentin died as he had lived and served, nobly and unselfishly; in the full strength and vigor of his youth, fighting the enemy in clean combat. You may well be proud of your gift to the nation in his supreme sacrifice.

I realize that time alone can heal the wound, yet I know that at such a time the stumbling words of understanding from one's friends help, and I want to express to you and to Quentin's mother my deepest sympathy and friendship. Perhaps I can come as near to realizing what such a loss means as anyone.

Enclosed is a copy of his official record in the Air Service. The brevity and curtness of the official words paint clearly the picture of his service, which was an honor to all of us.

Believe me, Sincerely yours,

Theodore Roosevelt wrote, "I am immensely touched by your letter of July 27th. I thank you for what you have said of Quentin. My dear fellow, you have suffered far more bitter sorrow than has befallen me. You bore it with splendid courage and I should be ashamed of myself if I did not try in a lesser way to emulate that courage."

12

Push Comes to Shove

The United States maintains a troubled 1,000-mile border with Mexico. It was as impossible to keep bandit chiefs, guerrillas, insurgents, revolutionaries, and refugees from crossing over that border between 1910 and 1916 as it was to keep "wetbacks" from slipping across it in the 1950s. For six years revolution swirled through Mexico, leaving in its wake desolation and civil war. American ranches, mines, and settlements on the Mexican side of the Rio Grande yielded horses, money, and guns, usually through robbery or extortion. Cities on the American side—Brownsville, El Paso, Columbus, Douglas—served as ports of entry for insurgent arms, ammunition, provisions, and recruits, and sanctuaries for fleeing revolutionaries.

A variety of men made the Mexican revolution—rich and poor, Indian and peon, bandit chief and intellectual, guerrilla and European-trained general—each commanding a loyal faction. More political parties and splinter groups circulated around this revolution and civil war than around any other of North America's political disaffections. But no matter what the passion or the tactic, each of these men and factions had the same goal: to take Mexico back from the foreigners. No matter what the Mexican government, it replied to the United States government's notes about expropriation and depredation that what was done had to be done, because the Mexican people wanted it done.

In Mexico's bloody agony of revolution and counter-revolution, not only American property was forfeit but, to an alarming extent, American lives. By 1914, American businessmen, investors, mining operators, and oil engineers in Mexico had formed a vocal lobby that demanded of Washington military protection. Receiving them, Navy Secretary Jonathan Daniels asked, "Why did you leave the United States and go to Mexico? You went there because you preferred to invest there rather than in the United States. Isn't that so? Well, then, you must take the risk of losing your property. You must not expect the people of the United States to pay taxes for the support of an army to protect you in Mexico."

This is a succinct statement of Woodrow Wilson's military policy vis-à-vis Mexico, when the border began to glow red hot. But Wilson also had a diplomatic policy by which he hoped to protect American "extrality" in Mexico. "Extrality" was a popular word in the second decade of the twentieth century denoting extraterritorial rights and interests of Americans. Wilson wanted to determine which chief of which faction could subdue the others in Mexico. Having made the determination, the Wilson Administration would extend United States recognition that would enable this chief to buy arms and supplies from America and also secure loans. In return, the Wilson Administration wanted preference for American rights and interests.

In August, 1914, the State Department suggested that General Pershing meet with Generals Álvaro Obregón and Pancho Villa. At that point, Woodrow Wilson thought Pancho Villa was the man who might bring peace to Mexico. He also owed Villa a favor. Villa had refused to move against the United States the previous April, when armed American forces occupied Vera Cruz. Not only had Villa stilled discontent in Chihuahua, but he had convinced Emiliano Zapata, who controlled a guerrilla army farther south, and Álvaro Obregón, who led the Yaqui Indians of northeast Mexico, that their future lay in tolerating this incursion and in cooperating with the United States.

Almost immediately Villa found he could buy and ship arms openly in El Paso despite the embargo. By August, 1914, Villa was at the height of his power. He was ready to move against Mexico City with 40,000 well-armed men; he had adequate artillery, 240 carloads of coal for his locomotives, which had been legally borrowed from American mining operators, and 300 carloads of provisions and supplies. For Villa this meeting with Pershing was of momentous portent. Secretary of State William Jennings Bryan had wired him, "Please accept the sincere thanks of this government for valuable service you have rendered in restoring order to Chihuahua and Sonoroa. Your patriotic labors in this matter are greatly appreciated."

Among other subjects Villa, Obregón, and Pershing discussed in the Mexican consular offices in El Paso was the plight of several hundred friars, priests, and nuns who had sought refuge in the United States from Mexican guerrilla bands. Many Mexicans were savagely anticlerical because the Catholic Church was a large landowner. Pershing had to remind Villa and Obregón that the Wilson Administration depended upon a large Catholic voting bloc. After the meeting Villa and Obregón said they had discussed ways and means of restoring six hundred confessors to their homes in Mexico.

Then the three generals watched a military review. Pershing must have found his Mexican companions curiosities. Obregón and Villa each owned his own revolutionary army, in the manner of an Oriental warlord. Both were accompanied by their staffs which, if not as numberless as the stars, still were as numerous as a regiment at mess call.

Obregón was the model of military dignity in a plain khaki uniform unadorned by medals. A canny and manipulative professional army man, with a waxed moustache, he knew all the details of what was going on around him. Villa, short and stumpy, saw the world through coal black eyes under heavy lids. He neither drank nor smoked, but he had chased enough women to make up for it. He was fiery, often unpredictable and unstable. He came to El Paso in a Norfolk jacket that bulged over the brace of six-shooters he habitually carried. He had disdained the traditional sombrero in favor of a Stetson, and he affected a crooked bowtie. Proudly he displayed a gold watch over his stomach, and was on his best behavior. He kicked his bodyguard, Rudolfo "The Butcher" Fierro, for bad manners. "Take off your hat," hissed Villa. "You brute. Animal!"

Many Americans, especially those living removed from the border, had found much to romanticize about Pancho Villa. The journalist John Reed had transformed Villa from an unsophisticated *bandido* into a knight-errant. William Jennings Bryan had compared Villa to Sir Galahad, because both were teetotalers. But Pershing was not much given to romantic inspiration and he had prepared himself for the meeting by reading Victor Poncelot's *A Little Biography of a Great Man*. The American Poncelot, who knew Villa, revealed that as a young boy Villa had found amusement by putting lighted firecrackers in horses' ears. Poncelot also disabused his readers of the myth that Villa had become a bandit after murdering a hacienda don to save his sister from dishonor. It was Villa, argued Poncelot, who raped a high-born lady and murdered her brother in his escape. Villa lived as a millionaire, extorting money from miners and ranchers. His brother, Hippolito, exacted additional tribute from the bull rings, gambling concessions, and brothels.

Obregón and Villa were serious and straight-faced when they posed for a photograph after shaking hands with Pershing on the International Bridge. Pershing, however, flashed one of his rare smiles for the photographer. Spurring their horses with wild cries and firing their six-shooters and rifles randomly, the two generals rode off. Pershing wondered to Tasker Bliss, his superior, why the State Department insisted on an ammunition embargo. "The Mexicans waste ammunition so fast, there will soon be none left."

Keeping his brigade in combat readiness occupied Pershing constantly. He complained of shortages in wagon parts, tent flies and helves, straw, blacksmith coal, mule- and horseshoes, and clothing and equipment for his soldiers. But he worked his command into combat alertness. Along the border, however, trouble continued.

The bandit leader Luis de la Rosa, whose guerrillas made their home in Matamoros, came over the line at Brownsville. The bandits seized the American cargo of a southbound train of the Gulf Coast Railroad.

Eighteen American cavalry troopers were wounded and one killed in Naco, Arizona, when one faction of Mexicans attacked another in Naco, Mexico, which was across the street.

Guerrillas in Ciudad Juarez amused themselves by firing into the railroad yards of neighboring El Paso.

Trouble intensified after November, 1914. Villa and Zapata did take Mexico City, but they did not move quickly enough to consolidate their gains. This gave Venustiano Carranza, the First Chief of the Constitutional Party, time to build up his own forces in Vera Cruz, and also enabled him to recruit Obregón by handing over abandoned though well-stocked arsenals.

Carranza was an old man, rickety, with a long white beard, who usually affected the white clothes of the peon and who looked for all the world like Don Quixote. But he was the first revolutionary able to rally different groups to his cause. While he was anything but a strong man, he was shortly to prove that he had no equal in statecraft. Washington began to see this, too.

Pershing was constantly dispatching small units to guard against the marauding bands of Quevada and Orozco, whose raids near the border became more frequent as the United States tightened its arms embargo. But he also saw in Carranza a possible resolution of the civil war. He wrote to Tasker Bliss, who had moved on to become the assistant Chief of Staff, "Mr. Bryan and the President are undoubtedly throwing their influence toward Carranza and the Constitutionalists. I hope they will let them go to Mexico City and fight it out. This is the only way we can have even the prospect of peace it seems to me."

When Villa came out of Mexico City, the Carrancistas led by Obregón beat him and drove the Villistas back to Chihuahua. A year from the time he had met with Pershing, Villa was in eclipse. Carranza, meanwhile, still had to stamp out revolutionary brush fires to his left and his right.

Woodrow Wilson declared, "If the Mexicans want to raise hell, let them raise hell. It is their government, it is their hell. After they have raised enough of it, it will sit so badly on their stomachs that they will want something else. They will get down to hard pan and make a government that will stay put." In the meantime, he said, his administration would adopt a policy of "watchful waiting."

Military men did not agree with the policy. General Hugh Scott burst into the office of the Secretary of War with a report of American casualties and in choleric anger said, "I can't stand this anymore. If Mr. Bryan won't do anything, I'll go down there and drive those Mexicans away myself." Nor did Pershing agree with administration policy. He thought Wilson worried too much about America's duty to the Mexican people and too little about Mexico's duty to the United States.

Woodrow Wilson's policy of watchful waiting came to an end in 1916, when the administration decided Carranza could secure Mexico. It clamped an embargo on arms for Villa and lifted the embargo that had stalled the Carrancistas. But Carranza also needed to reinforce the border garrison his followers held at Agua Prieta, a Mexican suburb of Douglas, Arizona. Not only was Agua Prieta a dagger at the Villistas rear, but Villa needed to capture it to smuggle arms for his forces. Carranza held the town, but Villa controlled the passes to Agua Prieta; the stalemated revolution went on. So Carranza prevailed upon Woodrow Wilson to let reinforcements take a shortcut from El Paso, Texas, across New Mexico to Arizona. It was a decision on Wilson's part that had neither congressional nor public sanction.

Pershing had to collect the rolling stock at El Paso that would transfer the Carrancista regiment commanded by General Plutarcho Calles. In the forty-eight hours it took the regiment to entrain and entrench, Pershing and General Frederick Funston reinforced the American garrison at the site and made its defensive lines coordinate with the Mexican lines.

The Carrancista regiment constructed an excellent trench system protected by coil after coil of barbed wire. Its machine guns were correctly positioned for a murderous crossfire, and searchlights powered by American current were installed atop telephone poles, to illuminate the front if Villa attacked at night. Villa was the only rebel general who had succeeded in directing night attacks. The Carrancistas possessed a remarkable variety of weapons, including small arms, 3-inch shells, shrapnel, a Hotchkiss revolving cannon, and rockets, as well as bugle calls of melodious and infinite multiplicity.

Villa came out of the mountains on the night of November 1, 1915, and learned within minutes what it had taken graduates of St. Cyr, Sandhurst, and the Imperial Staff School a year to learn: an assault against an entrenched position, aproned with barbed wire, defended by machine guns, backed up by artillery, cannot succeed. Though Villistas courageously pressed the attack, they were unnerved when the blinding searchlights spotlighted them. Half of Villa's force came streaming back, the other half lay dead. The failure to take Agua Prieta meant Villa was cut off from supplies coming from the north and from launching any operations to the east or south.

Villa, who had made many concessions to Woodrow Wilson, knew he was betrayed. One of the men who invented the concept of machismo, Villa burned with the lust for vengeance. Mexicans, not as enthralled as some Americans with Villa's boldness, considered him a man suffering from "Delirio de Grandessa"—dreams of an unapproachable glory. And it was this delerium that determined Villa upon the Columbus, New Mexico, raid. In *The Great Chase*, the definitive account of the Punitive Expedition, Herbert Mason Malloy quotes General Jaime Quinonez, a Villa intimate:

> The reason for the raid is simple. Francisco Villa, who I thought was a great man in many ways, was *muy hombre*. He felt deceived by the *Norte Americanos*. Villa was also quite unstable. He worked himself into a great anger, and it was this anger which drove him to Columbus. He was really very, very mad.

Pershing heard so many reports of intended raids on border settlements that he had to discount all of them. His only sources of information were Mexican scouts; the army was prohibited from sending intelligence units across the border. Pershing hired the Mexicans on a per diem rate, so it was in their interest to continually report the northern movement of heavily armed columns. The same scouts would be dispatched on following days to report the progress of the columns, which would eventually vanish. Pershing later commented that he had signed enough vouchers to have put a column in Alaska.

American diplomatic representatives, like Special Agent George C. Carothers, forwarded information that was reliable, but never up to the moment. American newspaper correspondents relayed tips they had received about suspected raids, but these raids never transpired. In addition, there was simply a limit to the rapidity and frequency with which Pershing could transfer troops from one point along the border to another.

Until early January, 1916, neither Pershing nor the scouts nor the correspondents nor the special agents knew where Pancho Villa was, other than that he was somewhere in the Sierra Madre Oriental in Chihuahua. But at noon on January 10, Villa marked his position with a bloody raid on a passenger train of the Mexican Northwest Railroad. The train was transporting American mining engineers and Mexican workers of the La Cusi Mining Company to Cusihuriac. General Obregón had convinced the directors of the company that the area was secure enough to recommence operations. Mining operations had been suspended the previous November when the State Department warned the company it was indulging a risky operation.

One thousand horsemen shouting "Viva Villa!" swept down upon the train at the watering station of Santa Ysabel, fifty miles west of Chihuahua City. The Villistas herded the Mexican workers out of their cars to the platform and robbed each of them. The eighteen Americans, hands held behind their heads, were lined up against the engine, systematically stripped of clothes and boots, and shot in the back of the head. Only one, Thomas B. Holmes, survived by feigning death in the chaparral. The Villistas, having looted the train of its cargo of ammunition, rode off, their ringing cries of *"Mueran los gringos!"* almost drowning out the caws of circling buzzards.

American anger was wild and unrestrained. Southwestern Senators, led by Albert B. Fall, demanded retribution and protection. First Chief Carranza of the *de facto* Mexican government promised vigorous and quick apprehension of the murderers. John J. Pershing ordered American troopers to return the fire of Mexicans shooting across the border. Diplomatic notes and assurances passed between Washington and Mexico City. Slowly the furor died down. Other American-owned mining companies decided to bide their time instead of opening properties in northern Chihuahua.

In the dark hours before dawn of March 9, however, five hundred Villistas quietly crossed the border three miles south of the New Mexican railroad town of Columbus. Columbus, a town of 330 people, was also the temporary home of the Thirteenth Cavalry, under the command of Colonel Howard Slocum. That very afternoon, uneasy about the quietude, Slocum had strengthened his defenses in Columbus and on nearby ranches.

Columbus was like a "plus" sign geographically. The railroad formed the horizontal bar running east and west, and Main Street the vertical bar north and south. Villa moved into the almost-deserted southwest quadrant and, at 4 A.M., sent out two converging columns in a nighttime attack, a difficult maneuver requiring a disciplined force. One column of horsemen galloped into the northeast quadrant, making for the safes in the post office, bank, and hotel. The other ripped across Main Street, making for the army barracks in the southeast quadrant, hoping to stampede four hundred horses toward Mexico.

Though Villa achieved surprise, it was by no means an overwhelming tactical advantage. Lieutenant John B. Lucas, preparing for a dawn inspection of his machine gun detachment, recognized the Mexicans by their sombreros. He strapped on his .45, picked his way in the darkness to the ammunition shack, and, with the men of his command who gathered there, got four machine guns to bear on the attacking force. Through it all Lucas was barefoot, having forgotten to put on his boots. Lieutenant James P. Castleman, the officer of the day, was on his rounds when he heard the wild cries and shooting. He got the men of F Troop in arms and led them across the railroad tracks, where, prone in a skirmish line, they began to pour a concentrated fire into the Villistas.

Unfortunately for themselves, the Villistas had set fire to the hotel and surrounding houses to light their way, and now they were outlined against the flames. The field officers of the Thirteenth, who lived in town, secured their families and quickly organized the troops and secured vantage points. Several Villistas, seeking cover, backed into the army mess, which was adobe and bulletproof. The cooks hurled scalding water on them and a KP fired a blast from a double-barreled shotgun kept handy for bagging game.

On Cootes Hill, the high ground outside Columbus, Major Frank Tompkins found Colonel Slocum. Both saw that the withering American fire was devastating the Mexicans. "Round up your troop and give chase," ordered Slocum. Tompkins and Captain Rudolph Smyser corralled enough horses in twenty minutes to mount H Troop. Riding hard out of Columbus, they were joined by Lieutenant Castleman with twenty-seven men of F Troop. The cavalry mounted a charge at rearguard Villistas on the International Line, killing thirty-two of them. The Americans plunged into the desert and twice more brushed by Villistas. By noon Tompkins was out of ammunition and water and he reined up. The troopers watched the Villistas racing south, huge billows of dust raised in their wake. On the way back to Columbus, Tompkins counted over one hundred dead Villistas. In the town itself, sixty-seven more dead Mexicans, piled like cordwood, were burning with kerosene. Eight Villistas had been captured, of whom seven would soon be hanged.

Villa had suffered another catastrophic defeat. He had lost more than a fifth of his force together with their mounts, had not succeeded in robbing the bank or the post office, and had gotten very little from the hotel. Nor had his men rustled any of the cavalry's horses. The tactical advantage of a nighttime surprise had been quickly dissipated by the discipline and smart thinking of the officers and men at Camp Furlong.

But this is not what the nation's press emphasized. George Seese, AP Bureau Chief in El Paso, had come to Columbus the night before, urged on by a sixth sense. By sunrise he was filing one of the greatest scoops ever to make headlines. What Seese told the country was that seven American soldiers had been killed in the fighting and five wounded; eight civilians had died, six of them summarily executed at the hotel, and twenty-two more were wounded, of whom three would die. In addition, Villa had executed Americans he had encountered in his march on Columbus. His men had also raped two women in Columbus.

"All the brutality in Villa's nature has come to the front," wired Special Agent Carothers to Woodrow Wilson, "and he should be killed like a dog." After a cabinet meeting on the afternoon of March 10, Woodrow Wilson issued a statement to White House reporters:

> An adequate force will be sent at once in pursuit of Villa with the single object of capturing him and putting a stop to his forays. This can and will be done in entirely friendly aid of the constituted authorities in Mexico and with scrupulous respect for the sovereignty of that republic.

Chief of Staff Hugh Scott and his adjutant, Major General Tasker Bliss, quickly decided who should command the expedition. The logical choice was Major General Frederick Funston, who had led the troops into Vera Cruz and had subsequently succeeded to command of the Southwest Department. But Scott and Bliss knew that Funston enjoyed drinking mint juleps in the lobby of the Menger Hotel in San Antonio every afternoon, so they chose Pershing. Scott knew that Pershing was acute, understood political consequences as well as developments, and that he could be trusted to obey orders. Pershing was ordered to invade Mexico but not to start a war.

In three days of concentrated work, Pershing not only assembled the expedition but mapped its campaign. In 1916, the army consisted of 170 regiments of coast artillery, all useless for this purpose, 6 regiments of field artillery, 31 regiments of infantry, and 15 of cavalry. Most of these were below strength by one hundred or more men. Two-thirds of the army was stationed in the Philippines, the Hawaiian Islands, and the Canal Zone, with fewer than 25,000 mobile forces inside the continental United States. Of this 25,000, one-third were support troops—medical detachments, supply units, administrative sections. From what was available, Pershing chose the Seventh, Tenth, Eleventh, and Thirteenth cavalry regiments, to which he added the Sixth and Sixteenth infantry regiments, to guard the line of communications and the camps. He included two batteries of the Sixth Artillery because he knew from his Philippine experience that the only way to get some guerrillas out of the mountains was to blast them out.

To this strike force Pershing decided to add two companies of engineers, an ambulance company and a field hospital, two wagon companies—27 wagons, 112 mules, 6 horses, 36 men—and a detachment from the Signal Corps that reported for duty with some hand-operated battery radios its officers had scrounged from other outfits along the Rio Grande. He also thought he could count on the First Aero Squadron of eight planes. Its antics during the coming weeks so discouraged him that he never truly believed in air power again. In all he had 4,800 men, 4,175 animals, and the promise he would be reinforced if needed.

Mapping the campaign was harder because neither the General Staff nor the War College had ever drawn plans for an invasion of Mexico from the north. In the event of war, the General Staff had plans for either a seaborne invasion at Vera Cruz, on the Gulf of Mexico, or one at Guayamas, on the Gulf of California. Pershing would have to find Villa by invading Chihuahua, whose Sierra Madre and Sierra Tarahumao mountains grow broader and more rugged as they proceed south. Though he was unfamiliar with the terrain, as an old cavalryman Pershing knew well enough what to expect from that hard country.

The plan Pershing and his staff devised called for two columns to enter Mexico: the First Cavalry and Infantry Brigade, which he would lead, were to march south from Columbus, while the Second Cavalry Brigade, under Colonel George A. Dodd, would move south from Culberson's Ranch in the southwest corner of New Mexico. These two columns were to snap shut like jaws at Casas Grandes, seventy-five miles south of the border, perhaps trapping Villa.

Pershing's staff was headed by Major John L. Hines, who would succeed Pershing as commander of the AEF in 1919. It included Lieutenant George S. Patton, a 1909 graduate of West Point. The Punitive Expedition transformed Patton into a soldier who wanted to look like, talk like, and be like Pershing. Other officers who would assume military prominence in the coming decades were Charles P. Summerall, Lesley J. McNair, Carl Spaatz, Courtney Hodges, Benjamin Foulois, who would command the Air Corps in World War I, and Ulysses S. Grant III. The expedition was always called "Pershing's Punitive Expedition," a distinction in an administration so thoroughly dominated by Woodrow Wilson.

The columns were to proceed into Mexico on March 15 at 12 noon. Pershing was to make for the small town of Las Palomas. Here the expedition would be interdicted if the Carrancista commander offered resistance. By early afternoon of the fifteenth Pershing wired that the local commander had not only communicated that Americans might cross the border in force, but that he would be glad to lead his men in the chase to capture Pancho Villa. When the column reached Las Palomas, however, the small town was completely deserted.

"Move out," said Pershing, heading his horse toward the moonlike landscape, pocked with craters, split by arroyos, across which sand storms cut like knives. In his initial report to Scott, which he filed that night, Pershing concluded, "Don't be optimistic." To this Scott replied, "But the whole country is optimistic."

13

"When Valour Strikes"

Newton D. Baker, Woodrow Wilson's newly confirmed Secretary of War, told Hugh Scott, Chief of Staff, "I want you to start an expedition into Mexico to catch Pancho Villa."

"Mr. Secretary," asked Scott, "do you want the United States to make war on one man? Suppose he gets on a train and goes to Guatemala or the Yucatan or South America. Are you going to go after him?"

"No I am not," said Baker.

"That is not what you want then," said Scott. "You want his band captured or destroyed."

"Yes," said Baker. "That is what I want."

This common-sense exchange reflects a more practical military policy than the one the newspapers formulated. "PERSHING ORDERED: GET VILLA ALIVE OR DEAD" was emblazoned on every Hearst newspaper from the *Atlanta Georgian* to the *New York Journal*, a headline composed by William Randolph himself. Other newspapers were not as pithy, but they informed their readers that Woodrow Wilson had deputized John J. Pershing to bring in Pancho Villa, the wicked centaur of Chihuahua.

It would seem that Woodrow Wilson had no choice other than to dispatch Pershing after the Villistas who had violated American territory, claimed American lives, and were keeping alive a revolution that cost American investors millions. But a few days before the Columbus raid, Woodrow Wilson thought he had other choices. To his press secretary, Joseph P. Tumulty, Wilson said,

> The gentlemen who criticize me speak as if America were afraid to fight Mexico. Poor Mexico, with its pitiful men, women, and children, fighting to gain a foothold in their own land. They speak of the valour of America. What is true valour? I would be just as much ashamed to be rash as I would to be a coward. Valour is self-respecting. Valour is circumspect. Valour strikes only when it is right to strike. Valour withholds itself from all small implications and entanglements and waits for the great opportunity when the sword will flash as if it carried the light of heaven upon its blade.

Despite these sentiments, Wilson sent an American army onto the Chihuahuan plain without a by-your-leave from the Mexican government, a serious mistake that came near bringing his administration to a sorry pass. Though Woodrow Wilson had taught history and had written definitive historical texts, he often lacked a historical perspective. That lack utterly confused his foreign policy on Mexico. Yet his Mexican policy was in counterpoint to the great fugue of the well-constructed world Woodrow Wilson wanted to orchestrate from Washington. To understand why his policy of intervention failed in Mexico is to understand why his policy of "peace without victory" failed in Europe.

Though Mexico gained its independence from Spain in 1810, Mexicans did not draw up a constitution until 1858. At that time Mexico theoretically became a republic with certain rights reserved for its states. The constitution established a central government with executive, legislative, and judicial branches, and it decreed the secularization of church property, land reforms, and an end to the abuses perpetrated by a military hierarchy. But Mexicans found precious little economic or political freedom under this constitution, because Napoleon III of France took advantage of the American Civil War to occupy Mexico and establish Maximilian of

Austria as its emperor. When, after Appomattox, General Phil Sheridan appeared on the Rio Grande with the cavalry of the Army of the Potomac, Napoleon quickly withdrew his troops, leaving Benito Juárez to depose Maximilian and become the president of the Republic of Mexico. Unable to consolidate his power, however, Juárez never instituted the constitutional reforms.

Juárez was succeeded by Porfirio Díaz, the first of the Latin American strong men, who used the constitutional provision for a president to make himself Mexico's supreme autocrat. Díaz maintained himself in power for more than three decades by judiciously overpaying both the army and the police. Men as diverse as Theodore Roosevelt, Leo Tolstoy, and Andrew Carnegie revered Díaz as a phenomenon akin to a natural force. Díaz suppressed peons, Indians, and workers, transforming the latter into the cheapest labor in the world. He cultivated and made wealthy the large landowners. Mexico became an Aladdin's lamp of profit for foreign investors, particularly American investors.

By the first decade of the twentieth century, the U.S. State Department calculated that in physical plant alone Americans had invested $331 million in Mexico. President William Howard Taft put the total investment at $2 billion. William Randolph Hearst, Meyer and Daniel Guggenheim, Edward Doheny, United States Steel, and Anaconda Copper owned three-fourths of the gold, silver, and copper mines in Mexico and one-half of the oil fields. Other Americans worked extensive sugar plantations, and along the border American ranchers owned spreads as big as Rhode Island.

In 1906, five thousand Mexican miners walked out on strike. Díaz machine-gunned them indiscriminately, but the miners were joined by the textile workers, and the oil field workers began to sabotage the wells. Villagers and peons joined into guerrilla bands that made the deserts and the mountains unsafe for Díaz's soldiery. By 1910, the disaffection spread into the larger cities and became revolution, spurred on by the rhetoric and patriotism of Francisco Madero, a wealthy landowner who was a reformer by conscience. Madero coaxed, stole, and extorted money from the investors who owned the cattle ranches, the lumber and cotton mills, the founderies and factories, and the oil distilleries. Soon Madero started an inexorable movement. When an army of Maderistas took Juárez, Díaz decided that, for the good of Mexico and the preservation of his health, he would yield power. He decamped for Paris with as much of the national treasury as he could transport.

Madero promised he would make Mexico truly democratic: he would educate all the children in public schools, unfetter the press, hold free elections, separate church and state, redistribute the land, and bring peace. He lasted only fifteen months, principally because by 1910 everybody in Mexico had gotten hold of the revolution. They had become more interested in the shooting than in what the shooting was about. Madero could not redistribute the land until the guerrillas disbanded and went back to work it.

Emiliano Zapata refused to disband his army until the land was divided among his followers. Pascual Orozco, who wanted dictatorial powers for himself, staged a garrison revolt in Vera Cruz. Eulalio Gutiérrez, who commanded a small army in the desert, declared himself ruler of Mexico. He stripped Zapata, Orozco, and Madero of their offices and tried them in absentia, with the cacti for jurors.

Beleaguered in Mexico City, impotent, Madero called upon General Victoriano Huerta to save the revolution from Zapata and Orozco. Huerta was an Aztec, as pitiless as the high priests who carved the hearts from living sacrifices on the pyramidal steps of Tenochtitlan. He moved into Vera Cruz and deposed Orozco, then dashed to the south, where he chased away the Zapatistas with machine guns. Huerta, however, burned with no revolutionary ardor. He was a tough who had earned his way in the army by strangling superior officers some of the junior officers did not like. He was also an alcoholic who downed two bottles of brandy every day. He was evil, he lusted for power, but he was brainy, gauging his chances through beady black eyes that glittered like a panther's.

He turned from Zapata and loosed his troops on Mexico City, which they secured after ten days of bitter street fighting against the loyalists of Madero. Huerta told Madero and his vice-president, José Maria Pino Suárez, they were dead men if they did not immediately resign. They resigned. Then excited platoons of soldiers began shooting at Madero and Suárez. Huerta kicked the bloody bodies to make sure they were dead, and wired President William Howard Taft, "I have overthrown the government. Therefore peace and order will reign."

It was a telegram that made American business hearts pump with delight. James Spreyer, whose bank held $101 million in Mexican notes, urged Taft to extend Huerta immediate recognition as head of the new government. Spreyer told the President that honest American businessmen were willing to go along with any government that could promise stability and the maintenance of the status quo. Anaconda Copper said that, while Huerta had never been a Boy Scout, still he was everything an American could want in a dictator. But William Howard Taft had different thoughts on the matter.

Huerta could not guarantee American lives and property; nor did he want to renew United States naval leases in Baja, California. And revulsion attended the murder of Madero and Suárez. The Mexicans themselves were far from unanimous in recognizing Huerta as a duly constituted president. What had been revolution now quickened into civil war, a fury of flame and blood. Governor Venustiano Carranza of Coahuila denied Huerta's authority, and his followers moved against Huerta's garrisons. In Sonora, Álvaro Obregón and Plutarcho Calles mustered small armies for war against Huerta. Francisco Villa gathered seven men in El Paso, Texas, crossed the Rio Grande secretly, and within weeks was to become the leader of a formidable guerrilla force. Having quickened, civil war spread. William Howard Taft saw clearly that what Huerta wanted was an American force to establish his rule.

Taft never subscribed to Theodore Roosevelt's doctrine of the imperial presidency. He had resolved not to use American force in Mexico unless authorized by Congress. He opted for American neutrality and abstention from Mexico's affairs. Taft wanted to protect American interests, and was sure that armed intervention would provoke Mexicans into destroying the very interests the intervention was supposed to protect. Having made his decision, Taft had to yield office to Woodrow Wilson.

The analytic Wilson saw the Mexican Revolution for what it was, not the revolt of one class against another, but a determined and ferocious attempt by the people to establish a welfare state. Mexican revolutionaries wanted to establish the right of a working man to organize and strike, to make known without fear his political sentiments, and to read what he chose to read in newspapers. The Mexican Revolution was the harbinger of the economic and social reforms enacted into law by Britain, France, the Scandinavian countries, and the United States later in the twentieth century. Woodrow Wilson was sympathetic to these aims. Intellectually, Wilson felt closer to the revolting workers and peons than he felt to the harassed American investors.

Woodrow Wilson determined to bring moral force to bear on the issue of recognizing a Mexican government, and said publicly he would not recognize a Mexican president who had come to office through murder. He said he would recognize the present government of Mexico only on the condition that Huerta called for free elections and abided by their result. The powers of the world, Wilson went on, expected the United States to act as Mexico's dearest friend. Until Mexico gave the civilized world a satisfactory reason for installing a nonrepresentative government, the United States would neither recognize nor send arms and aid to that government.

So where Theodore Roosevelt's foreign policy *vis-à-vis* Latin America had been "Speak softly and carry a big stick," and Taft's had been "Dollar Diplomacy," Woodrow Wilson's was to be spiritual colonization. He hoped to usher in a new order, one in which the great country would aid and instruct the weak country in the morally right way. Morality was the keystone of all Woodrow Wilson's foreign policy. He argued that self-interest alone could not strengthen America's dealings with other countries of the world; self-interest had to be consonant with morality, for soon morality would govern nations. The question before the American people was not whether Huerta's government could bring about internal stability, nor even whether Huerta's government was the only government with which the United States could negotiate to protect American interest, but whether Huerta's was a government the United States *ought* to deal with.

Huerta thought Woodrow Wilson was literally crazy. Sarcastically, Huerta always called Wilson "the Noble Puritan." He also said that an American president had no business telling a Mexican president when and where to hold Mexican elections. Huerta, however, needed United States loans in order to keep going, and needed United States recognition even more in order to deal with other nations; so he scheduled a national election for the fall of 1913. Having satisfied Wilson that the election machinery was operative, Huerta raided the Chamber of Deputies, arrested all who had ever opposed him, campaigned as the only candidate, and won a stunning majority.

"That scoundrel Huerta," said Wilson, outraged, "so false, so sly, so seldom sober." He promptly announced that it was clearly his duty to secure Huerta's retirement from the Mexican government and that he would proceed to employ such means as were necessary to facilitate this end. Plainly, Woodrow Wilson wanted nations to transcend past habits; and if Mexico would not do this willingly, then the United States would have to find some way to make Mexico do it.

Wilson believed he was the instrumental agent of a new era in which the moral principles of men who represent nations dominate all policy. National pride, traditional glory, and selfish interests would be secondary considerations for the peoples of the world. "The public opinion of the world," he said, "is the mistress of the world." And it was world opinion he was summoning in his attempts to rescue Mexico from Huerta and continuing civil war and revolution.

In April, 1914, six American sailors were arrested in Tampico when they put ashore to reprovision their ship, the USS *Dolphin*, part of a small task force watchfully waiting in the Gulf of Mexico. Within an hour, General Hermanilla Zaragoza, the local Huertista commander, released the six and sent a prompt apology to Admiral Henry C. Mayo. Mayo replied that the incident was an affront to the United States, and could be rectified only by a formal apology, quick punishment of the officers and men responsible, and the public hoisting of the American flag accompanied by a twenty-one-gun salute. Mayo gave Mexico twenty-four hours in which to comply.

Within twenty-four hours, however, the incident had become one of grave international complications. "I do not know how Admiral Mayo could have done anything else," said William Jennings Bryan, as the navy ordered all available ships at Hampton Roads to Mexican waters. Wilson extended Huerta's deadline from April 10 to April 13, then to April 16. He warned that unless Huerta complied, he would have to lay the whole affair before Congress, but Huerta did not comprehend what laying a matter before Congress portended.

Wilson was having a hard time with Huerta. First, the Mexican questioned the legality of the American landings; then he said Mexicans could not fire a salute during Holy Week; next he asked how Mexico could be sure the United States would return the salute according to the dictates of international protocol—perhaps it would be better to fire simultaneous salutes. Better yet, suggested Huerta, why not lay the whole matter before the tribune at The Hague. When Wilson proved obdurate, Huerta finally asked with some exasperation who was he, Huerta, to order the salute? If he represented the government of Mexico, why did the United States not recognize him?

Having extended the deadline three times, Wilson asked Congress on April 19 for authority "to use armed forces in such ways and to such an extent as may be necessary to obtain from General Huerta and his adherents the fullest recognition of the rights and dignity of the United States." Two days later a landing force of Marines and sailors moved to occupy the customs house at Vera Cruz. The Huertista garrison abandoned the city, taking with it arms, ammunition, and rolling stock.

When the Mexicans who populated Vera Cruz saw the landing parties, they began firing in defense of their homeland. Among these patriots were the cadets of the Mexican naval academy. Battle-savvy Marines took cover at the first crack of rifle fire, but American sailors, marching from the pier in parade formation, took a ferocious volley before dispersing. The USS *Chester* and the USS *Prairie*, anchored close inshore, turned their guns upon the naval academy and demolished it, killing many of the sixteen-year-old cadets.

From the vantage point of several buildings near the pier, other Mexicans picked up the fire. Marines played their machine guns like hoses against these structures, accounting for another fifteen dead Mexicans. Sniping continued. Squads of Marines chipped their way through the interior walls of houses and stores with picks to get at these Mexican sharpshooters. Nineteen Americans died in the landings and 71 were wounded, before 3,000 army men secured the city three days later; 126 Mexicans perished and 185 were wounded.

Every splinter-group leader in Mexico protested the occupation of Vera Cruz, with the exception of Pancho Villa and Álvaro Obregón. The strongest protest came from Carranza. Though the Carrancistas had the most to gain from the occupation, since it distracted Huerta from pursuing them, yet they proved the angriest and most intractable of any party.

A dozen Latin American countries protested the action vehemently and angrily. And so did Republicans in the United States Congress. "American children will go through life fatherless because of the action," cried newly elected Senator Elihu Root of New York. "And when these children grow to manhood, and turn back the page to learn in what cause their fathers died, are they to find that it was about a quarrel as to the number of guns and the form and ceremony of a salute and nothing else?" Root's protest was typical of those Republicans raised. Apparently a politician can sing one song about the Philippines when he is Secretary of War and another about Vera Cruz when he is in Congress.

The bloodshed distressed Wilson, who had expected no Mexican opposition. The protests convinced him that he had perpetrated one of the least defensible actions in American political history. Eagerly he accepted the offer tendered on April 25 of Argentina, Brazil, and Chile—the "ABC" powers—to mediate conflicts between the United States and Mexico. This mediation gave Wilson the chance to pull out of Vera Cruz in November, 1914, with as much dignity as possible under the circumstances.

The Vera Cruz adventure reveals one of the rents in Woodrow Wilson's idealism. In truth, he had good reason to go into Vera Cruz, but it was not a moral reason. The State Department had learned that the German freighter *Ypiranga*, loaded with 200 machine guns and 15 million rounds of ammunition for Huerta, was due to dock in Vera Cruz on the noon tide of April 21. Wilson sent the sailors and Marines ashore so that they could take the customs house and impound the *Ypiranga*, thus depriving Huerta of needed arms and seriously weakening him. But in the end, three thousand soldiers had to secure the city to insure the safety of the detachment in the customs house. Wilson did not tell either Congress or the American people about the *Ypiranga*. Instead he assured Americans on April 20, "There can be no thought of aggression toward Mexico. Its people are entitled to settle their own domestic affairs in their own way." He staged the operation under the guise of insuring American dignity rather than admit he was deliberately interfering with the outcome of the Mexican civil war.

In the face of German protests, however, the State Department found no legal way the United States could hold the *Ypiranga*. Three days after the sailors had impounded it the ship was released and unloaded its weaponry at Puerto Mexico, a small seaside wharf to the south of Vera Cruz. Nevertheless, the occupation of Vera Cruz weakened Huerta, if only because outrage against the United States united many revolutionary groups. Zapata, Villa, and Obregón coordinated their military movements against Huerta, and when Guadalajara fell in July, 1914, Huerta resigned as president and went into exile in Spain.*

*Huerta tried to return to Mexico in 1915, with German money, to finance a counter-revolution. He was caught and imprisoned in Fort Bliss, Texas, where drink finally got the better of him. He died during an alcoholic convulsion in January, 1916.

Huerta's resignation brought not peace, but even more bitter civil conflict. Every Mexican faction contended in bloody combat for Mexico City and its palace—and its treasury. American lives in Mexico were again endangered and investments increasingly threatened as *bandido*, *rurale*, and *Federale* robbed, extorted, and pillaged to keep small armies supplied.

Woodrow Wilson again offered Mexico a plan for mediation, promising that the United States would join with the ABC powers to bring a resolution of the conflict. He made a direct appeal to the Mexican people, pledging American support "to some man or group of men, if such may be found, who can rally the suffering people of Mexico to their support in an effort to return to the Constitution of the Republic." The plea had no effect. The Mexican people became more antagonistic to the *gringos* and sang in popular ballads of their willingness to go to war with the Norte Americanos.

Wilson should have expected no less. The Mexican revolutionaries were engaged in a struggle to the death that only complete victory by one faction could end. The outbreak of the European war distracted and preempted the attention of his administration, but Wilson was determined to restore peace in Mexico through American offices. He was forced to the conclusion that mediation, conciliation, and compromise would not work, that the United States would have to take sides with the strongest of the contending factions, now shaken down to the Villistas and the Carrancistas. When the ABC powers agreed among themselves to recognize Carranza as the head of a *de facto* government in October, 1915, Wilson did, too.

Congress knew and approved of the State Department's exchange of consular representatives with the Carrancistas; it knew and approved of Wilson's lifting the arms embargo; but it did not know and might not have approved of Wilson's giving the Carrancistas access across New Mexico on American railroads to beat Villa to Agua Prieta. No one ever blamed Woodrow Wilson for Villa's retaliation. But once Villa paid out his vengeance, there was no calling it quits. In its stormy ignorance, Congress was bent on passing a forceful resolution that would take Mexican—and European—foreign policy out of the President's hands. To save his prerogatives, Wilson had to bring Villa to justice.

Effective pursuit would have to start immediately. The national election for the presidency was only seven months away. To wait or to delay was to give the bloodthirsty Republicans an issue. Wilson dispatched Pershing.

Though he was an astute, even a profound student of history, Woodrow Wilson misunderstood the Mexican revolution because he confused its aims with those of the American Revolution. Consequently, he wanted Mexicans to enjoy the benefits of free elections. But the Mexicans did not care about free elections. And he presumed that the Mexicans, like the Americans, had revolted to make property inviolate. But the contrary was true. The Mexicans were in revolt precisely to violate property, because property belonged to the foreigners and to a small and haughty aristocracy. Wilson tried to instruct Mexicans in what they wanted by talking directly to them. But it is impossible for a nation to discuss options with itself. Nations depend upon parliaments or congresses or ministries or presidia to make decisions for them.

Woodrow Wilson subscribed to the credo that democracy was the wave of the future. The nineteenth century, he said, was the democratic century. That obdurate nations failed to see this only inspired in him the desire to teach nations about their future. He was to discover later that Europeans were as deaf as Mexicans to his pedagogy.

American foreign policy in Mexico displayed two fundamental shortcomings. Wilson never correctly gauged the aspirations of Mexican revolutionaries. He thought Villa, Carranza, Obregón, and Zapata prolonged the struggle through avarice and greed; he never assessed the force of nationalism that motivated these revolutionaries and their followers. Which is to say Woodrow Wilson did not understand that the Mexican Revolution was Mexican. Second, Wilson consistently overreached the means he was willing to employ in settling the civil war. He was never able to wield convincingly the threat of armed intervention. When he wielded it, he wielded it reluctantly, grudgingly, a Zeus who worried that the lightning bolt would hurt.

Many years later, Pershing asked, "Is it wise to interfere politically in the affairs of other nations unless we are ready to see the issue through if necessary by force?" He chided Wilson with regard to intervention in Europe, saying enormous naval and military establishments were required, and that Wilson "was averse to even adequate preparation." But he looked back on the Mexican intervention differently. "In the case of Mexico," said Pershing, "we had the force."

14

The Heaven-Lighted Blade

Left to his own devices, John J. Pershing would have collected every cavalryman and mount he could lay hands on and, within twenty-four hours, would have shipped these troops by Mexican Northwest Railroad to Guerrero, 230 miles south of Columbus, in Chihuahua. Here this cavalry force would have detrained and begun fanning northward over the plains and through the mountain passes. A reinforced column would have left Columbus a few days later, and perhaps the two cavalry commands would have caught Villa quickly in the nutcracker. But Pershing could not use available Mexican rail transport, which meant that his Punitive Expedition would have to chase Villa.

Villa's course wasn't hard to follow. Clouds of buzzards made swooping gyres over dead horses, and Pershing knew Villa would have to keep his force near water. Still, the advantage lay with the Mexicans. Villa had a running start into Chihuahua, the largest of the Mexican states, as big as New York, with a population of 327,000, all of them Villistas, at least in sympathy. Protected from the United States to the north by a forbidding desert and on the west by jagged mountain ranges, Chihuahua was an ideal hiding place for a bandit chief. There were wild ducks and geese, but a military force in search of provender was more likely to find lizards, horned toads, tarantulas, scorpions, and rattlers. Villa could supply his force from the villages, where his men could replenish their horses. His pursuers would have to depend upon a long supply line; and the deeper the pursuer drove, the more fragile the line grew.

Pershing had clear orders as to purpose and conduct from Woodrow Wilson:

> In view of the great distance between the seat of Government and the forces in the field, the President regards it as of the utmost importance that . . . all officers in command of troops of the United States clearly understand the exact nature of the expedition of our forces into Mexico, and he therefore directs obedience in letter and in spirit to the following orders:
>
> ONE. If any organized body of troops of the *de facto* Government of the Republic of Mexico are met, they are to be treated with courtesy and their cooperation welcomed, if they desire to cooperate in the objects of the expedition.
>
> TWO. Upon no account or pretext, and neither by act, word or attitude of any American soldier, shall this expedition become or be given the appearance of being hostile to the integrity or dignity of the Republic of Mexico, by the courtesy of which this expedition is permitted to pursue an aggressor upon the peace of these neighboring Republics.
>
> THREE. Should the attitude of any organized body of troops of the *de facto* Government of Mexico appear menacing, commanders of the forces of the United States are, of course, authorized to place themselves and their commands in proper situation of defense, and if actually attacked they will of course defend themselves by all means at their command, but in no event must they attack or become the aggressor with any such body of troops.
>
> FOUR. Care is to be taken to have in a state of readiness at all times the means of rapid communication from the front to the headquarters of the General commanding the Department, and, through him, to the War Department in Washington; and any evidence of misunderstanding on the part of officials, military or civil, of the *de facto* Government of Mexico as to the objects, purposes, character or acts of the expedition of the United States, are to be reported to the Department with the utmost expedition, with a view to having them

taken up directly with the Government of Mexico through the Department of State.

However, the orders did not specify treatment to be meted to Pancho Villa, if indeed the expedition captured him. Secretary of War Newton D. Baker later confessed that no one in the administration ever gave that prospect much thought. The chances are that, as the expedition continued its pursuit in the heat of mounting Mexican antagonism, Woodrow Wilson and his cabinet members covertly hoped Pershing would not capture the bandit leader.

The day after the Columbus raid, Carranza had notified the Wilson Administration of an old agreement between the United States and Mexico, dating from 1880, that provided for reciprocal border crossings by each country when its troops were in pursuit of Indians. Carranza wanted to activate this treaty in the event the Columbus raid *was repeated*. Wilson promptly accepted this reciprocal arrangement. In the exchange, Carranza did not describe how his government would secure the American border from the encroachments of Villistas, nor did Wilson mention that the Punitive Expedition was about to enter Mexico. Wilson and Carranza dealt with each other like two scarcely honest businessmen, each trying to win an exclusive advantage.

The two columns that crossed the border marched two days and a night over a Chihuahuan plain on which rain had not fallen for nine months. Within hours, the men were coated with a silver dust as fine as talcum. They looked as though they had been rolled in dough—from which the nickname "doughboys" is derived. The march was hard on the mounted troopers; harder on the infantry, who carried heavy packs and rifles; and hardest upon the mule skinners, who had constantly to stop to wrap wetted rags over the nostrils of their animals and soon fell behind.

The expedition found that the sun didn't set in Chihuahua, it simply vanished behind the horizon. With darkness came a numbing cold. Soon the troops were shrugging into their ponchos and rain slickers, for none of them had been issued coats. The water in their canteens froze by morning. It was obvious to Pershing and to every man in the expedition that the weather and the soldiering could only get worse, not better. Pershing's column found the body of an executed American, hands still tied behind his back, blindfold in place. He had been shot in the head and stripped of boots and clothes. The soldiers passed in oppressive silence, then the infantry picked up the step and the mule skinners made the air blue with their cursing.

On March 17, a week after the Villa raid, the two columns converged at Casas Grandes. Pershing marched both columns into camp a few hundred yards north of the town, at Colonia Dublan, a small, green oasis maintained by American-born Mormons. The war had claimed the lives of many of these Latter-Day Saints and even more had left. The survivors fell to their knees in prayer when khaki-clad troopers emerged from the clouds of dust. Pershing chose Colonia Dublan for his headquarters base because there was less chance of an incident there than at Casas Grandes. More important, Colonia Dublan was intersected by the railroad, and though Pershing was prohibited from using it, the Mormons were not. The expedition could receive supplies by rail as long as the supplies were addressed to residents at Colonia Dublan. And Pershing's supply problems were mounting.

Behind him in Columbus the supply depot was a maelstrom. Soldiers, animals, blankets, cannon, hay, hardtack, horseshoes, lumber, wire, boots, wagons, tools, and rations poured into a base that had not one warehouse. Fortunately for the expedition, Pershing had detailed Major William Sample of the Twenty-ninth Infantry as base commandant. Sample immediately hired civilian workers to build the mess halls, latrines, and barracks to accommodate the men, who soon constructed warehouses and stables, water lines and sewerage systems. Within a month, Sample had wrought from chaos not only an efficient supply depot, but a model installation of such manifold operations that the army brass found it necessary to replace him with a colonel. Two years later Pershing dropped stars on Sample's shoulders and put him in charge of a much greater, more complex base in France.

Pershing's tactical problems were unlike those ever encountered by an American commander. The pursuit of one army by another is often a military end in itself; pursued hard enough, an army often falls into disarray and surrenders when it runs out of space. But in this instance, Pershing could stretch his lines only so far in pursuit. He saw clearly that the harder he pursued Villa, the more the Villistas would disperse in the hopes of regrouping farther south. The more the Villistas dispersed, the harder they were to catch.

His plan was to send three columns south, like a trident spearing through the Chihuahuan plains, the Santa Clara Valley, and the mountain ranges. From each of the tines, smaller units would move east or west to flush Villistas, hoping to chase these bands to a place where the trident could pin them. Sooner or later, of course, the trident would splinter into dozens of units chasing badmen.

The Punitive Expedition might have quickly accomplished its objective if the eight planes of the First Aero Squadron, commanded by Captain Benjamin Foulois, had proved airworthy. These planes could have proved more efficient observers of Villa's whereabouts than troopers on horseback traversing unfamiliar territory at night. But the First Aero Squadron failed in a series of courageous misadventures.

The First Aero Squadron flew JN-2s—Jennies—the most unstable aircraft ever to leave the ground. The Jennies were equipped with 90 hp engines that were barely enough to lift them over the Palisades in New Jersey, let alone the Sierra peaks of Chihuahua. In the dry heat the propellers often splintered in mid-air. The planes had a limited cruising range, drifted constantly, and were likely to crash on landings or takeoffs. In 1916 the United States ranked fourteenth among the nations of the world in airpower, right behind still-feudal Japan. The emperor had expended $600,000 on his air force, Congress only $500,000 on ours.

The Jennies proved momentarily useful in carrying mail, flying between different advance bases with Pershing's orders, and transmitting needed intelligence for the expedition's staff officers. One Jenny flew Pershing's reports, taking off on nineteen such sorties in a single day. The First Aero Squadron, which lost all but two of its planes, provided only thirty-five days of use to the Punitive Expedition.

Colonel William C. Brown's Tenth Cavalry made up two of the three advancing columns. Pershing sent it west, where the regiment was to split in two, the first spearing south from Madera, the second from Babicora. While Pershing had no authority to use the Mexican railroad system, he was not prohibited from employing American locomotives and rolling stock. He asked for a dozen cars and a locomotive from the El Paso & Southwestern Railroad. The general manager sent what he had—an old wood-burning locomotive and twelve cattle cars whose sidings had no ventilation and whose interiors no flooring, the hoboes having burned them out with their fires.

The troopers disassembled nearby corrals for flooring; they repacked the wheel bearings under the guidance of the engineers; and they cut windows into the walls of the boxcars. Pershing warned the men to keep clean, boil their water, and stay out of Mexican dwellings. The train chugged off into the high mountains hoping to make Madera, a narrow mountain pass, in a day.

Halfway to its destination, the engine had almost exhausted its fuel. Uncoupled from the train, it went on ahead with troopers clinging to its sides, dropping off to scrounge for wood. The men on the stock cars waited through a cold night. Some of them wondered about setting fires on the newly repaired flooring. None of them dared. When the engine returned, Colonel Brown off-loaded the first column and led it himself toward Madera. The second column stayed aboard the rattler until Cumbre, when two of the horse cars jumped the rail and dropped troopers on the roof down a fifty-foot gorge. Eleven men were badly injured and a number of horses had to be shot. The men decided that they had had enough of trains and proceeded by mounts to Babicora, a ranch owned by William Randolph Hearst. There they learned that Villa was not in the high country, but to the east, in Namiquipa, forty miles away, on the other side of the mountains.

At the very moment that the Tenth Cavalry learned of his

whereabouts. Villa was routing a force of two hundred Carrancistas unlucky enough to run across him at Namiquipa. Villa
strengthened his army by forcibly impressing into it young men
who lived in the small villages he swept through. These draftees
rode with rifles pointed at their backs, the rifles cocked by Villa's
devoted bodyguard, the Dorados.

The column in best position to encounter Villa therefore was the
third tine of Pershing's trident, which moved out of Colonia Dublan under the command of Colonel James B. Irwin. Riding with
this third column, in order to coordinate the work of the other two,
was Colonel George A. Dodd, crusty, tough, and smart. This column ran into the remnants of the Carrancista force fleeing north.
Dodd asked its commander, Colonel Jorge Salas, Villa's whereabouts and Salas replied, "Namiquipa." Then Salas asked by what
authority American troops were in Mexico. Dodd produced the
document drawn up by the State Department outlining the reciprocal agreement between the United States and Mexico for the pursuit of Indians. Salas said he had never heard of such an agreement
and added that no Mexican officer had received formal notice of its
existence from his military or civil superiors. Dodd quickly reported this conversation to Pershing, and for the first time Pershing realized that his expedition did not have authority for its presence from the *de facto* Mexican government.

Dodd left the Carrancistas to their wounds and pushed the
Seventh through a gale of such ferocity that the men eventually
had to dismount, seek ground cover, and let the horses turn tail to
the wind. When the storm quieted, the Seventh led their horses
up a precipitous range. Marching through a forest of pine, cedar
oak, and juniper, they passed through Bachineva, where Dodd
learned that Villa had stormed the Carrancista garrison at Guerrero, thirty miles to the west. By a night march, Dodd reached the
plateau that overlooked the small town. On March 29 three squadrons of the Seventh launched an attack. Troops galloped as close to
the town as they could and charged on foot when their horses
dropped from fatigue. At first, the Villistas tried to repel the
charge, then fled in small bands. Troop E, which had worked its

way behind Guerrero, cut off the retreat for many. Guerrero fell at the cost of five wounded Americans. Fifty-six Villistas were killed, thirty-five more wounded. Dodd captured many of their horses, mules, and ammunition.

But the Seventh missed Villa by a few hours. During the fight against the Carrancistas, one of the forcibly impressed soldiers had seen the chance for a potshot at Villa, taken it, and felled the bandit chieftain with a .44 caliber bullet that shattered his shin-bone. In terrible pain, Villa had the wound dressed and splinted. He left Guerrero before dawn for Parral, where he could get medical treatment.

The action at Guerrero cheered the United States Congress. Wilson nominated Colonel Dodd for the Silver Star and for promotion to brigadier, actions promptly confirmed by the Senate. But Guerrero was as near as any of Pershing's columns ever came to capturing Villa, and the campaign was to last almost another year.

Having dispatched his flying columns, Pershing had to deal next with the endlessly threatened supply line. When Carranza learned that Pershing had used rail transport, he forbade Mexican customs from passing any train with American goods and supplies, no matter to whom addressed. The order effectively meant that the expedition must slowly but surely perish.

It took four mules to haul one disassembled mountain gun. Six mules hauled the gun's ammunition. A dozen mule skinners drove these wagons. Each mule and man had to be supplied by other mules and men carrying forage and food by wagon. In turn these men and animals needed supply. The problem expanded in a geometric progression that no commander could solve without rail transport. Pershing could hardly expect his command to live off the countryside, which had been devastated and stripped raw by revolution and civil war.

The State Department could not persuade Carranza to relax his prohibition. Consequently, the department washed its hands of the matter in early April. When General Hugh Scott howled at this ineptitude, the State Department apologized, but said if the army was going to use the rails in Mexico, it would have to use force to seize them. Hugh Scott asked Brigadier Henry G. Sharpe, quartermaster general, how many trucks were available at different army bases that could be used to supply Pershing. Sharpe said he didn't know, but he knew there were not enough. How much would it cost to buy enough trucks? Sharpe said it would cost almost a half-million dollars.

"All right," said Scott, "send right out and buy those trucks with the necessary traveling garages and mechanics. Put a chauffeur on every truck and send them by express to Columbus." Scott went over to Secretary Baker's office and confessed he had spent money without a congressional appropriation, a serious crime entailing a jail sentence.

"If anyone goes to jail," said Baker, "I'll be the man."

Army quartermasters bought more than six hundred trucks within the next month. Among the trucks, some of which were literally stolen from the New Jersey docks where they awaited shipment to England, were Whites, Jeffreys, Macks, Packards, Locomobiles, Peerlesses, Velies, a dozen tank trucks, six wreckers, and four machine-shop trucks. By June, when most of them were rolling in convoy, these trucks maintained a long line of communications deep into Chihuahua, over ground that was rutted and torn, where engines could boil over by day and the heads crack by night. The ingenuity of the drivers and mechanics kept the trucks rolling month after month without a stop. They found, for instance, that a mixture of gasoline, kerosene, and mule dung made a perfect radiator sealant when it coagulated.

The quartermaster general also purchased seventy-three passenger cars, most of them Dodge touring limousines. The Dodge car was the vehicle that took generals off horses and kept them off. The auto did work that astonished Pershing. The first photograph taken of the Punitive Expedition showed Pershing swimming a horse across the Rio Yaqui. Thereafter photos showed him in a Dodge touring car, although he still wore spurs.

The Punitive Expedition remains the poorest supplied of any American expedition. By the time it was concluded, there wasn't a piece of leather covering a stirrup, troopers having stripped their saddles for the leather to make soles for their boots. Pershing's furniture consisted of empty hardtack crates, his only concession to comfort a walled tent. He had purchased his own maps for the campaign in a New Mexico drugstore. One of his aides had to pay $3.50 for a small pad of lined paper so the general could send a report to Funston. Potatoes cost the mess officer $14.50 a bushel, and a small goat purchased for its milk cost $4.00. A disgusted mess sergeant described the goat as no bigger than a guinea pig.

The Mexican climate killed the animals. Troopers dared not mount a cavalry charge because the horses were so weak. On March 21, Maud, a mule that had hauled supplies for the Tenth Cavalry in Cuba, succumbed. The bugler blew taps. Veterans who also served in Cuba and later in World War I said the hardest campaigning they ever endured was in Mexico. Despite the hardship, Pershing said the Punitive Expedition added ten years to his life. The photographs taken of him during the campaign reveal a strong physical presence. Nevertheless, his experiences in Mexico implanted the first doubts Pershing ever had about his country's policy.

Pershing did not have the affection and respect for Woodrow Wilson that Grant had for Lincoln or George C. Marshall for Franklin D. Roosevelt. Pershing wrote, "I followed Wilson's policy despite the difficulty I had of understanding his mind." He went on in his autobiography:

> ... But though I followed instructions I often thought them wrong, and now that what happened is a matter of history it will do no harm to give the reasons.
> ... There have been a number of occasions when Presidents, led by Secretaries of State or leading them, have made strong protests on moral issues over the actions of other governments, even those as remote as Russia, China and Japan, but there has been probably no case more conspicuous or protracted than that of President Wilson in Mexico. Yet even in that country on our immediate frontier interference with only partial use of force was in my opinion a mistake. Instead of ending the trouble for the Mexican people, which was the declared purpose, our actions aggravated it. The

motive was right but the method wrong. Our government had two
well-cut alternatives, intervention or neutrality. If intervention was
chosen we should have gone in with adequate force and established
law and order—a very difficult task; and if neutrality, we should
have observed that in full. But we did neither. We denounced
factions in strong terms, imposed and lifted embargos on arms, made
demands and did not insist upon fulfillment, sent troops into the
country on two occasions for specific purposes and withdrew them
in each case before the object was attained. Not till we ceased
vacillation in regard to Germany did we cease it regarding Mexico.
Our entry into the World War took our attention away from the
revolution on our frontier and we left the Mexican leaders to fight
out their own rivalries.

When Pershing crossed into Mexico, two battered cars followed. In a rattling Model-T Ford were Floyd Gibbons of the
Chicago Tribune and Robert Dunn of the *New York Tribune*. Gibbons had bought the car in New Mexico by writing a check on a
piece of wrapping paper. Behind the Ford was a Hudson carrying
Byron C. Utrecht of the *New York World*, H. W. Blakeslee of the
Associated Press, and Frank B. Elser of the *New York Times*. These
correspondents made their press room wherever Pershing set up
his camp.

Utrecht publicized the sorry state of the First Aero Squadron in
a story headlined: "Risking Lives Ten Times a Day But Are Not
Given Equipment Needed." He also called the Jennies "suicide
buses." The story, which Utrecht slipped by Pershing's censoring
blue pencil, caused a furor back in the States. Secretary Baker
demanded an explanation from General Funston; Funston demanded one from Pershing; and Pershing from his inspector general, who asked the pilots how the story got into print. "Beats the
shit out of me," replied one of the flyers.

Gibbons filed exciting stories from Mexico, as well as stories on
the inadequacy of supply and organization that also created a furor.
Elser and Dunn kept diarylike accounts of Pershing's forays into
southern Chihuahua. Both of them later published these accounts
in popular magazines. The only lies these newspapermen wrote
concerned the "cooperation" the expedition received from the *de*

facto government. "Cooperation" was a necessary diplomatic myth.

Pershing found that his ability to communicate with his columns was negligible once they were on their way. The columns moved too fast for the couriers, and Mexicans had severed the telegraph wires. The wireless field radios, called "Telefunken," had a radius of only twenty-five miles. So Pershing resolved to move south as near to the columns as possible.

He had a small but extremely able staff at Colonia Dublan. Colonel De Rosey C. Cabell was chief of staff (to become a major general by 1919); Major James L. Hines was adjutant general; Major James A. Ryan was intelligence officer, his assistant Captain W. B. Burtt. These last two would both be general officers by 1918. They took over all detail and routine.

Pershing set off down the Santa Maria Valley in a gypsy caravan of five cars. He was accompanied by his aides, Lieutenants James L. Collins, Martin Shallenberger, and George S. Patton. Patton had wrangled the assignment by stalking Pershing's office in El Paso and convincing the general he was "in good with the correspondents," who found him fascinating copy because he had been an Olympic champion. Patton's endurance, stamina, and uncomplaining nature, his willingness to do more than ordered, and his initiative in seeing it done endeared him to Pershing. The other officers insisted that Patton was an imperfect cavalryman because he shot rattlesnakes with his .45 instead of severing their heads with his saber. Patton kept a diary and proved an able reporter of the expedition. Pershing knew about the diary and, when the expedition withdrew from Mexico, asked to borrow it as an aid for his final report. Patton was hard put to delete his comments about many of his superior officers.

Pershing left Colonia Dublan on March 20. In the lead Dodge, one fender decorated with an identifying red flag of headquarters and the other with the general's pennant, was Pershing, his orderly Lanckton, one of his aides, and the civilian driver. In the next two cars were eight enlisted men, two aides, and the general's cook, a black man named Booker, who once trailed a nervous hen into an adobe hut and waited for her to lay an egg for Pershing's breakfast. The newspaper correspondents brought up the rear in the last two cars.

The caravan traveled over brutal country, riven by ruts and arroyos, often with no road whatsoever, seldom bettering fifteen miles an hour. It bumped through the bottoms of 1,000-foot box canyons and over passes where flowers the size of pineapples bloomed. The newspapermen served as water bearers to quench the steaming radiators, lugging oat bags filled from small streams. Pershing paced quietly whenever the caravan had to stop to repair a blowout. They halted once at a hacienda, seeking a guide, but the inhabitants had smallpox. Speedily the cars pushed on. Another time Pershing stopped when the caravan passed a peon driving a rickety two-wheeled cart carrying brown lump sugar. Pershing paid the peon, picked up a lump, broke off a piece, and stuffed it in his jaw like a tobacco plug.

The caravan headed due south down the valley toward Namiquipa, a journey that lasted three days. They made camp the first night at El Valle. They ate slum—beef jerky boiled with potatoes and carrots, garnished with hardtack. Pershing, rubbing his chin, his characteristic gesture, stared toward the sere hills of the Sierra Madre. The night was cold, so cold that all Pershing took off before sleeping in his bedroll was his field glasses. He put on his slicker, pulled his campaign hat over his face, and slept deeply.

In the morning, he washed his face in a canvas bucket and shaved. He shaved every day he was in Mexico and expected everyone in headquarters to shave, too. He always wore a tie, even though his shirt was sometimes in its tenth day of wear. When there was a stream nearby, Pershing lathered himself with soap and dived in.

At Namiquipa, Pershing received reports from scouts and couriers. Having digested them, he settled into the Dodge with a flashlight to write orders. These he gave to Patton to deliver.

Pershing said, "Be careful, Patton, there are lots of Villistas. But remember, Patton, if you don't deliver that message don't come back."

This was the first chance the correspondents had to file dispatches. Bending before the car headlight, Pershing read Elser's optimistic conclusion that Villa might be killed or captured before the dispatch reached New York. Pershing looked up and said, "You fellows mustn't be too sanguine. It may require weeks, perhaps months. It's like trying to catch a rat in a cornfield."

Reports of Villa's death began to filter back to Pershing after Guerrero. As time went on, these rumors inundated the forward command post. The War Department had posted a $50,000 reward for Villa's capture and many a peon decided an old skeleton might pass for the bandit if decked out in a tattered sombrero and worn cowboy chaps. Patton went off on one of these details to ascertain if the corpse in a newly discovered grave was indeed Villa. He reported to Pershing, "If that was Villa, Villa was a runt."

From Namiquipa, Pershing moved farther south to San Geronimo. The headquarters detachment was now subsisting on hardtack fried in bacon grease. Reporters attended Pershing's first press conference in a light snow. Pershing had no tent, no table, not even a folding chair. To keep the fire from blowing out, the men stretched a sun-dried bull hide between two poles to serve as a windbreak.

"Our troops are pressing him," said Pershing to the correspondents, "but I won't hazard any predictions. Villa is no fool. It may be that the campaign has just started." With a pencil, he indicated on an imaginary map the directions in which the cavalry was moving. When certain units effected a second junction farther south, he said, they would have Villa surrounded. He paused for comment and questions. A lanky scout named C. E. Tracey, squatting on his haunches and chewing a straw, said, "Uh huh, completely surrounded, on one side." Pershing laughed along with everybody else.

Pershing also laughed one morning when he ran into camp and

excitedly exclaimed that he had found a nearby stream that was "choked with trout." Everyone followed him down to the creek bank, halted, and squinted. One of the guides spat. "General," said the guide, "them ain't trout, them're suckers."

One Sunday evening, when the valley was hushed, and the soldiers had piled the chaparral and brush for the fires, a mule wagon with four Mexican musicians, a woman, and three small boys creaked into the camp. The little orchestra had performed at a *felicitation* up the valley. The woman and the three boys remained in the wagon but the musicians got down and timidly began to strum and sing. The American detachment gathered round and the music became more spirited. The woman began dancing in the cart, her three sons singing the endless verses of "La Cucaracha."

The soldiers and correspondents applauded, crying, *"Mas! Mas!"* and the Mexicans passed around a sombrero to collect coins. Pershing had moved off into the gathering twilight, listening with arms folded as the group played "Adeleta." Then the woman began to sing the verses of "La Paloma." Lieutenant Collins rose and quickly shushed her. To the ring of soldiers he explained quietly, "It was her favorite song."

Pershing turned and came back to the group. "I liked that," he said. "Why did they stop? Tell them to play "La Paloma" for me, please." A little later, hand on his chin, he stood by the flickering campfire and watched the little wagon wobble into the darkness.

In early April, General Luis Herrera paid Pershing a visit. Herrera had been governor of Chihuahua province until Carranza assumed power. He had fought for both the Villistas and for the *de facto* forces, but had made no commitments to either after the Columbus raid. Herrera commanded an efficient cavalry. He was accompanied by these two hundred horsemen smartly outfitted in Carranza blue. His loyalties were no longer a secret.

The horsemen approached the camp, zigzagging across the floor of the mesa, testing whether they would draw fire. When they did not, they rode up the trail with a show of boldness. Herrera and his men wore a double row of cartridge belts over their shoulders, their boots were armed with cruel Spanish spurs, and the roans, pintos, sorrels, and bays were bitted hard.

Pershing's orderly, Lanckton, approached Herrera's horse and held its reins while Herrera dismounted and, with a fine show of white teeth, approached El General Pershing. The Carrancistas waited, mounted in a large semicircle, smiling, speaking so softly the Americans couldn't hear them.

The cook, Booker, swept the center of the area clean and provided a hardtack crate for Herrera and a gas can for Pershing. The Mexican was sizing up the Norte Americano and the American was thinking of the way the Mexicans treated their horses. Herrera asked if Pershing knew of Villa's whereabouts, or if he credited the rumors of his death. How many men had Pershing in the field? Where were they? Herrera said he was particularly interested in how much farther south the Norte Americanos intended going.

Pershing listened and asked Herrera what rumors he had heard of Villa. How many men did he have in his command? Where indeed were his men going?

Herrera flashed a big smile, rose, performed a sweeping bow with his sombrero, mounted, and with tumultuous shouts he and his men rode away, leaving Pershing on his gas can, hand stroking his chin. With his orders that day Pershing passed a message to his command: "All officers and enlisted men are cautioned against a feeling of overconfidence as to the final result to be achieved by this expedition."

The Punitive Expedition had now penetrated 450 miles into Chihuahua, almost to the Durango border, meeting more and more hostility from Villista and Carranza sympathizers and patriots. Supply lines were dangerously exposed to anyone who wanted to break them. Pershing had informed Funston and Scott that these lines were in fact stretched taut and bound sooner or later to snap. On April 14 he advised Scott:

It is very probable that the real object of our mission to Mexico can only be attained after an arduous campaign of considerable length.

It is possible that the truth of this statement may not be fully appreciated. . . . Our various forces have had to rely for their guidance upon the inaccurate knowledge of untried American employees, or else upon uncertain information of frightened or unwilling natives. Thus have well-laid plans often miscarried and the goal has moved further and further into the future. Almost the exact contrary is true as to Villa and his men. Villa is entirely familiar with every foot of Chihuahua, and the Mexican people through friendship or fear have always kept him advised of our every movement. He carries little food, lives off the country, rides his mounts hard and replaces them with fresh stock taken wherever found. Thus he has had the advantage since the end of the first twenty-four hours after the Columbus raid occurred.

As Herrera had issued an unspoken warning that the Punitive Expedition had gone as far as it was to go, so had Pershing issued a warning, which went unheeded. The Wilson cabinet was trying to resolve the Sussex Crisis: a German U-boat had torpedoed a passenger ship carrying twenty-five Americans. Baker, Scott, and Funston took the chance that the Carranza government would not break openly with the United States. They sent reinforcements to Pershing.

Pershing ordered this new force of artillery, engineers, and infantry to Colonia Dublan. The infantry began to move south along the extended supply lines and the engineers set to lengthening the roads. The artillery became a reserve. If the venture suddenly blew up in his face, Pershing had to order his cavalry to a point where it could consolidate and await relief or fight its way out. But he moved his headquarters still farther south to Satevó, eighty miles below Chihuahua City, one hundred miles north of Durango.

The Americans had by this time seen their last friendly face. Newspaperman Robert Dunn surmised that the worst had happened: Carranza had allied himself with Villa. "And Pershing took it on the chin. He never got a break. I shaved in his mirror, watched him work, but no word, act, mein of his gave away the gyp."

On his way to Satevó, Pershing passed through Bachiniva. He

came upon Major Frank Tompkins, who had chased Villa from Columbus and was commanding a squadron from the Thirteenth Cavalry. Before a campfire, Pershing suddenly asked, "Tompkins, where is Villa?"

Tompkins didn't know. He said he would surely like to find out.

"Where would you go?" Pershing asked.

"To Parral," said Tompkins. Parral was a small town on the Durango border.

"Why?" asked Pershing.

"Before he was a general," said Tompkins, "when he was just a bandit, he always holed up in Parral, in the mountains. He has friends there."

"What would you need?" asked Pershing.

"Twelve mules for transport," said Tompkins. "And the squadron. Villa might come out to fight a squadron."

In the morning Pershing said, "Go find Villa wherever you think he is." He gave Tompkins twelve pack mules and 500 silver pesos, and wished him good luck. Pershing and the members of his ever-mobile headquarters proceeded to Satevó in three days of hard driving. The touring cars bounced through the chaparral and the mesquite and past the cactus, trailed now by three trucks carrying gasoline for the remnants of the Aero Squadron. Pershing was dependent upon the trucks and the remaining two planes to carry messages. The caravan made its way through small village streets lined with Carrancistas, many of these troops as ragged yet as heavily armed as Villistas. These Mexicans suddenly began firing on the convoy. The caravan speeded ahead. In a cornfield outside Satevó, Pershing swung the cars off the trail. Soon the careening trucks drew up. The Americans had suffered no casualties but it had taken the mechanics and the guards an hour of determined resistance to beat off the attackers.

Pershing deployed the automobiles and the three trucks in a hollow square. The headquarters complement piled seats and cans, bedding and spare tires between the gaps and then set to digging an interior line of trenches.

Pershing held an inspection, checking rifles and side arms. The correspondents had been issued arms in San Geromino. Elser confessed to Pershing he had left his weapon behind him.

"Soldiers don't lose rifles," Pershing said.

"No, sir, they don't, soldiers," said Elser.

For the first time Pershing did not insist the newspapermen describe the cooperation of the Carrancista government. They informed their newspapers of the apparent attempt on Pershing. Elser noticed that Booker and some of the mechanics were on their knees in prayer. On closer inspection, however, he saw they were shooting craps. Not far away, the general slept, drawing deep, regular breaths, his boots standing like Paris chimneys beside his bedroll.

Major Tompkins was on the right track. Villa, soaking his wounded leg in potassium permanganate, splints completely covering it, headed south after Guerrero, probably reaching Parral, then seeking refuge in the Durango mountains. Tompkins might well have found the trail on which to run the bandit down, but Tompkins soon had all he could do to get his hundred-man squadron out of Parral alive.

General Ismael Lozano told Tompkins that Villa wasn't in Parral, that he hoped the Americans would find him wherever he was, but that Tompkins should never have come this far. Tompkins, who could see a large crowd of armed Mexicans collecting in the plaza, said he would get out as soon as he procured corn fodder for the horses. To hurry the squadron on its way, Lozano offered to lead them to a campsite outside Parral. It was a good idea, thought Tompkins, who loosened the flap on his revolver as the Mexicans in the plaza edged closer toward his men. No one was smiling. As the cavalrymen passed out of Parral, heading north, Carrancistas on a nearby hill opened fire, killing Sergeant Jay Richley. Lozano deserted, and Tompkins saw that the Carrancistas in Parral had mounted horses and were intent on giving chase.

Tompkins couldn't make a dash for it, the horses were too weak; besides, he had wounded now, so he kept his men at a steady trot, sending back small detachments to form a skirmish line and keep the Mexicans from charging.

The Americans moved briskly through the desert toward Santa Cruz, where Tompkins thought he could get them into a defensive perimeter. Six hundred Carrancistas pursued them, and were beaten back only by the cool discipline and courage of the rearguard, who consistently refused to panic, but kept pouring steady volleys into the ranks of the pursuers. That they were driving an invader from their land, however, was a concept that lent these Mexicans a new, determined courage.

Tompkins made it to Santa Cruz with the Mexicans close behind. The Americans had taken hard blows: two were dead, six were wounded, seven horses were killed, and sixteen more were bleeding. But the cavalry had taken a fearsome toll on the Mexican patriots. Probably forty were dead when General Lozano reined his troops a half-mile away and began readying them for a charge. Tompkins always thought that what prevented the complete devastation of his squadron was one of the American sharpshooters, who dropped a Mexican at almost a thousand yards. Lozano pulled his men farther back. Three cavalry troopers rode off for help. Tompkins thought he and his squadron had found another Alamo. Tompkins knew that he didn't want and was sure that Pershing didn't want another Alamo.

The messengers galloped on mounts near death from exhaustion and came across the rear of Colonel William C. Brown's Tenth Cavalry. Brown sent Major Charles Young, one of six black officers in the army, to Tompkins's relief. With Brown's arrival, trumpeters heralding the charge, flags whipping as the horses broke from the canter into the gallop, the Carrancistas withdrew.

Major Young relieved Tompkins on the night of April 12. Pershing learned of the fight on the morning of the fourteenth. The anger that welled within him was enormous. He called the correspondents, described the fight, and said in hot summation, "The lid is off. I want the American people to know the news. I want you to tell the truth." At that moment headlines became bullets, and

Pershing inspected the firing line of wildly typing men. Within the hour, Captain Foulois would fly the dispatches in the last of the First Aero Squadron's planes to Columbus (where the aircraft was destroyed—the squadron never re-equipped). Pershing stood over the newspapermen reading what they wrote as they wrote it. When Robert Dunn described Parral as an "ambuscade" Pershing stopped him and, in pencil, wrote "treacherous" ambuscade.

"Whole hog, sir?" asked Dunn and promptly typed in caps: "ARMY IN FULL RETREAT TO SALT LAKE CITY. PERSHING DECLARES ALLEGHANIES MUST BE DEFENDED."

Not a smile. The general was through laughing.

Elser wrote:

> The United States Punitive Expedition directed against Pancho Villa and his followers has come to a standstill. Whether the halt is to be permanent or not depends on circumstances beyond the control of General Pershing. But from a military standpoint he has for the time being come to the end of the line. . . .

Pershing asked if that was the way it looked to Elser, and when Elser nodded, Pershing said that was the way it looked to him, too.

What Pershing was looking at now was an armed crescent of Carrancistas, one tip of the crescent at Parral, the other below New Mexico, either tip capable of a scythelike cut that could sever the expedition's line of communication and supply.

15

Taking Orders

The day before Parral, General Funston had advised:

Villa's continued retreat makes our present line of communication and supply impossible. Only our advance cavalry which has probably reached Parral or is further south can have any effect on the chase. All the remainder of the thousands of troops are keeping up a line of communication that is unable to get supplies to the extreme front. In other words the line of communication is so long that the troops in the rear guarding it consume nearly everything that can be brought up along it.*

And General Scott had advised:

It seems to me that Pershing has accomplished about all he was sent for. It does not seem dignified for the United States to be hunting for one man in a foreign country. If the timing were reversed we would not allow any foreign army to be sloshing around in our country 300 miles from the border, no matter who they were.

From Namiquipa Pershing wired:

In order to prosecute our mission with any promise of success it is

*General Scott's armada of trucks was only now beginning to make runs.

therefore necessary for us to assume complete possession for the time being of country through which we must operate; and establish control of railroads as means of supplying forces required. Therefore recommend immediate capture of this command of City and State of Chihuahua.

He proposed to establish five military districts—Namiquipa, Guerrero, Bustillos, Satevó, and San Borja—each to be governed by a regimental cavalry commander, each commander to conduct independently the relentless search for Villa and the Villistas.

The advice and the proposal shocked Woodrow Wilson. The deteriorating situation finally engaged his full attention, and for the moment he had to forget the growing crisis with Germany. Parral had narrowed his options. To pull out after the incident was to cover his administration with shame and endanger his chances of reelection. Even after the Columbus raid there were several instances when American citizens on American soil were intimidated, robbed, or murdered by Mexicans who crossed the border and fled back into Mexico after their depredations. Pershing's presence in Mexico prevented any large-scale raids, because his cavalry could swing east or west to trap the raiding force.

Now, however, there were fifteen thousand armed Carrancistas in Chihuahua, under General Obregón, menacing this American force. These Mexican troops were trying to snake around Pershing's lines, and any sudden or impulsive move would bring on war. Wilson ordered General Scott to go to El Paso and confer with Funston, to see what the army could salvage from the situation. Scott was a big man with a white moustache, who always wore a campaign hat and affected a wool-lined sheep herder's jacket instead of the government-issued tunic. He was Wilson's man; his brother, a Princeton professor, was Wilson's dearest friend.

He and the diminutive Funston quickly outlined three choices for Wilson. On April 22 they wired that the Punitive Expedition could drive its way by force through Mexico and seize railroads to supply large reinforcements. Or Pershing could draw in his forces to Colonia Dublan, where there were water rations and considerable forage to support them into May. Their continued presence in Mexico could serve as an incentive to Carranza to kill or capture Villa. Or the Punitive Expedition could pull out, abandon Mexico, and patrol the border in force.

Scott and Funston recommended the second choice, with the proviso that the United States use the Mexican Northwestern Railroad, because the approach of the rainy season would make the road from Colonia Dublan to Columbus impassable. Wilson eagerly went along, and in a note to Carranza said the United States would maintain a police force in Mexico until the *de facto* government proved it was competent to guarantee the border.

By this time Pershing had established his five military districts, a rough parallelogram one hundred miles long by thirty miles wide. He asked Funston to delay orders to the expedition for a short time so that his command could flush several hundred Villistas who still inhabited this area. Pershing remarked that Carranza had no more control over what happened on the American border than "if he lived in London." While he was aware that the Carrancistas were hostile and bent on provoking his soldiers, he said, "I do not anticipate molestation unless they have overwhelming numbers coupled with every other possible advantage."

This stubborn, single-minded determination, which led Pershing to deploy his forces on the offensive against Villa rather than on the defensive against Carranza, stood his request in good stead. Funston delayed the orders for two weeks. In that time the cavalry fought sharp engagements at Tomochic, Ozos Azules, and Agua Caliente, the last notable because Captain Albert Phillips employed overhead machine-gun fire to advance attacking troops for the first time. Troopers flushed Villistas from mountain hideouts and village sanctuaries and, though threatened by *de facto* troops on several occasions, faced them down without incident. The deployment more or less convinced Carranza that it was indeed Villa the United States was after. When Pershing did start the withdrawal to Colonia Dublan, Carranza accepted an offer to send Obregón to confer with Scott and Funston at the Mexican customs house in Ciudad Juarez, on the southern side of the International Bridge.

At the end of April Generals Scott and Funston met with Obregón, the three soldiers talking over a round table in the center of a small auditorium, a gallery of Mexican newsmen above. They had, however, again come to talk about different subjects. Scott and Funston wanted the American border made inviolate, and Obregón insisted that the Punitive Expedition leave Mexico forthwith. Funston lost his temper. Shouting, he rose and banged the table, then promptly excused himself from the conference.

Scott and Obregón went at it alone. Fatigued and distracted because they got nowhere in formal talks, they adjourned and met secretly in a private room of the Hotel Paso del Norte, under the auspices of a mutual friend, A. J. McQuatters, president of the Alvardo Mining Company of Parral. In a conference that lasted from noon on May 2 until 3:30 A.M. on May 3, Scott and Obregón came to an agreement that they were able to communicate to their governments in 450 words. Their note said that, since the Punitive Expedition had accomplished its objective and the Mexican *de facto* government intended to maintain the pursuit of Villa, the United States would begin a gradual withdrawal of its troops, the withdrawal to commence immediately.

Scott said this simple agreement was reached only "after a continuous struggle of twelve hours duration which was not equaled by any similar struggle with the wildest and most exasperated Indian heretofore encountered." Back in Washington he put it succinctly to Wilson: "Get out now or be prepared to fight."

The United States thought that Obregón spoke for Mexico. He did not. Carranza spoke for Mexico. In the Wilson Administration's estimation Carranza was an intemperate, crotchety, addlepated old man, neither as moderate nor as acute as Obregón, a view far from reality. Carranza was a brilliant, visionary, resolute statesman who had seen that the United States had given ground at Parral and that, if pushed hard enough and long enough, the United States would withdraw the Punitive Expedition unconditionally. Carranza refused to sign the protocol because it indicated approval of the expedition's entry. "In refusing to be the base puppet of a Yankee felony," said Carranza, "we not only defend the national life, the honor, the dignity, and the independence of a people, but also those of a race—from the common mother who gave us her blood and her language." He warned Mexicans to prepare for war.

Carranza never dreamed that irregular Villistas would perpetrate another raid on the United States. But they did. On May 5 one hundred armed and mounted Mexicans crossed the Rio Grande at San Vincente, in the Big Bend. Splitting into two parties, they galloped north and south into the small settlements of Glen Springs and Boquillas. At Glen Springs the raiders killed two soldiers and a seven-year-old boy, and wounded several more Americans in the process of looting the general store. At Boquillas they kidnapped several Americans. If Woodrow Wilson had signed any agreement with Mexico on the morning of May 6, Texas, Arizona, and New Mexico would have seceded from the Union and started after the Mexicans themselves.

The Scott-Obregón agreement went for naught. General Scott advised calling out units of the Texas, New Mexico, and Arizona National Guard to reinforce the weak points along the border. But when these units assembled they numbered barely five thousand men.

"The whole country is given over to banditry," wrote Pershing on learning of the new raid. "The main purpose of the bandits is to live without work and have first call on all the young girls as they arrive at the age of puberty or even before."

Newspapers editorialized that Villa had outguessed and outwitted the expedition. Embroidering on the theory, the Hearst papers told their readers that Villa from his mountain sanctuary watched the United States Army pass in review every afternoon. To Elser, Pershing angrily insisted that no command that had ever left the borders of the United States more nearly ". . . represented the flower of the American Army or was better able to take care of itself in any emergency. They can't make this Expedition budge one inch unless so ordered. It stands ready to hold its ground, to meet all emergencies, face all contingencies."

In May, Patton distinguished himself while buying corn. In

three autos with ten men and two guides, Patton had purchased 250 hectares of corn at markets in Coyote, Salsito, and Rubio. In Rubio, however, the party came upon fifty horsemen identified by one of the guides as Villistas under the command of Julio Cardenas, the general who had personally led the Columbus raid. Patton set a course for San Miguel, the ranch owned by the Cardenas family. As he and an unarmed soldier approached the hacienda, three mounted caballeros bore down upon him. Unfortunately for these Villistas, Patton was the pistol expert of the United States Army. With three shots he dropped the horses, and, when the Villistas rose to fire upon him, dropped them. Patton lashed the three dead men over the radiators of the cars and drove back to headquarters. Afterward, Pershing always called Patton "The Bandit."

Pershing held on to Namiquipa with a small isolated troop although a *de facto* force of twenty-two thousand men was beginning to collect in Chihuahua City. This Mexican army had eighty pieces of heavy artillery—virtually every cannon in Mexico—and a hundred machine guns. Elements of this force were moving north toward Pershing's eastern flank. Pershing now commanded 10,500 men armed with twenty pieces of field artillery and twenty machine guns. But he felt confident that his force was better led and better organized.

"You are instructed to act conservatively," wired Funston. "If a breach does occur the responsibility must be beyond question on the Carranza troops." Though he was in a cramped tactical position, Pershing did not insist on aggressive deployment to protect himself.

On June 16, General Jacinto Trevino, commanding the Carrancista force at Chihuahua City, wired Pershing:

> I have orders from my government to prevent, by the use of arms, new invasions of my country by American forces and also to prevent the American forces that are in this State from moving to the south, east or west of the places they now occupy. I communicate this to you for your knowledge for the reasons that your forces will be attacked by the Mexican forces if these instructions are not heeded.

Pershing wired back:

> In reply you are informed that my Government has placed no such restrictions upon the movements of the American forces. I shall therefore use my own judgment as to when and in what direction I shall move my forces in pursuit of bandits or in seeking information regarding bandits. If under these circumstances the Mexican forces attack any of my columns the responsibilities for the consequences will lie with the Mexican Government.

To reinforce his point, however, General Trevino dispatched the Mexican commander at Casas Grandes to Pershing's headquarters to repeat the warning.

"I do not take orders except from my own government," said Pershing curtly, in a widely quoted remark.

In case of attack his orders from Washington directed him to wire Funston immediately and to move to destroy the attacking force, avoiding extended pursuit. The cavalry was to cut the railroads and secure the flank. General George Bell, Jr., would cross from El Paso and drive for Gallego, where Pershing would join him after taking Chihuahua City.

On June 17, 1916, Pershing received intelligence that a large Carrancista force was detraining at Villa Ahumada, ninety miles due east of Colonia Dublan. He ordered Captain Charles T. Boyd of Troop C, Tenth Cavalry, to make a reconnaissance of the area. Boyd was a West Pointer, a thoroughly capable and trustworthy officer who had published a book on tactics. Pershing also ordered Captain Lewis Morey of Troop K, who was midway between Columbus and Colonia Dublan, to join Boyd at the Santo Domingo Ranch, about twenty miles from the railhead, and assist the reconnaissance.

On the same day, Woodrow Wilson and Newton Baker regretfully came to the conclusion that the country would have to mobilize the entire National Guard, between 100,000 and 125,000 men, in order to free 30,000 regulars for what appeared to be an inevitable war with Mexico. Scott issued the order with the comment, "It looks to me as if the war will be on in a few days."

And Carranza called all male residents of Ciudad Juarez to the colors, issued rifles and ammunition to the populace of Nuevo Laredo, dismantled the Mexican vessels in Vera Cruz, and ordered the official records of every village shipped to the archives in Mexico City.

Captain Boyd, commanding the seventy-six officers and men of Troops C and K, approached the Mexican pueblo of Carrizal, three miles to the south of Ahumada, on the morning of June 21. The Mexican commander, General Felix Gómez, told Boyd he could not pass through Carrizal, that Mexico was honor-bound to oppose him. Though he could easily have skirted the pueblo, Boyd determined to breach it. "Goddamn you," Boyd said, shaking his fist at Gómez, "I've never disobeyed an order yet, and I'm not going to now. I'm going through your goddamned town."

"You will have to walk over the bodies of Mexicans," replied Gómez, whose two hundred men had already begun to take up defensive positions. In the next hour, these Mexican defenders killed fourteen Americans, including Boyd and Lieutenant Henry Adair, wounded between thirty and forty more, including Captain Morey, and captured twenty-five.

Though the Mexicans had sustained even more grievous casualties—Gómez died in the first volley—they had put the Americans to rout. Mexico City proclaimed a great victory. By wireless and telegraph Carranza broadcast the news to the world. Woodrow Wilson learned of Carrizal when he heard newsboys shouting "Extra! Extra!" on Pennsylvania Avenue. The War Department was provided with more details by the Mexican consul in El Paso.

While official Washington and its military hierarchy thought the war had begun and were preparing to aid the expedition's offensive developments, John J. Pershing knew nothing. His first intimation that a serious event had transpired came in a wire from General Funston: "Why haven't you reported?"

"Reported what?" Pershing wired back.

When he learned by the next wire that Captain Boyd's reconnaissance had been wiped out, he sent a detail of the Eleventh

Cavalry toward Ahumada to round up survivors. All of them were afoot, for during the battle their horses had stampeded.

Woodrow Wilson thought the fat was in the fire. He wrote Colonel Edward House, his personal emissary to the warring powers in Europe:

> The break seems to have come in Mexico. And all my patience seems to have gone for nothing. I am infinitely sad about it. I fear I should have drawn Pershing and his command northward just after it became evident that Villa had slipped through his fingers; but except for that error of judgment (if it was an error) I cannot, in looking back, see where I could have done differently, holding the sacred convictions I hold in this matter. Right or wrong, however, the extremest consequences seem upon us.

Funston, who believed Pershing guilty of a terrible blunder—a belief he had no inhibitions about expressing—also thought the fat was in the fire. He asked if he should dispatch General Bell's column to seize the railroad. Funston also wanted to move American troops across the international bridges immediately, to safeguard border towns from bombardment; and he wanted Pershing to attack toward Villa Ahumada, to beat off Mexican troops moving toward him. The War Department superiors ordered him to get the troops to the bridges, but to wait upon Bell's movement until Washington had confirmation that Pershing had moved. Wilson, Baker, Scott, and Funston waited for this news during the entire day of June 23.

But Pershing didn't jump.

He had provocation for the jump. And he had prompting. Major Charles Young, who had relieved Tompkins at Parral, and who was soon to become a lieutenant colonel, the highest-ranking black in the army, stormed into Pershing's tent when he learned that Mexicans had captured some of his troopers. He wanted to mount up and get his men back before the war made their rescue impossible. Pershing told Young he wanted to get the men back, too, more than Young did, but they would both wait.

Something had transformed him from a policeman into a soldier.

That something was the first sketchy testimony of the Carrizal survivors. Boyd had acted inexplicably—inexplicably and incredibly. Boyd had attacked an entrenched position over ground barren of cover. He had split his two troops so that one could not support the other. The captain could never have expected to gain a military objective; he was out to make history. For John J. Pershing, soldiers didn't initiate the historical process. Carrizal was Boyd's doing. Pershing filed his official report of the incident at Carrizal, and in it explained why he hadn't jumped:

Attention should first be invited to the fact that this Expedition having entered Mexico in pursuit of bandits, through the courtesy of the Mexican government, the *de facto* forces, in firing on our troops under these circumstances, committed a deliberate act of war. In declaring, through the military commander at Chihuahua, that the American forces were to be attacked under certain conditions, the Mexican government accentuated its own responsibility in the premises. So serious were the consequences believed to be that many did not think the *de facto* troops would risk committing such an overt act. Possibly this view may have had its effect upon Captain Boyd's mind, although there is no evidence to indicate that the thought ever occurred to him. Whether or not this be true, and regardless of Captain Boyd's attitude, the Mexican government itself was entirely responsible for the opposition offered to Captain Boyd's progress and, finally, for the culminating act of open hostility to the United States which started the fight at Carrizal.

With reference to Captain Boyd's action, I had known him a number of years, although not intimately, and considered him a capable and cautious officer who would faithfully carry out any orders he might receive. In giving him instructions regarding this reconnaissance, I told him, among other things, that the Mexican situation was very tense, and that a clash with Mexican troops would probably bring on war and for this reason was to be avoided. I pointed out to him that the country to the east was uninhabited and that he might have to go as far as Santo Domingo Ranch, a distance of about sixty-five miles, to get reliable information regarding the Mexican forces. I told him that at such a distance, should he clash with *de facto* troops, it would be impossible for me to support him. After my conversation with him, I felt confident that Captain Boyd fully understood the importance and delicacy of his mission. No one could have been more surprised or chagrined than I was to learn that he had become so seriously involved.

Due to failure of our aeroplanes, and the impossibility of verifying through native or other reliable sources the reported presence in the vicinity of Ahumada of 8,000 to 10,000 *de facto* troops, who had threatened to move against our line of communications, there was no other recourse than to send cavalry to reconnoitre in that direction. The hostile *de facto* commands at Ahumada and Carrizal were in a very advantageous position from which to strike our line at either Dublan or El Valle before we could concentrate at either place to meet them, unless by obtaining timely information we could anticipate their intentions. Under similar circumstances it had been necessary on several previous occasions to send cavalry as far as ninety miles away.

In view of the detailed instructions given Captain Boyd, the reasons for his action remain more or less a mystery. His decision to push on through Carrizal can be explained only on the hypothesis that, for some reason or other, he thought the Mexican troops would not fight, or that if they did fight he could easily brush them aside. In this view he was probably largely influenced by Lieutenant Adair's opinion. But it is even more difficult to comprehend why, after reaching the outskirts of Carrizal and talking with General Gomez, and seeing the large number of Mexican troops moving into position in his front and toward his flanks, Captain Boyd should have still adhered to his determination to go on. He surely must have seen that he was outnumbered and, if he thought there was going to be a fight, he could hardly have failed to foresee the dire consequences to his command in case of defeat. As to his mission, Captain Boyd had already obtained at Santo Domingo Ranch the information sought. Captain Morey had pointed out that his own orders did not contemplate going to any place occupied by *de facto* troops.

Arriving immediately in front of the Mexican position, his own command in an open plain, with mounted Mexican troops on his flanks within close range, it was a serious error to start a fight at all, but especially was it fatal to dismount to fight on foot under such disadvantage. Even though Captain Boyd had been directed to fight his way through to Ahumada, he would not have been in any way justified in deploying at such close range and engaging such a vastly superior force occupying such a strong defensive position. But every circumstance, from the time he arrived at Santo Domingo Ranch, up to the time he gave the command to fight on foot, including the note he wrote while there reporting that he had been to Ahumada and was on his way back, point to the conclusion that in Captain Boyd's mind there was slight probability of a fight.

As to the conduct of the fight, there is little that can be said in approval. The deployment was made very near the enemy's lines without cover or protection of any sort, and, under the orders given, the two troops from the start advanced along divergent lines. The right flank under Captain Morey, soon left in the air, was partially surrounded and turned, and, Morey being wounded together with several others, that part of the line gave way, broke and scattered. Boyd's own troops, urged on by himself and the dashing Adair, pressed forward into the town, but was itself soon decimated, several of its numbers were captured, and the attack failed.

The troopers in charge of the lead horses were left, in the first instance, in an impossible position. Later, after the fight started, they were ordered further to the rear, receiving a rather heavy fire during this movement, and, having no responsible person in charge, the horses became stampeded and the horseholders never recovered anything like an organized formation. The scattered groups of horseholders, pursued by superior forces of Mexicans, could hardly be expected to assemble. Under the circumstances, unfortunate as they were, it is not believed that any disciplinary action is indicated as advisable. There is no reliable evidence obtainable to sustain charges against any individual or group of these men for their conduct.

Notwithstanding the disaster resulting from this encounter, it must be said to the credit of this little body of men that they fought well as long as their officers remained alive to lead them and for some time after. The Mexican casualties were forty-two killed and fifty-one wounded, and thirty-seven horses killed. If Captain Boyd's force could have maintained cohesion among its parts, the results would probably have been far different. Too much praise cannot be given Boyd and Adair for personal courage in their gallant fight against overwhelming odds in which both died like the brave American soldiers they were.

Because Pershing waited, Wilson waited. To fill up the interminable time, the President and his Secretary of State, Robert Lansing, drafted a note to Carranza demanding the immediate release of the American prisoners. In part, they drafted the note to allay public demand for action. On receipt of the note Carranza agreed to release the prisoners immediately.

In the meantime, Wilson received thousands of letters, telegrams, and petitions from the constituency begging him not to start this war. The terrible magnetic attraction that had pulled two nations toward conflict was reversed.

Wilson had realized that the resources and reserves of the United States, resources and reserves the country might need for a war in Europe, would be drained off in Mexico. Once committed to a Mexican war, America's influence in demanding peace as the price for its neutrality would be a negligible factor in European considerations.

Carranza realized that a war with the "Colossus of the North" would imperil the Mexican Revolution. While his forces outnumbered Pershing's, Carranza had to tie up one army in the south in an ever-continuing skirmish with Zapata and string out another the length and breadth of the land to put down village mutinies and discourage ambitious opportunists.

With the return of the American prisoners, who crossed at Laredo, some of them barefoot, others wearing sandals, many with blankets for clothes, the two governments again bent to their tedious demands. Wilson asked for guarantees that the border be made secure. Carranza insisted that the Punitive Expedition pack up before he considered an agenda.

16

Home for Stone Wine

Mobilized on June 18, the National Guard sent 122,000 men to the border. The first Guard unit reached San Antonio on June 30 and the last reached Douglas, Arizona, on July 29. The Guard suffered shortages of transport, equipment, and weaponry, and hardly constituted a trained force, but its morale was excellent— with one or two exceptions. One lieutenant, detraining in New Mexico, asked in mounting terror, "My God, is this Columbus?" He reboarded the train, took out his .45 and shot himself. Guard units from the north were so unfamiliar with the Southwest that, when troop trains deposited them at campsites, their officers formed defensive perimeters on the assumption they were in the middle of Chihuahuan plain and could expect attack at any minute.

Assistant Chief of Staff Tasker Bliss made a detailed inspection of every Guard unit as soon as it set up. While he found much that was far from perfection or full efficiency, everything was better than the chaos of 1898. By the fall, the Guard became much more efficient; the troops trained over the summer and were adequately supplied and well armed.

Demobilization of the Guard began in January, 1917, but several units were still on active duty when Congress declared war on Germany in April. The dry run at the border, however, immeasurably instructed the army in mobilization procedures. Important, too, the dry run convinced Congress of the attendant dislocations in mustering men suddenly from civilian life for military duty. It passed a dependency act for the families of guardsmen called up. This act provided the precedent for similar legislation enacted during World War I and all subsequent wars of the United States.

Carranza's foreign minister, Candidio Aguilar, sent a note on July 4 that contained neither threats nor recriminations but stated directly: "The American Government with reason believes that the insecurity of its frontier is the cause of difficulty, and the Mexican Government considers that the continuance of American troops on Mexican territory is the immediate cause of the controversy." Aguilar proposed direct negotiations between the two governments. Wilson eagerly accepted the recommendation. He named three American commissioners to confer with three Mexican commissioners, neither side to adjourn without reaching an agreement.

The Joint Mexican-American Commission held its first meeting in a New London, Connecticut, hotel in mid-September 1916. It moved to Atlantic City in October. While the commissioners, in fact, could not agree on a protocol, their conferring gave their respective governments the time to find their respective accommodations.

At Colonia Dublan, Pershing's troops started to set up campsites on the wind-blasted plain. They were no sooner up than the rains changed Chihuahua into a morass, badly fouling the supply line. The troops were without heavy canvas for tenting. They were without rainwear. They had no tarpaulins. They endured the mud, which turned Colonia Dublan into a field of molasses; and. the heat, which almost turned the mud into bubbling lava; and the wind and the dust, which on dry days made the soldiers wish for rain. Army engineers, however, turned the road from Columbus to Colonia Dublan into a superhighway within months. Along it passed meat, flour, mail, coffee, and fodder. The troops learned quickly to make adobe huts from the soft earth. They reinforced these huts with straw and stretched their ponchos and their shel-

ter halves across them for roofing. They constructed a grid of
company streets, and white-washed the stones that lined the paths
to the mess, the headquarters, and the hospital. They had found a
Sahara and transformed it into a Switzerland.

Pershing kept them busy with simulated field exercises, fatigue
detail, and target practice, endless target practice. He had never
subscribed to the myth that there are natural-born marksmen. He
insisted that a man who is trained to shoot is without exception
more accurate than a man who is not. The infantry tramped endlessly, and the cavalry galloped in formation over the plains,
whether soggy or dry, and the men hated it and hated Pershing for
it. They griped that he was not only a martinet but a chicken-shit
martinet.

Yet he allowed the installation of a whorehouse in the center of
the compound. It was managed by an American madam and staffed
by an infinite variety of Mexicali Roses. The doctors inspected the
girls daily and the MPs made sure the clientele had the two dollars. The MPs also steered the sexually sated to a prophylaxis
station as soon as they exited. As a consequence, Pershing's Punitive Expedition had the lowest venereal disease rate in the army.

Pershing would not authorize the MPs or the officers of the day
to interrupt the nonstop evening crap and poker games. The men
were paid in silver coin, and for a week after payday Colonia
Dublan clinked as though it were a gigantic sleigh equipped with
bells. When Pershing and Patton went riding in the late after-
noons, they would often jump their mounts over high cacti, even
though they knew this innocent pastime brought out the gaming
instinct in the men.

Pershing devoted himself to the unpleasant duty of forwarding
professional estimates of his regimental commanders and their
field grade subordinates. He found three, two colonels and a
lieutenant colonel, wanting. Of one he wrote that the man knew
little of service in the field or else cared nothing. Another, he said,
was weak, vacillating, and dilatory. The third seemed "simply
asleep." "The sooner the Army gets rid of men like these three
mentioned the better it will be off," he wrote, in a sentence that is
impossible to parse.

These judgments were not gratuitously rendered by Pershing. Newton Baker had asked General Tasker Bliss to set up a committee of four generals to go over the army's list of field grade officers, indicating those who were to receive initial high command in the event of war, and those who were not. Some older officers would be asked to retire. Bliss's board took into consideration not only an officer's past record, but how fit he was physically and mentally to be elevated to the command of ten to twenty-five thousand men, when he had never before commanded more than five hundred. Bliss passed over officers with colorless records and always preferred the younger man to the older. Pershing lost three friendships. Bliss lost score upon score of friends.

Pancho Villa's gangrenous wound healed. In late August he appeared at Satevó with five hundred Villistas, surprised and killed two hundred Carrancistas, and put another two hundred to route. Then he disappeared into the hills, only to reappear a week later at Santa Ysabela, where he seized a military train and rolled its stock to San Andres. He also posted a letter on the walls of a dozen pueblos, promising to move on Chihuahua City and drive out General Trevino. Trevino considered the threat the empty promise of a braggart, an unfortunate judgment.

Villa's men galloped into Chihuahua on September 16 at 2:30 A.M., broke down the gates of the penitentiary, freed hundreds of convicts, and chased Trevino out of the governor's palace. Villa then delivered a speech from the balcony and departed with sixteen automobiles loaded with rifles, as well as some artillery hauled from the city by mules. His ranks were swelled by men recruited from the Carrancista forces. Behind him, in the streets of the city and in the alleys and around the plazas, he left six hundred dead men, half of them his, half of them Carranza's.

Villa was a sadistic, monstrous racist, who consistently attacked Chinese neighborhoods and murdered men, women, and children without mercy. The Chinese in northern Mexico left their villages and headed for the American encampment at Colonia Dublan. There they reestablished and reinventoried their small stores,

reopened laundries, and found the capital and the runners to operate their lottery.*

Villa's reappearance disrupted the touchy diplomacy between
the United States and Mexico. Carranza had been insisting since
late March that Villa was dead and that, therefore, the Punitive
Expedition had accomplished its mission. The attacks on
Chihuahua and Santa Andres, he said, were carried out by Huerta
diehards disguised as Villistas. But Villa was on the rampage
throughout Chihuahua with three thousand men, two thousand of
them well armed, all of them mounted.

American consuls in Tampico, Mexico City, and Monterrey
confirmed that northern Mexico was again invested with anarchy.
Trevino and General Cavazos admitted that the situation was beyond their control. Obregón and Carranza, however, airily dismissed these sentiments as subversive pessimism, and said that
peace had come to Mexico forever. The American commissioners
in Atlantic City said they could not accept this fantasy. The joint
Mexican-American Commission adjourned.

On November 2, Pershing outlined a campaign in which the
expedition would move quickly down the Santa Clara Valley to
seize Chihuahua City, from which he would dispatch his columns
east and west to hit and decimate the Villistas. This time he would
beard the "Lion of the North" in his den. Pershing argued that
chances for success now favored him, rather than Villa. His men
were trained and hardened, familiar with Chihuahua, eager and
pressing for the assignment. Such a blow, he insisted, would devastate Villa before he grew stronger and brought down the *de facto*
government. Moreover, argued Pershing, considering the disarray
of Carrancista troops, there was no danger of interception by the

---

*When the Americans went home, they took this Chinese colony with them, even
though Pershing had been informed that it was in direct contravention of the law.
Pershing replied that he could not leave the Chinese to be murdered and that
there were several ways to skin a cat. The State Department admitted the
Chinese as immigrants provided they never became public charges. A great many
of them found work laying ties and rails for the El Paso Railroad. At night they
were always penned up in their own stockade.

government. This time there was every expectation that the civilian populace would welcome the Americans.

Funston agreed. Bliss agreed. Scott agreed. But Wilson said no. Instead, the President coaxed the Mexican and American commissioners back to the conference table.

Pershing went into Mexico doubtful of the policy that sent him. Having realized his worst apprehensions, however, he became bent on tearing evil root and stump from the bare plain made desolate by Villa's savage and merciless depredation. Pershing made an existential decision that, because he had begun, only by finishing could he and his country sustain meaning and purpose from the whole affair.

Villa captured Parral, Torreon, and Camargo and again drove Trevino from Chihuahua City. He published *General Villa's Manifesto to the Nation*, in which, in richly rhetorical phrases and inflammatory slogans, he promised to take back the whole of Mexico and drive from the north "the abhorred Yankee."

"A swift blow should be made against this pretender," wrote Pershing to Funston after Woodrow Wilson's reelection. "Our own prestige in Mexico should receive consideration at this time. In the light of Villa's operations during the past two weeks, further inactivity of the command does not seem desirable."

But desirable it was. The Joint American-Mexican Commission had drawn up a protocol, which Secretary of State Lansing signed, stating that the expedition would leave Mexico forty days after Carranza added his signature, provided Villa did not menace northern Mexico at the time. The proviso really moved everyone back to square one, so the *de facto* government repudiated the protocol. Carranza mustered a large army instead, headed by the courageous Mugica. This army drew Villa from Torreon during the first week in January, 1917, and beat him badly.

The defeat momentarily lessened Villa's threat to the border, and Wilson took advantage of the situation to bring the Punitive Expedition home. Pershing later confessed that, when he received the order on January 12, he wept in the privacy of his tent.

Whether he shed tears is, of course, conjectural, but his heart wept.

On January 27, the Punitive Expedition struck its tents and abandoned its adobe huts. Ten thousand six hundred and ninety men, 9,307 horses, 2,030 Mexican and 533 Chinese refugees began marching toward Palomas. They crossed the border at Columbus on February 5. Pershing took the salute from troops who had long ago exhausted spit and polish to prettify themselves, but who were as tough and hard as the men of the old frontier cavalry. With some sadness, he watched the columns disappear into the huge cantonment of Columbus. The last posse had stabled its horses.

Some historians suspect that Pershing's Punitive Expedition was a covert military exercise to prepare the United States for its role in World War I. Others see in the expedition an aberration in American foreign policy. It was neither.

It is true that the Punitive Expedition tested equipment. The army discovered the value of motor transport in Mexico and, by 1917, had specified a standardized truck model. It also discovered that the regulation shoe would not do, and had given out contracts for new lasts long before the country entered World War I. Commissary officers, who improvised "rolling kitchens," found they could keep troops well fed indefinitely.

It is equally true that the experiences of the Punitive Expedition convinced military men that the cavalry still had an important role to play in modern war. During World War I the United States kept several cavalry divisions active. As late as July, 1918, Pershing asked for two cavalry divisions for the Western Front, a serious error in judgment that Chief of Staff Peyton C. March, an artilleryman, kept hidden from history by pigeonholing the request. Despite Pershing's misgivings, the Punitive Expedition uncovered the importance of the airplane. But no airplane of American manufacture ever flew in France.

What lends credence to the thesis that the Punitive Expedition was a preparatory military exercise for the European war is that, in the mobilization of the National Guard, the General Staff realized that it needed conscription to muster the army needed for a modern war. Indeed, Enoch Crowder, the Judge Advocate General, began preparing such a law as soon as the army realized this inadequacy of the Guard units. But the expedition was not dispatched originally to test mobilization procedures. And it was not the infelicity of the Guard's mobilization in 1916 that convinced Congress of the need for a draft law. What convinced Congress was that, by April 30, 1917, three weeks after it had declared war, only five thousand volunteers had enlisted. The army would need three million men to secure victory. Moreover, the Punitive Expedition did not test Crowder's well-written Selective Service law, which held up in the Supreme Court, or Newton Baker's decision that communities themselves, through appointed boards, would implement the draft.

What belies the insistence that America was preparing for a big war by indulging in a little one is Woodrow Wilson's avowed policy of neutrality. Wilson told the people that America was "too proud to fight," and that his administration would be neutral "in thought and deed." The voters returned him to office on the ground that he had kept the country out of war. In fact, early in 1916 Wilson had summoned Tasker Bliss to the White House and, in his cold, professorial manner, asked if it was true that the General Staff was preparing plans for a war with Germany. Bliss said it was so; that the General Staff and the War College understood it was their duty to prepare plans for war with England, France, Italy, Japan, and Mexico as well. In a fury, Wilson insisted that every officer involved in such plans be transferred immediately. In a cooler moment, he reconsidered and rescinded his orders for a wholesale transfer. What planning did go on was henceforth camouflaged. At the beginning of World War I there was not one combat-ready division in the United States.

Which leaves American history with the thesis that the Punitive Expedition was an aberration. Considered solely in terms of the Mexican Revolution, militarily and politically it was. The expedition's objective was the pursuit and dispersion of the band or bands that attacked Columbus. The expedition did disperse that band, killing 273 of its 500 members, including two of Villa's ablest generals, Julio Cardenas and Candelario Cervantes. But by August, 1916, Villa was once again a force in northern Mexico, and remained so for years. Even during its presence in Mexico, the expedition could not prevent minor raids on the American border.

Politically, Woodrow Wilson suffered a decisive defeat at the hands of Venustiano Carranza. Carranza sought to limit the dangers of future expeditions by persuading or compelling Pershing's to withdraw at the Mexican government's insistence. And Carranza won. Time and the vast open spaces of Chihuahua favored him. Carranza also played adroit politics. His threat of an oil embargo against Britain, until the expedition left, brought pressure on the State Department from London, for Britain was wholly dependent upon Mexican oil. The equally suggestive threat of a Mexican alliance with Germany made Southwestern Senators and Congressmen uneasy. Wilson's sanctimonious interference alienated Latin America; and his conviction that he knew what was best for Mexico, "with its pitiful men, women and children fighting to gain a foothold in their own land," was a fatal error. Wilson's perplexed and desperate Mexican policy cost over $150 million and the lives of more than one hundred soldiers.

But this Mexican policy was no more aberrant than the declaration of war against Spain to secure Cuba's independence; no more aberrant than maintaining an island garrison in the Pacific to secure nonexistent profits; no more aberrant than sending troops to Haiti, where they remained for nineteen years; no more aberrant than removing a combat regiment bound for the Western Front to invade Russia, late in World War I.

These policies of intervention reveal the American messianic determination that every revolution ought to conform to the American Revolution, which was waged by liberal and reasonable patriots. But most revolutionaries are neither liberal nor reasonable, nor do they make revolution in order to conform to the American model. Rather, they impose on their countries their own vision, which may range from the need to realize the prophecies of dialectical materialism to the need to free peons from serfdom to *gringos*.

Without the Punitive Expedition it is doubtful that John J. Pershing would have commanded the American Expeditionary Forces in World War I. At that it was nip and tuck. Woodrow Wilson heard rumors that Pershing was critical of his Mexican policy. Scott passed a warning to Pershing when the expedition came home. Pershing composed a "frank and manly" letter, in which he insisted that the reports were without foundation, that his remarks had always been guarded, and that he was neither a champion nor a critic of the administration, but an officer in the United States Army, bound in honor and conscience to obey his orders. Scott saw to it that Wilson read the letter. While Woodrow Wilson could not abide criticism, he considered his enemies to be critics who commanded newspaper and congressional prominence. Insinuation did not bother him. Scott later attributed the rumors to Pershing's rivals. Every major general in the United States Army would have given his right arm for command of the Punitive Expedition, but it had, by one means or another, devolved upon a brigadier noted for luck.

Without the Punitive Expedition, George S. Patton's career probably would have taken a far different turn. He emerged from the campaign as a Pershing protégé. And was to remain a protégé until he discovered that the tank was hardier than the horse.

And without the expedition Lieutenant Martin L. Crimmins probably would not have become a preeminent herpetologist, the world-recognized authority on rattlesnakes.

What remains important about the Punitive Expedition is that, because of John J. Pershing, it is the exemplar of the disciplined military effort in pursuit of an erratic and perhaps impossible national policy. When a Senate investigating committee asked questions in 1951 about President Harry Truman's dismissal of General Douglas MacArthur, George C. Marshall testified about the political inhibitions that restricted Pershing. "Pershing told me," said Marshall, "that he didn't mention [the orders to withdraw] to any of his staff, and that he walked around his tent, and around the bivouac there most of the night, and gave the order the next morning for the beginning of the withdrawal without any explanation whatever to anybody concerned. I think it was a very good model to follow in the Army."

17

A Worthy Army
for a Sacred War

Two protean struggles engaged the United States between August, 1914, and November, 1918, by which it hoped to influence and change world history. First was the struggle for a policy of neutrality in the Great War, and, when that foundered, the struggle to bring into the line an identifiable American army charged with a designated military objective. The first of these struggles was fought by Woodrow Wilson. The second devolved upon John J. Pershing.

When he campaigned for the presidency in 1912, Woodrow Wilson promised to invigorate the slackening United States economy by "readjusting" the tariff, making credit for investment more accessible, and building a merchant marine, all of which would increase American exports. The steady growth of the American economy would soon depend upon the nation's ability to secure world markets by competing with other industrialized powers. Wilson believed the country would win this race, because America was energetic, technically expert, and inventive, and also because America was morally determined to better the condition of the world.

"When an American comes into competition," he told the electorate, "he comes without arms that would enable him to conquer by force, but only with those peaceful influences of intelligence, a desire to serve, a knowledge of what he is about, before which everything softens and yields, and renders itself subject. That is the mission of America." Wilson wanted his country ruled by the Christian ideal of peace on earth and the Christian ethic of service to others.

"It would be an irony of fate," he told his wife, Ellen, on his inauguration day, "if my Administration had to deal with foreign affairs." Two years into his first term, however, the Central Powers of Germany, Austria-Hungary, and Turkey went to war against the Triple Entente of France, England, and Russia, also called the "Allies."*

The Great War did two things for America. Trade with the warring powers invigorated the American economy and made it mighty, conferring upon the nation an undreamed-of prosperity. Because of its highly charged industrial output and profitable wartime trade, by 1916 American banking reserves had $3 billion *more* than the combined banking reserves of England, France, Switzerland, Germany, the Netherlands, Russia, Japan, and the Reichsbank in Berlin. But the endless war also endangered that prosperity because the endless war weakened Great Britain.

It was this danger that inspired Woodrow Wilson's policy of neutrality. It was a positive policy, applied unremittingly in order to safeguard American interests. Wilson's neutrality aimed to stop the fighting in Europe before either side gained a decisive victory. In place of victory, Wilson tried to convince the European powers that their best interests could be realized by a negotiated peace, made lasting by the influence and economic power of the United

---

*Bulgaria joined the Central Powers in 1915. The Grand Alliance against them eventually numbered twenty-four countries, two of which, Russia and Rumania, did not last out the war. There were nine European states: Belgium, Britain, France, Greece, Italy, Luxembourg, Montenegro, Serbia, and Portugal; the United States and eight others from the Americas; Japan, China, and Siam from the Orient; and Liberia from Africa. No all were at war with all the Central Powers.

States. What Wilson saw beyond the war, and what he hoped to mediate by his neutrality policy, was an international community of civilized powers dominating the world, whose continued well-being would be guided by American liberal capitalism and moral hegemony.

"Somebody," said Woodrow Wilson in the 1916 election, "must keep the great stable foundations of the life of nations untouched and undisturbed. Somebody must keep the great economic processes of the world of business alive. Somebody must see to it that we stand ready to repair the enormous damage and incalculable losses which will ensue from this war." That somebody of course was the American people. Wilson, like Presidents before him, was giving voice to the messianic urge of America, channeling its impulses to end a major cause of imperialist conflict by a reform of world politics.

But Woodrow Wilson also insisted that, despite the war, America would not sacrifice any of its worldwide interests. The country would not join the fight, but it wanted the fighters to respect American international rights to trade and travel.

Neutrality meant something else as well—benevolence toward one of the warring combines, the Allies, whose trade and credit were encouraged by government decision. Loans to the belligerent Allies and the shipment of arms were not hostile acts, but reflected America's view of international law. Wilson could have opted for a policy of noninvolvement that would have entailed vast inconvenience for American enterprise. Noninvolvement was what the Mid- and Far West wanted. William Jennings Bryan, in fact, resigned as Secretary of State when he realized Wilson had abandoned a policy of noninvolvement.

Neutrality is always called "Woodrow Wilson's Neutrality" principally because he was its father; because he was its most eloquent and persuasive spokesman; because he made it his own by dispatching unelected emissaries, like Colonel Edward M. House, to the warring powers, emissaries responsible only to him; and because he managed the policy alone, typing out on his portable typewriter the official notes and proposals he sent to the heads of state and government in Europe.

Basically Wilson essayed three approaches to bring the warring nations to a compromise peace. In the first two years of the war, he tried to coax and persuade combatants to commit their war aims to an agenda. These aims were to be adjudicated in a conference presided over by the United States. Wilson acted on the presumption that world opinion would force the creation of such an agenda and the conference. This was far from an illusory hope. World opinion had led nations to institute the Hague Conventions of war, had established maritime principles, credit laws, and joint exploratory adventures. Though world opinion had not deterred the British in the Boer War, it had produced a division in British politics. But world opinion failed Woodrow Wilson in 1916, because only the opinion of the United States counted with the warring powers, and that opinion simply was not influential enough to make the Germans reconsider the case of Alsace-Lorraine, provinces claimed from France in 1871; or persuasive enough to force England to reconsider the independence of its colonies; or force France to reconsider its claims in Africa.

When he failed to persuade the warring nations, Wilson tried to coerce them. One example was the House-Grey Memorandum, negotiated by Wilson's plenipotentiary, Colonel House, and the British Foreign Secretary, Sir Edward Grey. The memorandum provided that, at a time propitious for the Allies, Wilson would propose a conference to end the war. Should Germany decline or reject these good offices and turn her back on a reasonable peace, the United States would "probably" enter the struggle on the Allied side. But the French and British never saw the immediate moment when this was to their interest. Their generals were never convinced that the war was stalemated or that their armies were beaten, and therefore neither government invoked the plan.

Last, Wilson tried to "light a fire behind governments" by addressing the warring peoples directly, through the offices of the League to Enforce Peace, and in the course of an address to both houses of Congress, in which he asked European nations to secure "peace without victory." This failed, because European peoples could in no way talk things over with themselves, and because they did not want "peace without victory."*

For these reasons neutrality failed. It may have been doomed from the start, for Woodrow Wilson only imperfectly saw the Great War. Wars are fought to realize state policy, and state policy can often be modified or compromised or adjusted. But this is not true in civil wars and the Great War was an unrecognized form of civil war. If there is any doubt as to this assessment, one has only to realize that the war destroyed orders of government that had existed for centuries; that it bankrupted almost all of the warring nations; that it ended the political, cultural, and economic domination of the world by Europe; that it provided the impetus for revolutionary socialism; that it inflamed nationalist patriotism and yearnings everywhere. One can ask no more of a civil war.

For Wilson to have understood the Great War as a civil war would have meant heeding the precept forwarded by Venustiano Carranza that "History furnishes no example of a civil war terminating by the union of contending parties." Had he known that the combatants in Europe wanted to fight to the death, Wilson might have realized the limited power of American moral and economic influence in bringing peace to such antagonists. In the long run, American intervention only helped prolong that civil war so that another generation could fight it.

Still, Wilson, despite his blindness (and millions of others were as blind), reached for the most worthy of goals: he wanted America to expand in an atmosphere of peaceful economic capitalism, knowing that no other atmosphere would be as enriching. Woodrow Wilson was one of the first to realize that neutrality has no

*In July, 1917, the war-weary German Reichstag, finally hearkening to Wilson's speeches, passed a peace resolution that forswore territorial annexations. But the Reichstag could not depose the German General Staff, and Wilson insisted that the Allies, now joined by America, would not negotiate with militaristic autocracies.

role in the twentieth century; that a war anywhere adversely affects those who neither fight nor have cause to fight.

The basic motive for American intervention in Europe was Wilson's intuition that America's security was menaced by a possible German victory. American intervention came in order to protect Anglo-American dominance of the North Atlantic, which submarine warfare came near destroying within a matter of months. A German victory would also imperil Wilson's hopes for the reconstruction of a world community. On April 2, 1917, Wilson told Congress he would fight Germany because Germany had attacked the United States and because a German victory would destroy the political values America affirmed throughout the world.

It was not, however, the trench-locked war that compelled American intervention; it was the blockade war. Though the weaponry used in the land war was capable of killing ten thousand soldiers in a day, the blockade was the most powerful weapon of all. The blockade of Britain, enforced by unrestricted submarine warfare, brought Germany, in the spring of 1917, as close as she ever came to victory. The British blockade of Germany, enforced by the fleet at the beginning of the hostilities, sapped the German will to fight. Eventually the British blockade broke German civilian morale, and the break precipitated the collapse of the German army. Both Germany and Britain conceived of their blockades as essential to victory.

The blockades were jugular grips. They were prompted by an emerging concept of war—"total war," in which a people warred against another nation's civilian population by warring against its economy. The blockade wreaked havoc on the economies of both Germany and Britain, and it also threatened to wreak havoc on the economy of the United States, whose industrial plant was equal to the whole of Europe's. British and German diplomacy both had as their goals the securing of the maximum of blockade that could be enforced without a rupture with the United States.

Both sides proposed a moral argument: each was bound to retaliate against the other on behalf of its people. But the moral argument was quickly diminished when Woodrow Wilson realized that it made little difference whether women and children are deliberately starved to death, as the British intended, or drowned, as the Germans intended. There was also a legal argument, which became the telling argument. Woodrow Wilson did not think international law was simply a rubric.

The blockade had been a weapon since ancient times, when Phoenician sailors blockaded the Minoans on Crete. The ships of one belligerent had frequently invested the harbors or ports of another to deny succor and aid from neutrals. It was a tested matter of international law that, just as neutrals had their rights, so did belligerents. Neutral shipping took its chances running a blockade. A warring power could halt a neutral ship at the mouth of a harbor, board it, search it, and impound contraband cargo, which was anything from canvas that could be used for sails to lead that could be used for bullets. The loss of a ship or cargo by neutrals was not considered *a priori* a hostile act.

In 1914, however, the British instituted the "distant" blockade, which was not a blockade of a harbor or a port or even a coastline, but of a whole country. The British blockaded the North Sea German ports of Bremen and Hamburg by laying an impassable mine field between Dover and Calais in the south and setting up a picket line of ships from the Orkney Islands to Iceland in the north.

The Admiralty violated the traditional precedents of the "close" blockade not only by stopping ships on the high seas in the northern latitudes for search and seizure, but by declaring as contraband all raw materials such as oil, rubber, copper, foodstuffs, and machinery. The Admiralty violated international law by seizing these cargoes as contraband and by impounding the contraband cargoes of ships bound for the ports of the northern neutrals— Denmark, Sweden, Norway, and the Netherlands. The Admiralty argued that these materials could be shipped into Germany by rail. It argued that herring was contraband because the civilian population could subsist upon it while German soldiers ate meat. Not only did the British stop ships on the high seas, but they forced these ships to an English port for search. The Admiralty argued that a sitting British cruiser was an inviting target for a U-boat torpedo. The English blockade was determined to stop the import of all commodities into Germany, and, rather than yield on the point, the British cabinet promised the Admiralty it would risk war with a neutral country.*

Though they rigidly enforced their blockade, the British found it did not appreciably diminish the efficiency of the German war machine, which the Kaiser could supply from within Europe. Nevertheless, the blockade shortened the war by starving the German people, who, toward the end, were so hungry they slaughtered the horses of the civil police and carried away the raw, bleeding flesh.

The Germans, too, relied upon a distant blockade, which they enforced with submarines against ships on the high seas. In the first winter of the war, the Germans had twenty-two U-boats on patrol in the North Atlantic; a year later fifty-eight, which sank one out of every four ships bound for British or French ports. The Germans, too, found they did not diminish the effectiveness of the Allied armies, though they produced serious dislocations within the British economy. England instituted food rationing, and the Admiralty worried about replacing sunken tonnage, which began to exhaust English monetary reserves. In 1916, the German admiralty too laid down the dictum that all raw materials and foodstuffs constituted contraband.

---

*The British had to practice some discretion. They could not, for example, deny the northern neutrals all trade, otherwise they would devastate their economies and reduce the population to such hardship as to make war inevitable. Nor did the British declare cotton contraband, though it can be turned into uniforms and into gunpowder. The British cabinet knew the South's cotton crop was in serious straits in 1914–1916, and to have visited a serious depression on one sector of the American economy was to lose the struggle for Woodrow Wilson's mind and sympathy. The British would also have invited economic retaliation from the United States. Eventually the cabinet solved this problem by reimbursing American shippers for cargoes of cotton seized. They paid for impounded cargoes with money borrowed from American banks.

The submarine could not, however, stop and search a neutral ship. Its crew was too small for such a task, and the submarine risked sinking from armed merchantmen. The U-boat was slow, fragile, and half-blind; it therefore sank ships on sight and without warning. This tactic made submarine warfare more efficient and more terrifying. These fifty-odd U-boats transformed the North Atlantic into a cemetery for combatant and neutral alike.

On May 7, 1915, the German submarine U20 torpedoed the *Lusitania*, a British passenger ship, off the coast of southern Ireland. One thousand two hundred and one passengers perished, of whom 274 were women and 94 were children. One hundred and twenty-four Americans drowned. With the *Lusitania,* the Germans also sank Woodrow Wilson's option for noninvolvement. The death of 124 Americans was intolerable.* If the Germans had any hopes of winning the propaganda war against the British policy of starvation, they lost it when the *Lusitania* began to heel over and plunge down.

Woodrow Wilson, in the name of the people, protested this hostile act. In his note he threatened to sever diplomatic relations unless Germany condemned the U-boat commander, abandoned its present practice of unrestricted submarine warfare, and held itself in strict accountability to the claims of the United States government. To the German explanation that its U-boat warfare was retaliation against the British blockade, Wilson said that "a belligerent act is *per se* an act beyond the law, and the defense of an act as retaliatory is an admission that it is illegal."

The Germans temporized. The Kaiser promised to suspend unrestricted submarine warfare and comply with the demands of the United States conditional upon Wilson's efforts to compel the British to lift their blockade. This, of course, the British would not

---

*Evidence culled from the British archives in the last decade suggests the Germans had every reason for sinking the *Lusitania*. It carried contraband. It was armed. But neither Woodrow Wilson nor the American public nor, for that matter, the Germans knew it at the time. Americans thought the *Lusitania* was innocently bound for a British port and that the Germans had wantonly sent her to the bottom.

do. And all the Germans did, consequently, was to warn neutral passenger ships before sinking them.

Woodrow Wilson could have accepted German U-boat warfare, as he had to accept British blockade entailments. In resigning, William Jennings Bryan asked why America should go to war so that rich people could travel in luxurious liners. But Woodrow Wilson did not accept U-boat warfare and did not accept it for good reasons. Both sides were violating what little was left of international law, the Germans no more mercilessly than the British. But as yet nobody was starving in Germany, while many were foundering in the sea. The Germans were violating international law unconventionally and seriously endangering important American economic interests. The United States had decided the British role in the war was beneficial to these interests. And having protested the *Lusitania* sinking, Wilson had committed American prestige to the issue. While economic interests and morality can sometimes be compromised, prestige cannot. Realizing this, Germany abated unrestricted submarine warfare. There were still incidents between Germany and the United States, however, and the U-boats still took a frightening toll of British shipping.

By the end of 1916 Germany had commissioned a new fleet of over three hundred U-boats, of which it could keep at least 125 constantly on patrol. And by this date, the German General Staff suspected it could beat the French if it knocked the British out of the war by denying them food and war matériel. Unrestricted submarine warfare could reduce Britain to starvation, could cut the British army off from all supplies and render it helpless. Moreover, submarine warfare could do this quickly, within five months according to the German admirals. Against a weakened British army, Germany could succeed in the conquest of Europe.

The German admiralty vowed to sink every ship on the high seas to the north and west of the British Isles. The Germans knew what they had in the U-boat; and the German people asked for nothing less than complete victory at whatever the moral, economic, or political cost. The German Foreign Office expected the United States to enter the war, but felt that before it could mount an army to tilt the balance on the Western Front, Germany would have beaten the British and French armies.

In April, 1917, the U-boats sank 516,000 tons of British and 336,000 tons of Allied and neutral shipping. By June, Germany had sunk 3,250,000 tons, more ships than the British or the world could launch to replace them in a year. Surely Germany must win the war.

The declaration of unrestricted submarine warfare was delivered to the State Department on February 1, 1917, with the warning that no ships on the seas would be spared on February 2. The *Algonquin* was sunk on March 2 and three more ships on March 18.

Unrestricted submarine war was coupled with the exposure of the Zimmermann telegram, in which the German foreign minister promised Mexico the states of Texas, Arizona, and New Mexico as a reward for declaring war on the United States. Within the same month, revolution broke out in Russia. The imperial czar was replaced by a parliamentary democracy that would not menace American interests in the Orient. The Zimmermann telegram and the February Revolution made the decision for war easier for Woodrow Wilson, but it was unrestricted submarine warfare that convinced him Germany could never be peacefully reintegrated into the liberal-capitalist international community. On April 2, he asked Congress for a declaration of war, which Congress voted on April 6.

Ostensibly, the United States went to war over a limited issue—neutral rights—and it could have fought a limited war to secure the rights of American shipping. Admiral William E. Sims had already devised the convoy system, and the American flotilla, with its large number of destroyers for escorts, was to blunt the effectiveness of the U-boat by the late fall of 1917. The United States Navy was also to lay a vast mine field across the 180-mile passage between Norway and the Orkney Islands, which by the end of the war would shut the U-boats from the high seas.

But Wilson had learned of the hazards of limited war with the Punitive Expedition: it is easier to lose a limited war than a total war. Nor did he want to "call through the crack in the door" at the peace conference; he wanted America to be there at the head of the table. Beyond the war lay the worldwide alabaster city, populated by civilized nations taking their direction from the moral and material expansion of America.

Woodrow Wilson was not propagandizing when he told the American people they were going to war to make the world safe for democracy. The war, he thought, would give democracy new strength, bring the world to a new flood tide of progress. The missionary spirit that inspired Wilson's neutrality paradoxically and sadly inspired an ideological cause for war which overreached itself.

To fight the war in Europe, Wilson chose Pershing.

In age, Wilson and Pershing were only three years and two weeks apart, Wilson having been born on December 29, 1856. Both came from areas ravaged by the Civil War and enduring depression. Wilson was born in Staunton, Virginia, and was raised in Augusta, Georgia, until his teens. Boyhood inspired in both a desire to study law as a means of bettering their lives and the lives around them. Both were admitted to the bar. Pershing never practiced and Wilson never gained legal acclaim.

In a time of burgeoning industrial and managerial skills, both were educators. The reputation upon which Wilson capitalized for his entry into politics was that of a professor of history and university president. In middle age both reached a point where their futures seemed behind them. Pershing was a forty-five-year-old regular army captain before he was suddenly swept forward by the comet of promotion to brigadier general. Woodrow Wilson was fifty-four in 1910, when the Dean of Princeton, Andrew F. West, out-thought, out-manipulated, and out-maneuvered him in a bitter quarrel about the graduate college. Wilson's humiliation was so complete that he resigned the presidency of the college and fortuitously fell into the role of reformer in a New Jersey gubernatorial election.

Both suffered the grievous wound of personal loss. For Wilson, in fact, the wound of losing his wife, Ellen Axson, cut deeper. He loved as romantically as Pershing and for a longer time. An inflexible man, Wilson doted on the company of women because he needed intelligent assurance without attendant argument. Which is what he got from Ellen and his three daughters. Her death in 1914 shattered his way of life, robbed him of a feminine dependence he not only needed but craved.*

Both men were literary in an uncompelling sense of the word. Pershing was a pedestrian writer, though among generals only Eisenhower published more. Aware that his delivery was not only flat, but unendearing, Pershing avoided any but absolutely necessary public statements. When Captain Charles E. Stanton included the phrase "Lafayette, nous voilà" for delivery at Lafayette's tomb, Pershing struck it out as "uncharacteristic." On reflection, however, he told Stanton to deliver it himself at the ceremonies.

Wilson, on the other hand, was facile, though he did not always say what he meant. When Woodrow Wilson said there was such a thing as a nation "too proud to fight" what he meant was that there was such a thing as a nation too proud to fight with its fists, but which would seek instead other means to redress injustice and inequity. But that is not what he said. And when Wilson included in his Fourteen Points for a European peace the rule of "open covenants openly arrived at" he meant that international agreements should be made public, not that the public should make them.

While Wilson and Pershing did not enjoy a large personal sympathy with each other, they had a mutually deep sympathy about the aims of the war. Pershing wrote:

This war brings us face to face with the greatest calamity, as I view it, that we have ever been called upon to meet. Personally, I am glad to participate in the great conflict between democracy and autoc-

---

*Within the year, however, Wilson fell in love and married Edith Bolling Galt, a Washington widow, who provided him with the same security, though she was more ambitious than Ellen Axson Wilson. Ellen wanted Woodrow Wilson for the world; Edith for herself.

racy, for that is what it means. Wars like this would be impossible if the people of every nation ruled themselves. So we are fighting for universal peace, strange as it may seem. It is the only way to get it.

And in every one of his communications to the troops of the AEF, Pershing unself-consciously always called their cause "holy" or "sacred" and described it as guided by "divine providence."

Some complex considerations dictated the choice of Pershing as commander of the AEF. On the occasion of announcing the appointment, Newton Baker told the press he had diligently studied the efficiency reports of every U.S. general. In these records, Baker said, he found each officer's history recorded year by year from the moment he entered the service. Every detail was noted by a superior, as well as the quality of performance. Efficiency reports assessed intelligence, character, tact, industry, energy, capacity to lead, and physical power and endurance. Pershing's record revealed that he had never failed an assigned task. With the concurrence of Generals Scott and Bliss, Baker had forwarded Pershing's name to the President.

After the armistice, Pershing asked Wilson why a Democratic President should have chosen as commander a good Republican, one intimately associated with such Republican leaders as Charles E. Dawes, Charles Magoon, Senator Francis E. Warren, and ex-President William Howard Taft. Wilson replied, "General, when you were down in Mexico you showed you could obey orders."

Still, the administration had picked the junior major general of the United States Army (Pershing's recess appointment of September 25, 1916, was confirmed by Congress in January). There were five senior generals. But of these, four—Hugh Scott, Tasker Bliss, Thomas Barry, and J. Franklin Bell—were in their sixties and near compulsory retirement. The fifth general, Leonard Wood, was considered the obvious choice for the command of the AEF. Though younger than Pershing, Wood was several years senior to him in grade. Wood was popular, the best known and the most widely admired army man. He had served as Chief of Staff between 1910 and 1914. But when he was reassigned from Washington to command of the Eastern Military District in 1914, Wood strengthened his old alliance with Theodore Roosevelt and the two became the foremost advocates of "Preparedness."

Together Wood and Roosevelt established the first of the Plattsburg Camps where young businessmen and college students underwent six weeks of military training during the summer at their own expense (camps, incidentally, which became the template for the army's Officer Candidate Schools). In their genuine concern to alert the country to the need for emergency military measures, Wood and Roosevelt even forced Woodrow Wilson's hand: their criticism of the country's military inadequacy prompted Wilson to include a preparedness plank in his 1916 election platform. Not only did Roosevelt and Wood give the Republicans a campaign issue, but they were as well readying themselves, one or the other, for a try at the presidency in 1920.

It was perfectly reasonable for Roosevelt to criticize the President in this process; but it was another thing for Wood to criticize his commander-in-chief. Yet he did. Wood saw a higher priority in criticism than in obedience. In December, 1916, for example, addressing a dinner of Vigilantes, a writers' organization devoted to Preparedness, Wood said, "Gentlemen, I have just received word today that the President had despatched another note to the German government. In his note he states that so far as he can see, the aims of Germany and the Allies are the same. Gentlemen, we have no leadership in Washington."

Wood was the most esteemed soldier of his day because he was a spokesman not for the military, but on behalf of what the military should be about. Wood said the army was not an instrument; first and foremost it was "a collection of men, gallant and wonderful human beings who might be craven or glorious according to their leadership." To bring them to the fight was only one of a general's duties. It was equally important to instruct them in what they were fighting for, equally important to make them into true and devoted citizens of the republic.

When war came, the alerted Eastern constituency wanted Wood to have the top command because events had proved him right. But in his heart of hearts Woodrow Wilson had steeled himself; it would be anyone but Leonard Wood. Wood was not the first or the last soldier to be punished for being right. It is always important to be right. But it is equally important to be right for the right reasons. When a general is right for Theodore Roosevelt's advantage at Woodrow Wilson's expense, then he is right for the wrong reasons. Woodrow Wilson told Newton Baker he would not nominate Wood for command of the AEF no matter what the pressures. So Baker explained to the public that the administration could not nominate Wood as commander because the general had an occasional limp—Wood had banged his head against a hanging lamp some years before which left him with a slight neurological impairment. No one chose to remind Baker that the French were employing one-eyed, one-armed, and one-legged generals, that several British generals were as overweight as Marshal Joffre and that a seventy-year-old once-retired Hindenburg commanded the German General Staff.

When several important Republican politicians argued that Wood had several more years of seasoned experience, that Pershing drove men by enforcing a fierce discipline while Wood led by kindling their spirits, Baker replied that Pershing was the only active general who had ever commanded a force of ten thousand men.

Pershing was hardly an unknown quality when Newton Baker read his name aloud to Tasker Bliss and Hugh Scott. They knew Pershing was ambitious, but so had they been ambitious. Pershing had an instinct for doing the right thing. Ambition was his friend. They knew he inspired confidence in his political superiors. They knew he was an inexorable taskmaster, a martinet of boundless proportions, but he had never proved ruthless in his use of men. If he was minutely exacting, still he knew the rules of fair play. He was austere and graceless, but his troops had always obeyed him. He was hard-boiled, but he was patient. If he had military genius, it barely exceeded anyone else's, yet he was brave beyond measure.

Perhaps Pershing after all, rather than Leonard Wood, was the soldier Woodrow Wilson needed to prove to the Germans they had miscalculated. The Germans had not guessed wrong about the United States entering the war. They were sure unrestricted submarine warfare would force America to side with the Allies. But the Germans miscalculated in how seriously the United States would wage war. The German General Staff was convinced the United States would come too late with only a token force to stem the blitz that would sweep through the French and English trenches. If the Germans thought the canny Junkers were the only professionals hardened, intelligent, and relentlessly ruthless enough to seize victory in the trenches, then Woodrow Wilson would let them take their chances with a West Pointer as equally hardened, who did it by the numbers and who believed men must agonize before they could become the military machine that would, without question or hesitation, brave the sheets of German flame.

Pershing's first intimation that he would command an American force in the European war came from an old friend Major General J. Franklin Bell. In a letter Bell described the possibility of war with Germany and speculated that the United States would send an army to France. In that event, Bell predicted, Pershing would command it. Bell was so strongly convinced of this eventuality that he asked Pershing for an assignment.

Pershing took the prediction to heart. Tight-mouthed and taciturn, nevertheless he took the newspapermen in Columbus, New Mexico, into his confidence, among them S. L. A. Marshall. Marshall was at the press conference Pershing called the day after the Punitive Expedition returned. When he had finished with the briefing, Pershing said, "We have broken diplomatic relations with Germany. That means we will send an expedition abroad. I'd like to command it. Each of you must know some way in which you can help me. Now tell me how I can help you so that you can help me."

In April, Pershing was commissioned the Commanding General of the Southern Department. In May he received an order from Hugh Scott directing him to select a division for service abroad which he would command. But Pershing had to extemporize. There was not then a division that met the army's table of organization. If there had been, still it would not fit into the trench system of the Western Front or into the European system of railroad transportation.* Fortunately for combat efficiency, the War College discovered in the National Defense Act authority for the President to change prescribed organization if the needs of the service required it.

Pershing selected the Sixteenth, Eighteenth, Twenty-sixth, and Twenty-eighth Infantry Regiments and the Sixth Field Artillery. He had to flesh these out with recruits and he had to create on-the-spot auxiliary units by transferring officers and men into them. This was the nucleus of the First Division—"the Big Red One"—which was the first to arrive in France, the first to see action, the division that always held first place in Pershing's heart.

Pershing was in Washington by May 10, where Hugh Scott ordered him to take this provisional force to France as soon as he judged it ready. Whatever Pershing's excitement, it was quickly subdued by his realization that, though a state of war had been declared a month before, scarcely a start had been made toward waging it.

"The War Department seemed to be suffering from a kind of inertia," he wrote, "for which perhaps it was not altogether responsible." Congress had not yet allocated the funds to build the wartime army; the General Staff had not yet determined where it would fight; and the War College had never drawn up a plan for transferring an army from the United States to a foreign field of battle.

Two days later Pershing reported to the Secretary of War, Newton D. Baker. Pershing found him younger and smaller than he

---

*An infantry division on the Western Front needed much more artillery than the cavalry organizations of the United States. In 1918, an American division in the trenches consisted of two infantry and artillery brigades (a brigade was composed of two regiments); one engineer regiment; one machine gun battalion; one signal battalion and trains; the division fired with 72 big guns, 260 machine guns, 17,666 rifles. It numbered 979 officers and 27,082 men commanded by a major general. American divisions were double the size of French, German, and British divisions.

had expected, almost diminutive behind the broad expanse of desk, virtually buried in his chair. Baker told him his orders had been changed. He was not to command the division but to precede it as Commander-in-Chief of all American forces in Europe. Baker told him to select his staff accordingly. Later that day the new European Commander-in-Chief met Woodrow Wilson for the first time. The President only remarked, "We seem to be laying great tasks on you, General," to which Pershing replied, "It is what we are trained to expect."

The elevation of Pershing's command came because great and momentous decisions were forced upon the War Department by the arrival of the French and British military missions. The French mission was headed by Marshal Joseph Joffre, the Hero of the Marne, and the British by Arthur Balfour, the Foreign Secretary in Lloyd George's cabinet.

The Allies wanted money. The war was costing France $133 million a month in armaments alone. The British, who were lending vast amounts to Italy and other Allies, were spending more— £60 million every thirty days. Both countries were near bankruptcy. They succeeded in securing American loans totaling $218 million a month apiece—more than $16 billion in all—at 3½ percent interest over twenty-five years.

Marshal Joffre and Lieutenant General G. T. M. Bridges of the Balfour mission were unanimous in their opinion that the United States "could not raise, train and transport an army of sufficient size to have any effect in the European Theatre." But Joffre added, "It will cheer our people if you send over a token force."

Which is not to say that the Allies did not want men. Indeed they did. But they did not want the American military organization. The Allies wanted all the men America could send them, but nothing above a battalion organization.

Joffre arrived in the United States attended by the same enthusiasm that had greeted Lafayette on his return visit almost a century before. Americans remembered that Joffre was the general who had brilliantly shuffled defeated and demoralized French troops into an army that turned back the right wing of the Germans in 1914. But Frenchmen in 1916 knew that he was falling asleep in the afternoon over his maps. The French General Staff made him a Marshal of France and replaced him as commander with General Robert Nivelle, who produced the Plan de Nivelle for ending the war in April, 1916. The Plan de Nivelle committed every soldier, every gun in even greater concentration along even lengthier lines for a mighty offensive along the Aisne. Even as Joffre talked to Wilson and Baker, however, the offensive had foundered and Nivelle was about to be replaced by General Henri Pétain. Yet the Plan de Nivelle remained to guide French military efforts during the rest of the war. That plan called for American participation to take the form:

—Of sending thousands of laborers, road gangs, railroad workers, miners, chauffeurs, foresters, stevedores, carpenters, nurses and doctors to free more and more Frenchmen for combat;—Of sending American fighting troops as much as was necessary for morale and American pride as replacements for devastated French battalions and divisions, such troops dependent upon French leadership and control.

General Bridges of the Balfour mission cherished similar sentiments, arguing that American troops should be used with the British armies since few French officers spoke English. An American army in France, Bridges argued, would only create one more weakening joint in the Allied line. Producing a memorandum signed by Sir William Robertson, Chief of the Imperial General Staff, and Sir Douglas Haig, commanding the Western Front, Bridges asked for a levy of 500,000 American recruits which, upon arrival in Britain, would be issued Enfield rifles and British uniforms and, after seven weeks' training in trench warfare, receive a week's orientation in France before joining the line in Flanders. It was, Bridges added, precisely the training and preparation Britain gave her own.

These suggestions occasioned anger and alarm in Room 223 of the War Department, where Pershing and his newly selected Chief of Staff, Major James G. Harbord, were putting together the skeleton of the AEF staff and formulating its myriad operations. That the question of brigades, divisions, the proportion of artillery to infantry, of auxiliary troops and medical detachments was one that might not concern them at all was a suggestion that shook their empire. Their alarm welled from the conviction that, under such a system, American troops would not fight. It was, thought Pershing, unreasonable to expect a German from Minnesota and an Irishman from Brooklyn to fight with the same determination under a British flag as they would under an American.* Harbord and Pershing realized that the Wilson Administration would lose its political support for the war if it allowed American citizen-soldiers into foreign military units.

Additionally, they pointed out that the Plan de Nivelle did not guarantee that Americans would fight only against Germany, the one declared enemy.† The British and French were fighting elsewhere in the prosecution of aims bound up in treaties of which no American was aware. To insure that our manpower was used solely for the purpose of defeating Germany, it was absolutely necessary that an American commander control it. The Plan de Nivelle, they argued, was folly, in that it took no account of the differences in national customs or diet; nor did it take into account national pride, or the history and traditions of the American military services, which had twice beaten the British.††

Pershing and Harbord might have saved themselves their alarm.

---

*They might have been wrong in this. American forces who did fight with the French acquitted themselves with distinction in World War I. French units fought valorously under the British in World War II, and the units from several nations waged heroic war against the Chinese Communists in Korea under the United Nations flag.

†War against Austria-Hungary was declared on December 7, 1917.

††In this they were right. Americans could not abide the ration of sour red wine relished by the French *poilu,* nor could the British understand why Americans would waste tonnage transporting chewing gum. The war-weary British soldiers were already singing, "The bells of hell go ding-a-ling-a-ling for you but not for me," and French soldiers were singing "The Internationale," while Americans sang "K-K-Katy" and "Over There," and shouted in battle, "Retreat, hell! We just got here," and "What's the matter with you sons-of-bitches? You want to live forever?"

Woodrow Wilson and officials of his administration quickly intuited that the Balfour and Joffre missions were presenting the views of governments fighting a war where position at the moment of victory determined annexations. Britain and France wanted to win the war without American combat help so that they could make peace without considering Wilson's views. Though they were initially enamored of Joffre and impressed by Bridges, the Americans were not invincibly naïve. When Joffre could not tell Pershing which was the most practicable port in France for the disembarkation of American troops, the War Department realized that Britain and France had given no thought at all to a concerted Allied plan.

The British and French were not lunatics in their proposals. They had raised armies totaling five million men since 1914, so many millions of whom had been lost that now they were hard pressed to maintain a million and a half men in the trenches. The British and French were dependent upon seventeen- and fifty-year-olds in the face of growing German strength, growing because German armies were being released from Russia, which was leaving the war. From the British and French view, all that would stem the German tide was superiority in rifles and machine guns.

Wilson informed the Allies that American troops would fight only as an independent army, reminding them that when Louis XVI sent a French army to fight with Washington, he ordered General Rochambeau to insure that the Frenchmen fought as an independent force.

Baker told Pershing, "I shall give you two orders. One to go and one to return." A Virginian by birth, Baker was a serious student of the American Civil War and he accepted its principal lesson, that the government must pare its interference with the military to the narrowest essentials once the fighting has begun.

Pershing's orders directed him to proceed at once to Europe with his staff and, after consultation with the French War Office, to establish all necessary bases, lines of communications, and depots necessary for active American participation at the front. Paragraph 5 read:

In military operations against the Imperial German Government, you are directed to cooperate with the forces of the other countries employed against that enemy; but in so doing the underlying idea must be kept in view that the forces of the United States are a separate and distinct component of the combined forces, the identity of which must be preserved. This fundamental rule is subject to such minor exceptions in particular circumstances as your judgment may approve. The decision as to when your command, or any of its parts, is ready for action is confided to you, and you will exercise full discretion in determining the manner of cooperation. But, until the forces of the United States are in your judgment sufficiently strong to warrant operation as an independent command, it is understood that you will cooperate as a component of whatever army you may be assigned by the French Government.

On the drizzly afternoon of May 28, Pershing and 190 officers and enlisted men left New York bound for Liverpool. This pioneer staff of the AEF wore civilian clothes and stole silently aboard the tender that cleaved through the harbor fog to the transport *Baltic*. But Pershing noted an unusual number of quartermaster officers on the pier as well as a skyscraper of boxes and crates addressed to various chiefs in his care. The batteries on Governor's Island fired a salute. He thought to himself there must be a better way to keep a secret.

He was able to consult with the British Imperial Staff in London before landing at Boulogne on June 13. He spent the next three weeks in France at Grand General Headquarters, in the trenches, and at the training camps. He met Pétain. Together they visited the military hospital at Souilly where Pétain pinned the Croix de Guerre on a nurse, wounded a few days before. When he introduced Pershing, she said, "I am glad you are here, General, to see how a French woman can suffer for her country."

That night, however, Pétain took Pershing aside and told him in detail of the grave military situation that faced the Allies. The Nivelle offensive had failed. It had cost the French 200,000 casualties. Manpower was almost depleted. The tremendous losses over the past three years, all for no gain, had finally driven the soldiers in the ranks to mutiny. Men in ninety divisions had refused to fight. Pétain had all he could do to hold the line and he had prepared no offensive operations except for small, limited goals. Pétain had visited each of the mutinous divisions, building up the shattered morale of his armies, trying to dispel defeatist propaganda among his men, correcting abuses on the spot, promising the *poilus* (the word means "hairy ones") that the Americans would come to win the war.

Morale in both French and British armies was low. Manpower resources were at point zero. Finances were depleted. When the Central Powers could withdraw divisions from the Russian and Rumanian fronts they would have a heavy superiority.

Pershing's lifelong admiration for Pétain was probably established at this moment. Even when Pétain had become notorious as the Vichy collaborator, Pershing still considered him a fine soldier.

Dorothy Canfield Fisher met Pershing again shortly after his arrival in France. She waited for him for breakfast on the balcony of the Crillon, observing a group of nattily dressed American officers below. She had been in France for two years and the situation on the front depressed her as it depressed her French neighbors. She wondered if Americans could turn the trick. She wondered no longer after Pershing arrived. In the midst of the glittering, gilded, Old World decoration of the dining room, she asked him what would happen. He alarmed her by bringing his fist down on the table. "I'll tell you one thing. I'm going to jump down the throat of the next man who asks me again if I think the Americans will fight. *Fight?* Americans?"

On July 6, Pershing wired the War Department outlining a General Organization Project. "Plans should contemplate sending over at least 1,000,000 troops by next May, the smallest unit which in modern war will be a complete, well-balanced fighting organization." The United States needed twenty divisions and their supporting troops, and it needed as many more men to move the supplies. This was beyond anything Wilson had dreamed of when he promised the Allies to employ the full power of the United States.

Pershing informed his Washington chiefs that the French and

British armies were near moral disarray. Both armies were writing off their lists divisions that had been annihilated. The French had lost the cream of their manhood at Verdun and the British were throwing what manhood they had left into the slaughter pits of a new offensive that even now the Germans were grinding down. It was left for American reinforcements to beat the Germans and the first million men "should not be construed as representing the maximum force which should be sent to or will be needed in France."

Pershing had determined as well where this American army would fight—on the battlefront from the Argonne Forest to the Vosges Mountains, from which it could strike a blow to achieve a decisive military goal, the captured French iron-ore regions of Longwy-Briey and the coal fields of the Saar. The line in 1918 would put the British on the left in Flanders, the French in the center defending Paris, and the Americans on the right in the south.

These determinations should have silenced forever the hopes of the Allies to implement Plan de Nivelle. They did not. The Allies had a wedge. They were compelled not only to transport but to arm the American Expeditionary Forces. The American merchant marine had never replaced its great loss of ships in the Civil War, and to fill out its merchant marine had depended upon charter, lease, rental, and impounding. Shipping was now in short supply throughout the Western World, except for Britain, whose merchant marine was seriously endangered by U-boats as it strained to keep the home islands supplied with food and raw materials. America would have to draw on some of this shipping, however, to transport its army. And that army would have to use French weapons.

At the beginning of the war, the United States Army had fewer than 1,500 machine guns and these were of four different types. It did not have enough artillery ammunition to provide for more than nine hours' bombardment, firing at the rate of an ordinary barrage. It had 55 training planes, 51 of which were obsolete and 4 obsolescent. It was unable to put a squadron in a European airdrome, although to support a million-man army it would need 300 squadrons, each of 18 planes with reserves for replacement.

The United States could not quickly make up these deficits. No less than the army needed retraining and reorganization, industry needed retooling. The United States never sent an airplane of American manufacture to France, and American combat divisions moved forward under the protective barrage fired by French big guns.

For ships and armaments, the Allies wanted a *quid pro quo*.

The French never ceased complaining about the lack of American troops in their line. They railed at Pershing as the author of this danger. He was the man they had to bend, and they importuned from the lowest to the highest levels for his compliance. In his *Secret Letters to General Pershing*, collected in the archives of the United States Military Academy, Colonel Paul Clark, liaison officer at French General Headquarters, reported to Pershing that the French staff wanted to send American officers and noncoms to French training schools; that the French General Staff thought it wiser and more instructive if the Americans took their training from French tankers rather than lend Pershing nine tanks; that the General Staff did not want Pershing to consider any part of the front as the "American sector"; that American officers spent too much time walking through the trenches and mingling with the men and too little time attending to the lessons of the French General Staff.

When Pershing established his temporary headquarters in Paris, the French General Staff detailed Marshal Joffre as his consultant. This appointment was a polite but determined attempt at subordination. Pershing quickly intuited that the French intended tutelage. He informed the French General Staff that the addition of Joffre and his assistants only complicated matters by adding another channel through which requests must pass. "Pershing," remarked one of his aides, "had no thought of engaging any nurse for himself, not even so eminent a one as Joffre."

Many French generals thought the American army a bushwhacking army, while Pershing and Harbord were capable of referring to the staff of Grand Headquartier Général as "fuzzy little Frenchmen."

In December, 1917, Pershing wrote a formal reply to General Pétain in which he declined to commit American regiments or battalions to French command. Annoyed, French Premier Georges Clemenceau took matters into his own hands by communicating with Woodrow Wilson. Through Ambassador Jean Jules Jusserand, Clemenceau represented that serious differences had made difficult the relationship between Pétain and Pershing. The French premier wanted to create doubt in the President's mind about Pershing's management of the American military effort. Clemenceau wanted a more amiable and compliant replacement.

The War Department snitched to Pershing. Black Jack promptly bearded the Tiger of France. He wrote to the premier directly, quoted the Jusserand cable, and insisted he and Pétain had no differences. Pershing concluded:

> May I suggest to you, Mr. Premier, the inexpediency of communicating such matters to Washington by cable? These questions must all be settled here, eventually on their merits through friendly conferences between General Pétain and myself and cables of this sort are very likely, I fear, to convey the impression of serious difficulty between us when such is not the case.

Amazed at the boldness of American generals, Clemenceau replied that such was not his intention. British Prime Minister David Lloyd George and Clemenceau never hesitated in trying to go around Pershing. French and British ambassadors in Washington suggested from time to time the wisdom of replacing Pershing, and political leaders and generals whispered as much to Colonel House as he tiptoed through their capitals.

However, Pershing rather liked Clemenceau, admired him, and found that he and the premier had something in common. Pershing asked the sixty-seven-year-old Clemenceau how he kept such vigor and Clemenceau replied he exercised every morning. A man after the Pershing heart. A member of Pershing's staff recalled looking out of headquarters' window early Christmas morning to see the Commander of the AEF in his bathrobe and slippers jogging in the snow.

Pershing had to stand to America's allies in place of matériel and an army. Though a draft act had been passed by Congress, it was not until June, 1917, that able-bodied Americans registered for Selective Service and not until September that the first men were called. Of the 650,000 subject to military duty, only 500,000 were mustered, because that was all the new cantonments could accommodate. The army-in-becoming waited while masons and bricklayers and carpenters finished the new arsenals and bulldozers leveled hills for the rifle ranges. As these recruits were formed first into companies, then into battalions, and finally into regiments, they were shipped piecemeal to France.

The French and British wanted to claim them for the trenches as soon as they disembarked, which Pershing would not permit. He wanted these regiments to form brigades and divisions, and he wanted to train these divisions in a manner the French and British had forgotten. Pershing wanted his divisons to fight a war of movement once they had breached the German trenches. He wanted his soldiers able to deliver heavy and effective rifle fire, for Pershing had seen French soldiers chase Germans until near enough to throw a grenade; he had seen the men in the trenches rely so heavily on the mortar and barbed wire and poison gas that they were rendered helpless and confused when forced out into the open. Troops in the trenches did not know how to take advantage of concealment and cover, how to support one another, how to bring coordinated fire upon an objective. Pershing wanted to commit new divisions to quiet sectors of the line along the Lorraine Front, but he would not put them in combat until he judged them ready.

He was as hard with his own officers as he was obdurate with his allies. They measured to strict standards and, if they were found wanting, he relieved them without compunction. He believed that, if a division commander lacked energy and aggression, so did his troops. When one commander told him his troops were tired, Pershing said there was no reason for their exhaustion, since they had been in the line only a short time. He relieved the commander and appointed another who was tireless and efficient. When Pershing discovered that his good friend J. Franklin Bell suffered from diabetes he sent him broken hearted back to the United States. Without sadness or regret he sent the inept, the inefficient, and the emotionally unprepared to Bloise or Cannes for reassignment (from which derive the vernacular expressions "Things went blooey," meaning they went to pieces, or "He got canned," meaning he got fired).

Under conditions without historical precedent, in a foreign country nearly drained of its own power, Pershing created and molded an army. Despite the urgent appeal of the allies demanding that he hurry to their rescue lest they die, he kept control of a force whose power would be all the more telling because it was American.

The British were more subtle than the French in their demands for American replacements. They dealt with the matter in a low key. British generals told Newton D. Baker, on a visit to the front, that they found General Leonard Wood a great soldier and hoped one day soon to be working with him. They had proved superb propagandists in convincing the world of the Hun's ruthlessness, and their offhanded requests for American amalgamation persuaded important Americans.

After the defeat of the Italians at Caporetto in October, 1917, the Allies formed the Supreme War Council, in Paris, to which diplomatic and military representatives came to coordinate the efforts of their armies. General Tasker Bliss came as the American representative.

Before Bliss took his seat at the council table, Sir William Robertson and Field Marshal Sir Douglas Haig got his ear. Robertson was an anomaly. Always called "Wully," he was a Cockney who had risen from the rank of private to become chief of the Imperial General Staff. He lent the English language a memorable phrase in 1914 when he was sent to Mons to relieve General Horace Smith-Dorrien. "'Orace, you for 'ome," said Robertson. Haig was an impeccably dressed cavalry dragoon, devious often, and ambitious. Many times a millionaire, Haig usually seized the upper hand in personal relationships by his superior snobbery.

Robertson and Haig told Bliss that, if the United States would agree to the infiltration of American troops within British divisions, the Admiralty could scrape up the tonnage to transport infantry and machine gun units to the amount of 120,000 men a month. At his first meeting of the Supreme War Council, Bliss presented the proposal and gave it his whole-hearted support. Pershing reacted with the sullen anger of a man who suddenly realizes he's been slipped a bum card from the bottom of the deck. He asked for an adjournment.

That night, in a suite in the Hotel Crillon, Pershing firmly informed Bliss he was against the plan. Bliss said he saw the plan's merit. He suggested he and Pershing cable their views to Washington for a decision.

Pershing said, "Well, Bliss, do you know what would happen if we did that? We would both be relieved from further duty in France and that is exactly what we should deserve. It is not my policy nor will it ever be to put anything up to Washington I can decide myself in France."

Bliss knew an old army game when it hit him and he said, "I think you are right and I shall back you up in the position you have taken."

Now Pershing studied the bum card. The British had admitted they could "scrape up" the tonnage to accelerate American troop movements. He made the card sharpers bargain. Pershing, Newton D. Baker, and the American Chief of Staff, Peyton C. March, asked the British for this tonnage. The British agreed to a compromise. They would provide ships to transport 120,000 men every month if Pershing would include only infantry and machine gun troops to comprise the elements of six divisions. These elements would train with the British army in reserve areas and fight with British troops if necessary—which they did, notably the Forty-second Rainbow Division. Once the six infantry components were across the Atlantic, the British would provide the tonnage for their artillery, engineer, and signal corps complements. With the arrival of these components, the divisions were to be rounded out and sent to the American sector under Pershing's command.

Pershing added one more detail: every American regimental and battalion commander with the British had a telephone that connected directly to Pershing's headquarters in Chaumont. These commanders were under strict orders to report the actions of their units day by day.

This agreement between the United States and Britain broke the worst of the shipping impasse. Additionally, the convoy system was containing the submarine menace, and this provided more tonnage. More than 49 percent of the AEF sailed to France aboard British ships, 44 percent aboard American, and the remainder aboard Dutch and Norwegian ships. The British saw that it was ultimately to their interest to put an American army in the line. They, too, were to become as down-hearted as the French when they had to fall back from Vimy Ridge, for which they had sacrificed the army Lord Kitchner had assembled, the last great volunteer army mustered in the history of warfare.

When the French learned of this Anglo-American shipping agreement, they demanded that they, too, receive 120,000 men a month. Pershing asked the French General Staff to provide the tonnage for transport and guarantees that the divisions would be returned to his command. The French could not provide the shipping, so the second condition was pointless.

On March 21, 1918, General Erich Ludendorff launched a series of massive offensives by which Germany hoped to win the war before the preponderant weight of the American armies was brought against it. Able to employ one hundred divisions newly arrived from the Russian Front, Ludendorff deployed 265 German and 45 Austrian divisions against the French and British. For the first time the Germans breached the allied trenches and broke into open country. If he could have exploited this tactical victory, Ludendorff would have split the British and French armies, penned the British into the Channel ports, and chased the French past Paris. If the Germans could have occupied Paris the Clemenceau government would have fallen, probably to be replaced by another determined upon a separate peace. Then the British would have been forced to go home.

Ludendorff's first thrust was against the British, who lost 150,000 men stemming the advance, using up all their reserves. By March 27, the Germans had penetrated thirty-seven miles past the British lines and were moving on Amiens, the capture of which would separate the British and French armies.

In Paris to meet Secretary of War Baker, Pershing was almost caught up in the panic at the Gare du Nord railway station. Terror-stricken villagers were joining with the Parisians in a flight from the city to the south. From the Crillon, Pershing and Baker heard the German big guns drawing nearer. To save the situation, the French would have to lend the British their own reserve divisions.

On the afternoon of March 28, Pershing drove to Clermont-sur-Oise in his Locomobile to see General Foch, newly appointed Allied Supreme Commander. No one at French headquarters knew where Foch was. Pershing and his aide, French-speaking Colonel Carl Boyd, were directed by a French noncom to the edge of town. Following a line of tall poplars, Pershing and Boyd finally came to a small farmhouse ringed by automobiles. Pershing waited under a blooming cherry tree while Boyd announced him.

Inside, Pershing found Foch, Clemenceau, Pétain, and General Loucheur bent over a map spread on a kitchen table. When Pershing said he had come to see Foch, the others withdrew. To Foch Pershing said, "I have come to tell you that the American people would consider it a great honor for our troops to be engaged in the present battle. I ask you for this in their name and my own." In the flush of the moment, Pershing delivered the offer in fluid if simple French, even promising that which he did not have: "Infanterie, artillerie, aviation, tout ce que nous avons est a vous."

Foch heard him out, still as a statue. Then gripping Pershing by the arm, Foch sped to the others and bade Pershing repeat what he had just said:

"Je suis venu tout exprès pour vous dire que le peuple americain serait fier d'être engage dans le plus grand bataille de l'histoire."*

Pershing had five divisions under his control to lend to the French. These divisions went into quiet sectors along the line and freed ten French divisions for the relief of the British. More troops arrived in the coming weeks, but Pershing sent them to training areas, his generosity, as the French later remarked, cooling faster than the situation, although in all the Allies got nine American divisions.

Operation Michael, the German offensive against the British, had succeeded too well. It moved so fast that its troops were exhausted when they ran up against stiffening Allied resistance. Ludendorff called off the drive against Amiens. In two weeks, however, the Germans had claimed 1,250 square miles of French territory, battered one British army, shaken another, and captured ninety thousand men and a thousand guns. Though the Germans had expended what was virtually one field army, Ludendorff still had enormous reserves. These he hurried against the French in another great offensive, this time farther south along the Aisne. Again the Germans made headway, again they threatened Paris.

Allied military and political chiefs met at Abbeville to determine how to stop the drive. The meeting was chaired by Marshal Foch, who had been confirmed on April 3 as Supreme Allied Commander. The Allies had charged him with the "co-ordination of the action of the allied armies on the Western Front." But each commander of the British, French, and American armies had full control of the tactical employment of his own forces. Foch was the author of many books on strategy and tactics and was devoted to the theory that only constant attack can succeed in war. He was a staff man rather than a field commander, and invariably remarked

---

*Authorities such as Barrie Pitt and S. L. A. Marshall regard the report as a mythologizing on Pershing's part. They point out that not only did he not have airplanes, he did not have artillery. Perhaps, but in crises people often transcend themselves and act uncharacteristically. It was uncharacteristic of the intellectual Tasker Bliss, who was fluent in French, to say in English to French generals, "We've come over here to get ourselves killed. If you want to use us what are you waiting for?" But he said it.

"Bon!" to the details of any military situation, no matter how grave, until on one occasion Field Marshal Haig snapped, "C'est n'est pas bon du tout!"

At Abbeville were Clemenceau, Pétain, Lloyd George, Haig, Lord Milner, Prime Minister Vittorio Orlando and General di Robilant of Italy, Pershing, and Bliss. Lloyd George told the conferees that Operation Michael had cost the British ten divisions that could not be reformed. The British could not reinforce the French in repelling this new offensive launched over the Chemin des Dames—the "Ladies Road" once traversed by the carriages of the mistresses of Louis XV.

Without reinforcements, Foch doubted the French could stop the offensive. The Allies needed American reinforcements. They needed every American in France. Foch, with a tear, recalled that millions of French and British soldiers had already died. But although there were 500,000 Americans in France, Pershing had contributed only driblets to the fighting.

"Are we to understand that the American Army is to be entirely at the disposal of the French and British commands?" Pershing asked.

The conferees said no, not exactly.

Pershing admitted the military emergency. He noted also that American divisions were serving with both the British and the French. To propose adding untrained American units for French and British deployment would neither relieve the emergency nor win the war. Trained Americans units would not be ready until August.

"You are willing to risk our being driven back to the Loire?" asked Foch.

"Yes," said Pershing, "I am willing to take that risk. Moreover, the time may come when the American Army will have to stand the brunt of this war, and it is not wise to fritter away our resources in this manner. The morale of the British, French and Italian armies is low, while, as you know, that of the American Army is very high. It would be a grave mistake to give up the idea of building an American Army in all its details as rapidly as possible."

"The war might be over before you are ready," said Foch.

"The war will not be saved by feeding untrained American units into Allied armies," said Pershing.

In a stage whisper Lloyd George muttered to Lord Milner, "It's no use. You can't budge him."

Pershing pounded the table. "I have thought this program over very carefully and will not be coerced."

He was accepting a grave risk and probably knew to the last detail how grave it was. He risked the chance of being cursed to the last generation if the Allies lost and blamed the loss on American failure to cooperate. It was a hazard he accepted, as generals before him had accepted hazards. Tough, inflexible, unrelenting in the presence of an enveloping disaster, he was a genuinely realistic military man. He knew that the French needed the Americans for a great psychological lift, that it would buoy the morale of three peoples, but that the lift in itself was not a military determinant. It would not blunt the German offensives. Brave men, well trained and organized and fearlessly led, would accomplish that. But he could not persuade Foch, who was dominated by an *idée fixe*.

Pershing had done more than feed driblets to the fighting; he had committed his nucleus. The Forty-second Division was in the lines with the British, joined now by the Twenty-seventh and the Thirtieth—and these last two would still be in the British lines when the armistice was signed. On April 26 the First Division stormed Cantigny and held, despite fierce counterattacks and galling artillery fire. The Third Division hurried to the Marne to deny German bridgeheads at Château-Thierry, while the Second Division helped blunt the German drive through Belleau Wood. These three divisions were sooned joined by the Thirty-second, the Twenty-eighth, and the Twenty-sixth.

Both Allies were perfectly capable of betraying Pershing's cooperation. The French were demanding and the British fussy. Pershing sent four black National Guard regiments, the infantry of the Ninety-third Division, to French command and was unable to retrieve them. When he detached the Ninety-second Division, also black, to British training areas, Haig said these troops would cause problems. To which Pershing replied, "These Negroes are American citizens. Naturally I cannot and will not discriminate against them."

If the German drive had continued, Pershing probably would have had no choice but to feed American units into the battle as soon as they arrived. Wilson and Baker were wavering, not because they were alarmed men, but because they were not military men. Pershing gambled that the German drive, which extended German lines by hundreds of miles, was still using up German soldiers, spreading German reserves thin. Unless Ludendorff secured victory quickly, the reserve must fail him. Pershing bet that Ludendorff would realize this before the French and British.

But it was more than this gamble that nerved Pershing. Pershing believed an army was the most active of all democracies. Soldiers cast an inarticulate vote to move at the order "forward!" Discipline, morale, and leadership contrive to make the vote unanimous, but what truly carries the motion is the assent of the man on the soldier's left and the assent of the man on his right. A soldier must understand the virtues of the men with whom he fights, for those are the virtues that ennoble him, and he cannot comprehend these virtues if the man on his right and the man on his left do not speak his language, or hold precious his traditions, or make reverent in the same way the cause for which he fights.

And there was something else at the root of Pershing's insistence: his realization, shared with many others, that the War of 1898 had not been *opéra-comique*, with Spain as the buffoon. Eighteen-ninety-eight marked the emergence of a great world power, a fact not everyone discerned. A power becomes great by virtue of its ability to lord it over other powers. The American economy without question lorded it over the other economies of the world. This regency could be diminished only by making of the American soldier a casual replacement for British and French commands.

A day after the Abbeville conference, Lloyd George argued, "If the war is lost it would be lost honorably by France and England as they would have expended their last in the struggle, but for America to lose the war without having put into it more than Belgium would not be in compatibility with American pride and traditions."

Pershing replied, "The United States will put troops on the battle line when it shall have formed an army worthy of the American people."

When Pershing finally assembled his army, in August, and ordered it to attack its first objective, Foch still tried to dissipate the force into the French mass. To attack and reduce the Saint-Mihiel salient to the south of Verdun, which throbbed in the Allied line like an infected tooth, Pershing massed thirteen divisions. He had journeyed to the British front at Wiry-au-Mont to ask Haig to return his five American divisions, four of which were actively defending the line. Pershing realized how disheartening it was for Haig to comply now that the British were turning to the offensive.

"Of course you shall have them, Pershing," said Haig. "There can never be any differences between us." Haig, thought Pershing, was an honest man.

Marshal Foch visited Pershing shortly thereafter. Foch came to American headquarters, momentarily a railroad coach, at Ligny-en-Barrois on August 24 with the news that plans had been changed, plans which had taken Pershing and his staff months to prepare. Foch wanted only a limited attack at Saint-Mihiel with a few American divisions, the rest to be shifted north to join the French II Army, which was going to attack toward Mézières.

Patiently, Pershing inspected Foch's plans, which threatened the movement of the army he had so patiently formed. It is important to remember that in 1918 the British and the French faced the Germans to the east, the line running north to south. But below Verdun the line curved sharply and the Americans faced the Germans to the north, the trenches running east to west. If the Americans breached the line they could proceed either northwest, toward Mézières, or northeast, toward Metz, the bolder move, and Pershing's plan.

"Well, Marshal," said Pershing "this is a very sudden change.

We are going forward as already recommended by you and approved by you and I cannot understand why you want these changes. Moreover, I think to make an attack in a salient with limited objectives will cost little less than to carry out the original idea which will put us in a better position."

Foch replied that he disliked dividing the American army but it couldn't be helped. Then he mistook Pershing's silence for assent and began further trespass. Foch asked Pershing to assign Generals Degoutte and Malcor to the American staff.

"This is only a roundabout way of assigning General Degoutte to command our forces," Pershing said. "Many Americans who served under Degoutte consider that, because of his orders, troops were unnecessarily sacrificed."

The argument proceeded. Foch said the French plan unleashed an immediate offensive. Pershing agreed with a plan of immediate offense, but objected to the way he was ordered to carry it out. Why is it necessary, he asked, to move some Americans around the curve, put others at the salient, and leave still others unattached in the Champagne area? Foch said there was no other way. Pershing said yes there was. His troops would take over as their sector not only the trenches that ran east to west but those around the curve that ran north and south. "Each time we are about to complete the organization of our army some proposition like this interrupts it."

"Do you wish to take part in the battle?" Foch asked.

"Most assuredly," said Pershing. "But as an American Army and in no other way. Assign me the sector and I will take it at once."

"There is no time," said Foch, "and you have no artillery."

Pershing reminded him that for months America had been shipping only infantry and machine gun units in accordance with Allied demands. "You promised you would furnish the auxiliary troops," he said to Foch. "Now furnish them."

Foch said he had to maintain the French plan. "I must insist," he concluded.

"You may insist all you please," said Pershing, slamming the desk. "Marshal Foch, I decline absolutely to agree with your plan. While our army will fight wherever you may decide, it will not fight except as an independent American Army."

Pale and exhausted, Foch picked up his maps and left, bidding Pershing study the plan, sure he would come to a different conclusion. Pershing compromised: but his First Army would fight intact. It would reduce the Saint-Mihiel salient. It would then take over the Argonne section of the line to undertake its role in Foch's strategy of "Tout le monde a la Bataille!"—alternating attacks at different points swelling into a general all-out offensive.

Two months after the beginning of the Argonne offensive, the war ended. The armistice was signed with a toughened and ever-strengthening American army in the field, an army that could have crossed the Rhine and plunged knifelike into Germany to cut off the retreat of Ludendorff's shaken and defeated soldiers. It was an army of heroic proportions and its deployment was one of heroic proportions, too. That army was Pershing's achievement. "It is sufficient to say," writes B. H. Liddell Hart, one of the most authoritative of all modern writers on war, "that there probably was no other man who would or could have built the structure of the American Army on the scale he planned. And without that army the war could hardly have been saved and could not have been won."

18

The Four-Star General
Carries a Pack, Parley-Vous?

The War Department's inertia, which appalled Pershing, its in-
ability to produce plans for mobilization, armament, supply, and
transport of an army, was not wholly the fault of the General Staff.
The National Defense Act of 1916 had provided a new organization for the army. In the process it emasculated the General Staff
by limiting its duties to "non-administrative matters." At the same
time it provided that only one-half of its personnel could serve in
Washington, D.C. These provisions reflected the influence of the
bureau chiefs, the generals who ran the Quartermaster, Ordnance,
and Signal departments and the rest who still struggled against
usurpation of their authority by the General Staff. As a consequence of this bill, the General Staff numbered only nineteen
officers in the spring of 1917. It is probably an impossibility for
only nineteen men to formulate the manner and means of mustering
a massive modern army.

These nineteen men might not have been on duty if Newton D.
Baker had not made the fatefully important decision that the new
bill in no way impair the authority of the General Staff. "Congress
did not intend to inaugurate a race for power among the bureau
chiefs or erect the bureaus of the War Department into a system of
co-ordinated impediments to one another," he ruled. "The policy

277

of the War Department will remain as before, the Chief-of-Staff speaking in the name of the Secretary of War will co-ordinate and supervise the various bureaus."

Baker's decision, however, hardly relieved the Commander-in-Chief of the AEF from a monumental operation. A seasoned general, John J. Pershing realized that he could not venture to France without an efficient and capable staff, one that was able to produce cohesive plans for an American military operation greater than any previously attempted. Ultimately, he realized, events would force Congress, the President, and the War Department to repair to a General Staff, but in the meantime he would have to create his own. The creation of that staff was his heroic contribution, a task that took mind and will, skill and imagination. Pershing's General Staff was, in an Aristotelian sense, the final cause of the AEF's success. It was, moreover, along with compulsory conscription, one of the two military innovations to emerge from the war as continuing American institutions.

For his Chief of Staff Pershing picked Major James G. Harbord, who, after enlisting as a private in 1889, had come up through the ranks. Though Harbord and Pershing had never served together in the same command, their relationship went back to the Spanish-American War. As quartermaster for the Tenth Cavalry, Pershing was held monetarily responsible for the horses left in Tampa and for those drowned off Cuba. Lieutenant Harbord, as acting quartermaster general, devised the accounting procedures that saved Pershing ten years' salary. On two other occasions they had traveled aboard the same ship back and forth to the Philippines.

Sarcastic critics always insisted that Pershing chose Harbord for his strong, pugnacious jawline. When asked the reasons for his choice, Pershing himself answered, "What difference does it make why I picked him? I picked the right man, didn't I?" Nor did Harbord know why he was chosen. Because he was not a West Pointer and because he was a "Leonard Wood man" he was thunderstruck when Pershing said he might take him along as chief of staff. Whatever the reasons, it was an inspired choice, the best Pershing ever made. In fact, when Pershing refused to designate his successor in the case of his own death, Baker covertly determined on Harbord.

The relationship between a commanding general and his chief of staff has been likened to the relationship between spouses: there are no secrets in a good marriage, but one doesn't tell the children everything. A commanding general needs neither a courtier nor an opponent. He needs a chief of staff with ideas of his own, unafraid to give argument, but who nevertheless can see things the general's way once they leave the tent with the lines of attack inked on the maps.

At the time, Harbord wrote:

General Pershing is a very strong character. He has a good many peculiarities, such I suppose as every strong man accustomed to command is apt to develop. He is very patient and philosophical under trying delays from the War Department. He is playing for high stakes and does not intend to jeopardize his winning by wasting his standing with the War Department over small things, relatively unimportant, though very annoying as they occur. He is extremely cautious, very cautious, does nothing hastily or carelessly. He spends much time rewriting the cables and other papers I prepare for him, putting his own individuality into them. He is the first officer for whom I have prepared papers who did not generally accept what I wrote for him. It is very seldom I get anything past him without some alteration, though I am obliged to say I do not always consider that he improves them, though often he does. He edits everything he signs, even the most trivial things. It is a good precaution, but one which can easily be carried to a point where it will waste time that might better be employed on bigger things, but is probably justified in the preliminary stages in which we are.

He thinks very clearly and directly; goes to his conclusions directly when matters call for decision. He can talk straighter to people when calling them down than any one I have seen. I have not yet experienced it, though. He has naturally a good disposition and a keen sense of humor. He loses his temper occasionally, and stupidity and vagueness irritate him more than anything else. He can stand plain talk, but the staff officer who goes in with only vagueness where he ought to have certainty, who does not know what he wants, and fumbles around, has lost time and generally gained some straight talk. He develops great fondness for people whom he likes and is indulgent toward their faults, but at the same time is relent-less when convinced of inefficiency. Personal loyalty to friends is strong with him, I should say, but does not blind him to the truth.

He does not fear responsibility, with all his caution. He decides big things much more quickly than he does trivial ones. Two weeks ago, without any authority from Washington, he placed an order one afternoon for $50,000,000 worth of airplanes, because he thought Washington too slow, and did not cable the fact until too late for Washington to countermand it, had they been so disposed, which they were not. He did it without winking an eye, as easily as though ordering a postage stamp, and it involved the sum which Congress voted for National Defense at the beginning of 1898 just after the *Maine* was blown up, and which we all then considered a very large transaction.

Pershing and Harbord went to work in Room 223 of the War Department, a small, square room with a desk, a flat table, and two chairs, later a telephone. Their first official order named the new command the "American Expeditionary Forces" under which it passed into history. Their next duty was to grasp the magnitude of the undertaking. They knew the peacetime organization of the United States Army must give way to one that could work in harmony with the organization of the Allies. In planning for an eventual war with a European power, American military men had always imagined it would be fought on native soil with American armies disposed in defensive alignments, the line of communica-tion leading back to the sources of supply in the interior. Now Pershing and Harbord had to recruit the staff to begin planning for a new and infinitely more complex military undertaking. By virtue of the country's unpreparedness and his unique command, Pershing became his own chief staff man, Harbord his principal assistant, both bent on devising the agencies and commands to implement their own strategy and tactics. The work in Room 223 concerned not who would carry out the orders, but who, and in what capacity, would issue them.

For this, the War Department allotted Pershing only two officers from the General Staff: Dennis E. Nolan and John McAuley Palmer, both light colonels, destined for stars. Pershing hardly scrounged for the rest. He had a memory that would have done credit to Plato's philosopher king. He remembered Captain Hugh Drum's plan for tactical reorganization and, after asking Drum for a copy of it, added him to the staff. From his ill-fated year as a "tac" at West Point, he remembered the brilliant cadet Fox Conner, who was to become his chief of operations.

He wanted efficient, imaginative, courageous men—above all, loyal men. To a general, loyalty is not that especial emotion evinced toward one's country, the devotion to its interest and the willingness to die for its cause; loyalty is the quasi-political acknowledgment that the commander is divine. Pershing had proved and would continue to prove a loyal "Wilson man," and in his turn he wanted loyal "Pershing men," a designation, incidentally, that followed many of these younger men throughout the whole of their military careers. He satisfied this concern for loyalty while exercising a catholicity in selection (for he had to appoint not only a General Staff, but an Administrative and Supply Staff) that was unusual in a professional soldier. That staff was a tribute to him as well to America; they were men who could think big. Though his General Staff, like most General Staffs, labored mightily and anonymously, still three of them were themselves to become Chief of the United States General Staff—Charles P. Summerall, Malin Craig, and George C. Marshall. Aboard the *Baltic* in May-June, 1917, this small group made the crucial decisions about America's military role.

The Pershing staff made the Air Force independent of the Signal Corps; assigned heavy construction to the Engineers, instead of the Quartermasters; decided to use the French 75 instead of the American three-and-a-half field piece; adopted the English Enfield rifle for the infantry, though urging the War Department to begin heavy manufacture of the Springfield '03, which used the same ball ammunition; and decided to equip Americans with the English steel helmet.

Realizing that the Channel ports were exerted to their utmost in supplying British needs, the staff chose the western ports of Saint-Nazaire, Brest, La Pallice, and Bordeaux, which had comparatively uncrowded rail lines running northeast to the trenches. Brest and Cherbourg were to be used for emergencies.

Sherman's troops needed thirty-nine pounds per man per day to march to the sea. The British Tommy needed fifty pounds per day in 1917. To supply an army of one million, Pershing's staff estimated that every soldier would need 100 pounds of freight per day, 350,000 tons every week. It considered the additional rail lines the army would have to lay, as well as the standard locomotives, rails, and freight cars that would have to be transported to France. This staff also planned the necessary docks and port improvements and determined which harbors would need dredging. It set up one board of officers to draw up the instruction for the management of ports; another for the report on machine guns, types, organization and distribution in units; another to prepare the prototype instruction for the management of training camps. It drew up the plans for the establishment of officer training schools in France; the program to bring over generals to study trench warfare with British and French units before returning to America to complete the training of their divisions; special schools for unit commanders and noncommissioned officers; schools to train instructors and other corps schools; and the gem of this educational system, the General Staff School, which was founded at Langres and graduated 537 staff officers, still a minuscule number by European standards.

Aboard the *Baltic* Pershing importantly remodeled the infantry division. French, German, and British divisions numbered 12,000 men, the maximum number European military men believed a general could manage. In combat, however, these divisions were usually no stronger than 8,000 and sometimes as weak as 5,000 men. It took three European divisions to carry an objective, which often meant imperfect coordination between three division commanders. Pershing, therefore, constituted the American division at 28,000 men, to give the American division a capacity for sustained attack.

In Paris, a French general asked, "Is this your personal staff?"

"No," said Pershing, "it is my General Staff."

When the general persevered, explaining to Pershing that it took thirty years to form a competent General Staff, Pershing snapped, "It never took America thirty years to do anything."

"War," wrote the theorist Alfred Thayer Mahan, "is business." Pershing was his man. He brought to the American army unsuspected managerial and organizational skills, which enabled it to fight at the crest of its potential proficiency. By September, 1917, Pershing had molded a General Staff the equal of any staff among the warring powers. He described the organization in his *Final Report* to Newton Baker:

> The General Staff is naturally divided into five groups, each with its chief, who is an assistant to the Chief of the General Staff. G-1 (General Staff-1) is in charge of organization and equipment of troops, replacements, tonnage, priority of overseas shipments, the auxiliary welfare associations and cognate subjects; G-2 has censorship, enemy intelligence, gathering and disseminating information, preparation of maps and all similar subjects; G-3 is charged with all strategic studies and plans, movement of troops and the supervision of combat operations; G-4 co-ordinates important questions of supply, construction, transport arrangements for combat, and the operations of the Services of Supply, and of hospitalization and the evacuation of the sick and wounded; G-5 supervises the various schools and has general direction and co-ordination of education and training.

The General Staff's European duties were multiple and diverse. It planned to provide tenting for the AEF cantonments assigned to the rear, and to billet troops moving to the front in French homes, barns, schools, and museums. But it knew that hospitals would have to be built, because French and British hospital facilities were overcrowded and overextended. The AEF needed timber not only for hospitals, but for portside piles, for telegraph poles and for fuel, timber in excess of any amount British or American tonnage could transport. It had to come from French forests, which only reluctantly did the French government permit. But to cut it, the General Staff had to organize an American forestry operation with loggers to fell and clear the woods, engineers to build the sawmills, lumbermen to mill timber into lumber, and laborers to throw down the roads for transporting the millions of running feet.

To save tonnage the General Staff planned to have the army issue the soldier his clothing and equipment, which formerly he had purchased as his own. When the infantryman came out of the trenches, he stripped himself at the delousing and bathing stations and received a complete clean issue. Salvage crews retrieved the discarded clothing, boiled it, stored it, and issued it to the next contingent.

During Ludendorff's spring offensives of 1918, Major S. T. Hubbard, of the General Staff's Order of Battle section, came to the clear conclusion that the next German attack against the French army would have to come along the Aisne River over the Chemin des Dames. Hubbard came to this conclusion by analysis and deduction, but he was deducing from neither small nor insignificant events. He reasoned that the German offensive would begin during the week of May 25, reasoning that convinced his French counterpart, Colonel de Cointet. The tactic called for was to man the front line only with machine gunners, and withdraw the mass of troops to trenches in the rear, so that the attackers encountered strong resistance as they themselves were running down. Unfortunately, General Denis Auguste Duchene held the American staff in contempt and crammed his forward positions with *poilus*. Thousands of them were dismembered by the German artillery, thousands more suffocated in a gas attack, and thousands more were convulsed by panic.

The supreme achievement of Pershing's General Staff was the shift of troops from Saint-Mihiel north to the Argonne. Two hundred and twenty thousand French and Italian troops had to move out of the line to admit 660,000 Americans, 400,000 of these coming from the mopped-up Saint-Mihiel sector. Three thousand guns with 40,000 tons of ammunition accompanied them. The entire movement across the rear of their own attacking army took place at night to preserve secrecy. The staff had to establish nineteen railheads and eighty supply depots. Fifteen thousand trucks moved over only three roads. To keep traffic moving when trucks broke down, or horses foundered in the mud, or tractors hauling artillery stalled, one thousand officers kept reporting from different checkpoints along the routes. Despite rain and rutted roads and trains switched to the wrong tracks, despite the inexperience of the Americans and the desperate haste in which the operation was carried out, every element reached its place on the scheduled date, one day earlier than Pershing had expected, a week earlier than Foch thought possible.

The staff officer who initiated the plans was Lieutenant Colonel George C. Marshall, assisted by Fox Conner, chief of the Operations Section, and Hugh Drum, chief of staff of the First Army.

When the General Staff lacked experts to implement its operations, Pershing drafted civilians. Professor Henry Graves, chief of the United States Forestry Service, recruited the men and engineers for the large-scale timbering in France. Pershing accepted the offer of the Pennsylvania Railroad to detach to his command Wallace W. Atterbury, its operating vice-president. Atterbury volunteered to join Pershing provided he could cut red tape. Pershing explained to Atterbury that red tape was the work of civilians in the Treasury and War Department who insisted on an accounting from the military. With a crew of railway men from many American carriers, Atterbury rebuilt the antiquated French railways into a model of supply efficiency, and brought into being the new Army Transport System.

The great work of the Pershing General Staff was to produce a cohesive effort. It was this fact that made Pershing the dominant military figure of the war, not only because he supervised the effort, but because he insisted the effort be his alone. When the War Department, alarmed because of the congestion in supply services, suggested it assign Major General George W. Goethals as a coordinate commander, responsible to Newton D. Baker, rather than Pershing, the result was predictable. Pershing, who had rewarded Harbord with a front-line command, pulled him out from the Second Division and installed him as chief of the services of supply. Pershing wrote Baker that as a principle of military organization, the suggestion did not meet with his approval. He was in control of his General Staff, which handled directly the questions immediately vital to military success. In order to work, the system could not afford divided authority or responsibility. The man who directed the armies had to control their supply.

The truth was that, by mid-1918, there were two General Staffs, one in France and one in Washington. Nominally, Pershing was subordinate to the one in Washington, commanded by Peyton C. March. Actually he was not, a situation that caused March concern and annoyance, for March was as ambitious as Pershing. March was no mean empire builder himself, and Pershing knew as much. So Pershing added to his letter to Baker, "The officer or group of officers who proposed such a scheme to the Secretary could not have had the success of the High Command in France very deeply at heart or else they lacked understanding of the basic principles of organization."*

Some of the Pershing staff's success can be laid to the distance it enjoyed from Washington. Authority was centralized in Washington, as it was in France, but it was centralized among hundreds of officers. Many of them were often at cross-purposes with each other, so that problems had to be bucked upstairs for a decision, which took time. Another factor in the amazing facility of the Pershing staff was that neither Wilson nor Baker interferred with its plans.

The Pershing staff not only guided the military effort, but influenced subsequent American military history. This influence derived from the men Pershing charged with responsibility. There are two notable examples.

One is provided by Colonel, later Brigadier General, John McAuley Palmer, one of six men who constituted Pershing's skele-

---

*Goethals's skills were hardly wasted. As Quartermaster General, he sent the mass of American troops to France well equipped. When he retired, at the end of the war, he had established a consolidated service of supply for the army, an achievement, if not as dramatic, at least equal in effort to the building of the Panama Canal.

ton staff in May, 1917. Because it had taken the United States more than a year to put its forces in the field, a delay that could have proved catastrophic to the Allies, Congress began to consider in 1918 substantative proposals to remedy such delay. It asked Pershing for his opinion. Pershing detached Palmer from his staff to present his views to congressional committees. Palmer, the son of a Civil War general, was an anti-Uptonian, the first to suggest an alternative to Upton's demand for an "expansible" regular army. What Palmer urged was a regular army organized and ready for immediate use as an expeditionary or defense force, a regular army capable of stemming an enemy force or successfully engaging it in the first stages of war until the citizen-soldiery mobilized, trained, and made ready for deployment. Though this policy has been modified and altered in many respects, it remains into the 1970s the military policy of the United States.*

The prime reason Pershing wanted this policy advanced was that he had learned what generals who preceded him had also learned about the citizen-soldier. After the Mexican War, Ulysses S. Grant said that if the volunteers don't run in the first five minutes, they never run at all. Though Pershing himself went to war with the professional soldier's doubts about the volunteer, he learned quickly enough that the ordinary Joe was a complete and valorous fighting man. The potential he saw in the cadets at Nebraska he happily realized in millions of draftees.

The second example was Pershing's appointment of then Lieutenant Colonel Charles G. Dawes as general purchasing agent of the AEF.

Before he left Washington, Pershing enjoyed luncheon at the Metropolitan Club with Dawes and Charles Magoon. Dawes confided that he was trying to wrangle a commission in one of the engineer regiments and asked Pershing for a good word. Pershing asked him what he knew about engineering and Dawes replied that he had carried a surveyor's chains in Ohio for a month thirty-five

*Brigadier General Palmer later wrote two innovative books on American military policy: *Washington, Lincoln, Wilson: Three War Presidents* (New York, 1930) and *The Experience of the United States with Military Organization* (New Haven, 1941).

years before. Not much impressed with these credentials, Pershing, nevertheless, spoke to Baker, saying the army could find some use for a man who had amassed several million dollars on his own.

Almost as soon as he set up his headquarters, Pershing found that use. In the beginning of the war every army supply department had its own purchasing officer. When that department needed supplies, the officer bid for them. Consequently the AEF often paid different prices for the same thing. Army officers bid against each other and against their Allied counterparts. Supplies needed in one area were often surplus in another. This catch-as-catch-can process resulted in ruinous prices for the AEF and inflation for the French. Inevitably the process produced more shortages than satisfaction.

To correct this, Pershing set up a General Purchasing Board and told Dawes to run it. Actually, Dawes did none of the buying, nor did he have monetary accountability. But he staffed the board with a purchasing officer from each supply department who reported directly to him. Dawes provided these officers with the needs collated by the General Staff and tried to insure that the army got good value for every dollar. Dawes also had to supplement each twelve tons of goods the United States shipped with another eight purchased in France and neutral countries.

Pershing soon gave up the attempt to make a military man of Dawes, although he promoted him to brigadier. Dawes found military amenities exaggerated and satirized them. Yet he never ruffled Pershing. On one occasion Pershing broke off a conversation with Foch to walk across a muddy road and button up Dawes's overcoat. On a surprise visit to Dawes's headquarters at Tours, Pershing returned the salutes of the hastily assembled Purchasing Board. Dawes rendered as snappy a salute as any of his fellow officers, though unconsciously he continued puffing his cheroot. Pershing went up to him and whispered, "That's a pretty fair imitation, Charlie. But the next time you salute, remember to put the cigar on the other side of your mouth."

The establishment of the General Purchasing Board was the

admission of one of the first agencies into what has since been termed the "military-industrial complex." And the establishment of this board in mid-1917 taught something to the staff back home. Though the stateside General Staff exercised authority over the army bureaus, the bureaus continued to make their own procurements. Each of them spent so recklessly that together they began to disturb the American economy and inhibit the war effort. These bureaus, for example, managed to place orders for thirty million pairs of shoes when only nine million were ever used. Manufacturers began to renege on one army order to fill another that promised higher profits for quicker delivery.

Eight army bureaus procured independently, each with its own purchasing staff handling its own funds, storing its own goods, and transporting its own supplies. Determined to meet their own needs, these bureaus foolishly competed with one another. In lieu of established bidding procedures, they passed out cost-plus contracts like mimeographed pamphlets. They commandeered facilities without plan or program. They usurped the rails to the point where one freight train transported enamel tubs for aviation personnel not even in France.

Part of the distress lay with the vainglorious bureaus and part lay with Congress, which had often considered marshaling American military might, but had never considered marshaling the American economy. The difficulties persisted until finally Congress gave Wilson the power to reorganize the government under emergency measures. Wilson established and organized a variety of government boards and commissions, which began to regulate every sector of the economy from railroad traffic to munitions. Along with Pershing's General Purchasing Board, Wilson's War Industries Board, headed by Bernard Baruch, became another forerunner of the complex.*

With this economic revolution under way, Newton D. Baker realized once and for all that the army bureaus would have to go,

*Since these boards were empowered with statutory powers, they also became the forerunners of Franklin D. Roosevelt's New Deal agencies.

that he needed a strong Chief of Staff to turn the General Staff into a competent central planning agency. He found this chief in Peyton C. March, who took over his duties in March, 1918. The army began to regulate its stateside military needs even more extensively than Pershing organized its overseas needs.

In devising a General Staff, Pershing can take part of the credit for establishing a military-industrial complex. For such a complex is possible *only* with a General Staff system.

It was not until after the war that the part Pershing's staff played in winning the victory became crystallized. With this crystallization, congressional sentiment favored the organization of the War Department along the lines marked out by the Commander of the AEF. As Chief of Staff under Warren G. Harding, Pershing, following the template of his European model, made the new General Staff an organic part of the postwar army. It has been argued that Pershing, in realizing that war was a managerial enterprise, is less the prototypical soldier and more the founder of the modern American military tradition.

19

The War Under
the Chandeliers

When the war began, in August, 1914, five German armies rolled into Belgium and spilled across the northern countryside of France thundering like apples from a barrel. To the south, three French armies attacked on the Lorraine Front. The French expected that the ferocity and *élan* of their charging troops would brush aside the defenders, after which the *poilus* could rush through Lorraine to the Rhine.

To the command of *"En avant!"* and *"A la Baionette!"* perfectly disciplined French armies advanced, officers twenty yards ahead of their men, the bands playing "La Marseillaise." Shrapnel and machine guns began knocking them over like rabbits. Time and time again, Frenchmen advanced against entrenched Germans; time and time again the machine guns and the artillery exploded old theories of war. Far from brushing the Germans aside, the French themselves were repelled. The more the French pushed in the south, the more they freed the German right wing in the north. Here the Germans planned to sweep west of Paris, curve south and proceed east. The French would be forced to turn and fight with their backs to their own frontiers.

The German right wing in the north made dangerous headway, but it was unable to destroy either the 100,000-man British Expeditionary Force or the two understrength French armies that tried to halt it. Though the Germans drove them back, the French and British retreated in order. Then, because German soldiers were exhausted from their dash and because unforeseen logistical problems began to impede their advance, the German generals took a short cut. Instead of continuing west of Paris before curving south, they swung down east of Paris, a move that exposed their flank. Transported by taxis, a French army sped from Paris to the attack. The French engaged the invaders before the five German armies crossed the Marne River. This delay allowed the defeated French armies from Lorraine to move into defensive positions from which they halted momentarily the mighty German right wing. When a space opened between one German army and a second, the British Expeditionary Force plunged between them. The Germans, far from being able to continue their advance, were hard pressed to save themselves.

The Battle of the Marne was a draw and both sides dug in. The Germans tried to flank the French by turning around and moving north, there to seize the high ground for another offensive. But before they could launch it, the French appeared below them. Then the French moved north in an attempt to flank the Germans, but they moved a day and a corps too late. Now the French were extended, and the Germans made a last dash to the sea. This time, however, the British Expeditionary Force, transported hurriedly by rail from the Marne, met them. By October, 1914, both sides realized that neither could turn the other's flank. The two armies faced each other from ditches that stretched from the Swiss border to the North Sea. This line of trenches "separated the speakers of vernacular Latin from the speakers of the German dialects."

Each side began to fortify its trenches with rolls and rolls of barbed wire, to guard the approaches; with sand-bag parapets, so that soldiers could keep up a continual sniping; with listening posts and machine gun nests in front and redoubts behind. Engineers and labor gangs began to extend the trenches in depth to the rear. The firing trench, which overlooked no-man's-land, was closely supported by a cover trench. Two hundred yards behind the cover trench was the support trench, and two hundred yards behind that the reserve trench, these last two beyond the range of the artillery. Troops in the forward trenches retreated quickly to the support and reserve trenches at the beginning of an assault. Frontal assaults never succeeded. Trench warfare presented the generals with a new complexity in which old tactics could not succeed.

Yet in itself trench warfare was nothing new. It had made its appearance in the American Civil War. It was directly attributable to the development of the rifled bore, which gave the infantry great distance and accuracy in firepower. General Robert E. Lee became a pioneer in trench warfare when he saw that a small number of entrenched defenders could decimate an attacking force that had to move over open ground. The bullets of the attackers were uselessly spent against the entrenchments while the bullets of the defenders more easily found bulking targets. Attacking Cold Harbor, Ulysses S. Grant lost eight thousand men in four hours and Union soldiers quickly built their own entrenchments.

In the same way the trench system of World War I was directly attributable to the development of the machine gun and the magazine rifle, which lent a defending force such concentrated firepower that the attackers had to go underground to save themselves as soon as they came within range. The attackers not only had to advance chest-to-machine-gun, but their forward movement was impeded by barbed wire. Though the attack was preceded by an artillery barrage, often lasting for weeks, the defenders who had retreated rose up in the rear as soon as the assault lost momentum. Geographically the North Sea and the Vosges Mountains fixed the trench lines permanently. Still this 400-mile distance was short enough to insure that neither defending army was ever overextended. Soldiers in sufficient mass, well supplied in matériel and weaponry, guarded every foot of the trench lines in depth.

The Allies believed that attack was a moral imperative. The German trenches cut across French territory. Now Germans worked French iron and coal mines, fired French steel mills, and plowed fruitful French farmland. Germans occupied Belgium and Luxembourg. To dislodge them, the British and French deployed a great mass of attackers and moved in frontal assaults, hoping somehow that one of these attacks would breach the line and, by exploiting the breach, "roll up" the trenches. Allied generals lost the manhood of several generations in these futile assaults. In 1915 alone, in killed, wounded, captured, and missing, the British and French lost two million men.

Everything Ivan Bloch had predicted in *The Future of War in Its Technical, Economic, and Political Relations* had come to pass: the opening of battles from great distances; the loose formation in attacks; the strengthening of the defense; the widening area of the battlefield; and the dreadful increase in casualties. War, as Bloch had warned, had become impossible except at the price of suicide. So two great armies besieged each other. The telling factor in a siege is famine, and both sides spent years trying to inflict this scourge on the other before one succeeded.

In 1916, the Germans ventured a second monumental assault. General Erich von Falkenhayn, the chief of the German General Staff, decided to "bleed white" the French army by attacking at Verdun, a fortified city with twenty concrete and steel forts that jutted into the German lines. Verdun was a point on the line that, for strategic and psychological reasons, the French could not give up. A smashing surprise attack here would force Marshal Joffre to throw in every corps, every division, every man as though onto an anvil where the German army would hammer them to death. Here the French could not fall back but would have to defend the city where they stood. Forced defense under unfavorable conditions would give the Germans victory and Verdun would become the pivot on which the armies could swing north, flushing the Allied soldiers from the rear.

In four months of continuous battle, the Germans felled 410,000 Frenchmen. For France, the Battle of Verdun was a trauma from which the nation never recovered, just as Stalingrad was a trauma from which Germany may never recover. But von Falkenhayn had made a serious mistake in forgetting that it is the anvil that always shatters the hammer. Verdun held, and in June the Germans abandoned the offensive with the loss of 210,000 men and concentrated on stopping the great British assault along the Somme River in the north. Here British soldiers went over the top against German positions that not only commanded the high ground, but gave the defenders a thirty-mile-wide tableau of the attacking force. A cataclysm of fire descended on the Tommies and the Canadians, who pushed on. Sir Douglas Haig added reserves without stint until, at last, he had expended 500,000 men and gained only a few hundred yards.

The Somme offensives were succeeded in 1917 by the Nivelle offensive, which cost France another 125,000 men. And still the lines remained unchanged. The generals had learned only that a vast preponderance in attack could win limited objectives that measured at best 1,500 yards. For these objectives thousands of men had to perish. It would have cost the Allies millions of men and billions of dollars over several decades to have inched into Germany by winning limited objectives.

The hellish irresponsibility of the generals was not that they failed to devise the strategy to break the stalemate, but that they kept on trying to break it by frontal assault. They kept throwing men against machine guns when it was obvious that the machine gun must win. Historians have described World War I as a war of attrition, a truth the *poilus* and the Tommies knew, but their generals and statesmen did not.

It was impossible for the Allies to win a war of attrition, but it was in the cards for a starving Germany, its morale weakening, to lose one. The Allies eventually won because the Germans, though they had learned the value of defensive warfare at Verdun, changed their strategy. By mid-1917, Germany had become a military dictatorship ruled by the proto-Hitler, General Erich Ludendorff, who called himself the First Quartermaster General of the German General Staff. He determined on a last, great German offensive for two reasons: a three-million-man American army would give the Allies the ultimate preponderance of attacking forces; and the British blockade was beginning to enfeeble Germany, and with enfeeblement comes hopelessness.

Drawing off one hundred divisions from the Eastern Front

(though he still left one million German soldiers in Russia, who ventured farther than Hitler's armies in 1942), Ludendorff staged three major and two minor offensives in the spring of 1918. The first of these tried to separate the British and French juncture; the second tried to drive the British into the Channel ports, forcing them to evacuate France; the third aimed to seize Paris, where the Germans would dictate peace. The minor offensives simply failed.

Ludendorff lost more soldiers than he could afford. Though he extended German lines deep into France, there were too few troops to defend them. Generalissimo Ferdinand Foch found the reserves by which to mount an Allied offensive in the summer of 1918, and in September a million Americans began an advance in the Meuse-Argonne sector. To stop this dangerous threat, Ludendorff withdrew the last of his reserves from the British Front. And the British crashed through. Then everybody came crashing through.

Trench warfare killed soldiers as no war before or since has killed soldiers. Ten million men died in World War I and another six million lived on as cripples.* The trenches became canals in the winter, in which rats as big as cats surfaced. They fed on the dead bodies disinterred by shelling. The duty of burying those who died in the attack was entrusted to their buddies, a supreme test of nerve. Men impaled on barbed wire groaned in agony for days. Soldiers moving forward drowned in the mud. Men died blistered by gas. Their toes rotted off with trench foot. The British punished a dozing sentry by tying him to the wire in no-man's-land for twenty-four hours. The French shot *poilus* after a summary court-martial when their division did not carry the objective.

Trench warfare left such a scar on the British, for example, that the one serious disagreement they had with the United States in World War II was over the advisability of a cross-Channel invasion. The British were sure the Normandy invasion would result in trench warfare once more. The memory of the trenches insured

---

*Eighty-three thousand Americans perished in combat or from wounds received in combat and several thousand perished from influenza. One hundred and twenty thousand more were casualties.

French defeat in June, 1940. The French entered World War I ardent believers in the attack and ended as profound believers in the defense. They committed their postwar military energies to the construction of the Maginot Line.

But trench warfare was not John J. Pershing's war. His war was fought under the chandeliers and on the parqueted floors of French mansions, in the rococo suites of the Crillon, and aboard railway coaches with gilded appointments.

Whenever in Paris, Pershing occupied the palatial estate of Ogden Mills, at 73 rue de Varenne, a three-story palace with a garden that rivaled the Tuileries. These premises had once been the palace of Jean Lannes, one of Napoleon's marshals. The great dining room could accommodate one hundred guests at a long marble table, a single slab over thirty yards in length, supported by only two legs at each end. One night, when Pershing, Harbord, and Dawes were finishing their meal, Dawes looked around the baronial rooms and said, "John, when I contrast these barren surroundings with the luxuriousness of our early life in Lincoln, it does seem to me that a good man has no real chance in the world."

"Don't it beat hell," said the meditative farmboy from Laclede.

His headquarters in Chaumont was in a fertile countryside with beautiful avenues of trees, gleaming stone causeways, and red-roofed tile dwellings, undisturbed and peaceful. His office was sparse, but bay windows admitted generous sunlight, and the room itself was spacious and warm and its floor always polished.

But he fought the war where he had to fight it. The American war effort has often been characterized as fifteen months of fighting in the rear and two months of fighting at the front. World War I demanded of army chiefs intricate and protracted planning. To mount a barrage preparatory for an assault on the Western Front, months of speeded-up shell manufacture was required in order to build up stockpiles. There was no husbanding of shells, because neither the Allies nor the Germans conceived of interludes in trench warfare. The trenches were part of an ever-continuing battle, and enough ammunition was expended during static months between offensives to claim the lives of 1,500 soldiers daily. Moving an army to its forward positions for an offensive meant moving dozens of divisions along limited and often inadequate rail lines and accumulating fleets of motor transport that had to transport supplies over unlit narrow roads at night. The forage for draft animals was in itself a mighty supply task.

The achievements of the military staffs were always more impressive than those of the line commanders, who quickly lost control over units in combat. This loss of control stemmed from poor communications, the irregularity of the terrain, and the disfigurement of battle formations obscured by fog, smoke, gas, and clouds of dirt.

Staff officers soon learned that every remembered detail contributed to victory; every neglected detail could lead to a loss. American ships took on sand at Saint-Nazaire for ballast on their return trip. When, on one occasion, the sand was not off-loaded at Baltimore, tons of vital supplies were left on the wharves.

French farmers did not want to sell horses to the quartermaster. The farmers realized that if the Americans transported horses from the States, Frenchmen could purchase the animals cheaply after the war was over. It was up to Pershing to authorize the bribes that saved the tonnage.

More than logistics and strategy were worked out beneath the chandeliers. Generals and statesmen were constantly trying to secure a political advantage for their nation at the expense of another. While the French and the Americans agreed that the war could be won only in the trenches of the Western Front, the British did not. For reasons of empire, the British wanted to win the war in Mesopotamia or Palestine or Salonica. They wanted to keep an army stationed in India, threatened by the collapse of the Russian Front. Constant cajoling, threatening, and persuading was needed to make the English see that the war came first and empire second. The Italians importuned for British, French, and American divisions to bolster their front against Austria.

But these decisions were never reached quickly; rather they were reached in formal proceedings that consumed time and demanded considerable skill and expertise in argument. Not until

October 12, 1918, for example, when he formed his Second Army, was Pershing recognized at Allied councils as an army group commander, coequal with Haig and Pétain. Until then he took his orders from Pétain, under whom he commanded the American contingent of the French army group.

The Allies found much to criticize in Pershing. He was late in coming to the fight, and they were sure at one point too late. Throughout his life he was notorious for tardiness. His demerits at West Point had accumulated from his arriving late in formation. In France he would arrive at midnight for a dinner with Pétain and Clemenceau that had been scheduled for six. There are many reasons why people are always late; in Pershing's case it was an absorbing interest in detail. He would sooner polish his shoes to a final shine at West Point than be first in place when his squad mustered; and he could not tear himself away from Chaumont while a chance remained to inspire his staff to think and act as replicas of himself. His allies thought his policy of "slow but sure" was time blindness writ large. He insisted that it took a year of training to make a soldier, even when Newton Baker wrote that the excitement of the war made the recruits appreciably more responsive and ready sooner.

His men complained he was a martinet. He was, indeed, sometimes needlessly a martinet. His order of October 4, 1917, read:

> The standards for the American Army will be those of West Point. The rigid attention, the upright bearing, attention to detail, uncomplaining obedience to instruction required of the cadet will be required of every officer and soldier of our armies in France.

Doughboys chafed under this as cadets chafed under his discipline when he was a "tac."

He later wrote:

> In a new army like ours, if discipline were lacking, the factor most essential to the army's efficiency would be missing. The army was composed of men representing every walk of life, from educated

professionals and business men to those of the various trades and callings, and practically all were without military experience. In the beginning our army was without the discipline that comes from training.

West Point discipline was the only discipline he knew. He wanted an aggressive spirit to grow "until the soldier feels himself, as a bayonet fighter, invincible in battle."

The discipline, though severe, was hardly pointless. Pershing knew the terrible crucible through which his men would have to pass. The novelist F. Scott Fitzgerald, viewing the battlefield of Verdun, remarked that it took a thousand years of Christmases to make men move through it. It took incredible love of country, incredible willingness for self-sacrifice, and incredible discipline to make men go over the top.

"When you stumbled upon a lost American doughboy in a God-forsaken hamlet," wrote reporter Frank Simonds in *They Won the War*, "his bearing, the set of his tunic, his salute, all authentically recalled the general who sat in Chaumont." As he created his staff into a replica of himself, so he wanted to make every private into a Pershing.

Americans hate military discipline. Citizen-soldiers quickly see the futility of make-work projects, and they always prove ingenious at devising efficient shortcuts, which puts them at odds with the military mode. Popular novels of both postwar periods are filled with a rage against authority.

Where Pershing failed as a great commander is precisely where the other Allied commanders failed. He did not devise tactics that could overcome the lethal effects of the machine gun. His insistence that troops train for a war of movement was, in the long run, idealistic, not realistic. Yet when his failure was brought home to him, as it was when the Meuse-Argonne offensive began to falter, when he realized he was not giving life to new tactics, but seeing old ones fail, he had the moral strength to persevere. He persevered not because it was the only thing to do, but because he determined that, though the AEF paid exorbitant costs in the attack, his men were drawing off from the British Front the last of Germany's reserves.

The tank alone could break the stalemate of the trenches, a truth politicians like Winston Churchill and junior officers like George S. Patton perceived. The Germans were the first to use poison gas, a dangerous risk, because the prevailing winds of the Continent blew from west to east; they were the first to bombard and bomb cities, and the first to use flamethrowers; but none of these was as effective as the tank, a British invention of which Falkenhayn, Hindenburg, and Ludendorff thought little. The tank could cut a swath through barbed wire in minutes, where it took the artillery months. Supported by infantry units, the tank could flush a machine gun nest quickly and traverse the trenches without pause, where it took soldiers hours to clear them with bayonet, pistol, and hand grenade. Though Pershing did not suspect that the tank could end the stalemate, nevertheless he saw enough of its tactical value to establish the American Tank Corps under Colonel S. D. Rockenbach in January, 1918. He gave in to Patton's pleas and assigned him to the command of the Tank Center at Langres, and later made him the commander of the 304th Tank Brigade at Saint-Mihiel.

Enmeshed in a war whose victories were always celebrated as miracles—"the Miracle of the Marne," "the Miracle of Verdun," "the Miracle of the Meuse"—Pershing still commanded troops who would bleed for him as old troopers were supposed to bleed. He got what he wanted from them because a good soldier convinces his troops that risk is the soldier's stock-in-trade. No one could ever doubt that he, too, was a soldier to his marrow, and no one ever saw him as less. When, in June, 1917, he and his small staff visited Napoleon's tomb, the old French attendant creakily removed Napoleon's sword from the case. The natural inclination of an American is to take the sword, handle it, appreciate its weight and balance, and flash it once or twice. But without a second's hesitation, Pershing bowed from the waist, hands at his side, and reverently kissed the blade.

20

A Good Man
Among Enthusiasts

On October 3, 1918, Germany asked Woodrow Wilson to arrange an armistice on the basis of his Fourteen Points. Three weeks later, on October 25, the Allied military chiefs met at Senlis to discuss terms. Pershing's opinion then was that, if the German people were sincere in wanting to end the war, they would have to withdraw their armies from Alsace-Lorraine as well as captured French and Belgian territory, return captured railroad equipment, surrender the submarine fleet, and accede to the continuing transport of American troops and matériel.

However, five days later, in a letter delivered to the Supreme War Council, Pershing suggested that the war should go on:

> We should take full advantage of the situation and continue the offensive until we compel Germany's unconditional surrender. To allow Germany an armistice now would revivify the low spirits of the German Army and enable it to reorganize and resist later on, and would deprive the Allies of the full measure of victory by failing to press this present advantage to its complete military end. A cessation of hostilities short of capitulation postpones if it does not render impossible the imposition of satisfactory peace terms, because it would allow Germany to withdraw her army with its present

strength, ready to resume hostilities if peace terms were not satisfactory to her.

It is the experience of history that victorious armies are prone to overestimate the enemy's strength and too eagerly seek an opportunity for peace. I believe the complete victory can only be obtained by continuing the war until we force unconditional surrender from Germany.

It was a letter that made no one at the Supreme War Council happy. Politically, Clemenceau and his generals doubted that France could continue now that peace was a near prospect. Haig and Lloyd George thought the British armies were too exhausted to take another step. Colonel House, Wilson's representative, did not want a sweeping victory, but only one sufficient to check Teutonic ambitions. It was not so much that the members of the Supreme War Council did not know what to make of Pershing's insistence as that they did not want to make anything of it at all. Colonel House confided, "Everyone believes Pershing's letter is a political document and a clear announcement of his intention to become a candidate for the Presidency in 1920."

Potential candidates worried Woodrow Wilson, who was planning a third term only to discover, midway through his second, that he was sailing in troubled waters. At the beginning of the war Wilson had asked for a bipartisan war policy, to which Congress pledged support. In the congressional elections of 1918, however, Wilson campaigned strenuously for the election of Democrats, an effort the voters apparently found so discreditable that, on the day after the election, Wilson found himself a Democratic hostage to a Republican Congress. Some of Wilson's trouble was his own fault. He did not see the armistice as the supreme moment of the American present, but looked forward to the peace he would facilitate. And some of Wilson's trouble stemmed from the voters' dissatisfaction with the hortatory goals of the war.

What House feared was that, if the Commander of the AEF stood in opposition to the President, the insubordination was bound to inspire controversy. Controversy affects popularity, and in this case could influence popular opinion for Pershing's gain. On an auto trip from Versailles to Paris, House took Pershing to task for the letter to the War Council. He accused the general of inconstancy, of approving one policy with the military chiefs and another with the prime ministers. Pershing replied that he had given his views on an armistice because the military chiefs had asked for his views on an armistice, but that there are other ways to end wars. Wilson, Pershing said, had invited his counsel and advice by wire, urging him to feel free to bring to his attention any consideration he had overlooked. Pershing proceeded to do this and had submitted his letter to the War Department, where apparently no one had thought it significant enough to show to the President. If House and Wilson wanted the matter closed, Pershing agreed to close it then and there.

He was, indeed, in serious disagreement with his commander-in-chief, but it was not for the purposes of enhancing his own candidacy. Wilson's initial response to the request for an armistice was to propose one with moderate terms, suggesting, among other conditions, that the German army retire unmolested to its 1914 borders. Militarily, however, this would have enabled the Germans to secure a defensive position with lines only half as long as those they held in October. Wilson wanted terms that left Germany free to negotiate at the peace conference. Allied generals wanted an armistice that attested to their victory on the battlefield, an armistice by which Germany confessed she had lost the battle.

Professor Bullitt Lowry of North Texas State University, in his monograph "Pershing and the Armistice," in *The Journal of American History* (Summer, 1970), writes that Pershing's recommendation to press the war without quarter was motivated principally by his desire to circumvent the soft armistice Wilson wanted:

When he received [Wilson's] telegram of instruction from Washington, Pershing had three options: he could support the President's express wishes; he could defy the President and continue to support the terms he had already proposed; or he could find some other alternative that would allow him to seek harsh terms but which would not leave him open to the charges of direct disobedience. Pershing took the last choice.

Pershing chose this because an American general has a harder time impressing his views on government than do French or British generals. France had a head of government in Clemenceau and a head of state in Poincaré, and Foch was the Supreme Commander-in-Chief; Britain had a head of government in Lloyd George and a head of state in King George V, and an Imperial General Staff that participated in the political decisions anent an armistice. But Woodrow Wilson was not only head of government and head of state, but Commander-in-Chief as well. When the President chose, he could stand in for Pershing as the military spokesman of his people.

The Grail pursued by the American military man is Unconditional Surrender. It is his tenet of faith that only unconditional surrender wins wars, and unconditional surrender means *Occupation*. American generals have often accepted conditional terms—Grant was generous at Appomattox, because Sherman already occupied the South. General Douglas MacArthur did not insist on deposing Emperor Hirohito, because the Japanese had acceded to a military occupation of their home islands. To European generals, however, unconditional surrender often meant the chance for their governments to annex territories and demand reparations. Americans are not in the game for land or money, they are in the game to carry the good news of liberal democracy to bitter foes, to convert them, as indeed MacArthur converted the Japanese and a succession of American High Commissioners converted the West Germans after World War II.

Having heard the proposals of the Allied generals at Senlis on October 25, Pershing knew the general nature of the harsh and stringent conditions they wanted to impose on Germany, but military occupation, except for limited beachheads, was not among them.

Instead of requiring the German forces to retire at once [Pershing wrote in his memoirs], leaving matériel, arms and equipment behind, the Armistice terms permitted them to march back to their homeland with colors flying and bands playing, posing as the victims of political conditions. If unconditional surrender had been demanded, the Germans would, without doubt, have been compelled to yield, and their troops would have returned to Germany without arms, virtually as paroled prisoners of war. The surrender of the German Armies would have been an advantage to the Allies in the enforcement of peace terms and would have been a greater deterrent against possible future aggression.

If Pershing's views on unconditional surrender had prevailed and an American military force occupied Germany, it is possible that the Weimar Republic would have proved more durable.

But it was shortly apparent that Allied generals would dictate the armistice. World War I was waged for so long, with such intensity, with such disregard for life, that it is not surprising that military policy subdued political judgments. The generals convinced their governments to impose hard terms, and their governments persuaded Wilson. The generals demanded:

—Immediate evacuation of all occupied territory—including Alsace-Lorraine.
—Evacuation of the western banks of the Rhine by all form of German military force, and establishment of Allied bridgeheads on the east bank of the Rhine at Mainz, Coblenz, and Cologne, these bridgeheads to be as much as thirty kilometers radius.
—Repatriation of all Allied prisoners of war, without immediate reciprocity, and repatriation of all civilians of Allied nations.
—Surrender, in good condition, the following materials of war:
  5,000 guns (2,500 heavy, 2,500 field);
  25,000 machine-guns;
  3,000 trench mortars;
  1,700 aeroplanes, including all night-bombing machines, in the
       possession of the German forces;
  all German submarines.
—The internment in British ports, with only German care and maintenance parties on board, of the following German Naval vessels:

6 Battle-cruisers;
10 Battleships;
8 Light cruisers (including two mine-layers);
50 destroyers of the most modern types.

In the last clause of the armistice, Clemenceau added:

With the reservation that any subsequent concessions and claims by the Allies and the United States remain unaffected, the following financial conditions are imposed:
Reparation for damage done.

No general was later consulted at Versailles about the peace, though many generals were in attendance. When Foch tried to explain the military importance of boundaries, Clemenceau snapped, "Keep silent! It is I who represent France." Before he reached Paris with Colonel House, Pershing probably realized he had offered as much about ending the war as he was expected to offer.

"He has been a good President to me," Pershing remarked as he awaited Woodrow Wilson's arrival in Brest on December 14, "but I fear he has his hands filled now." Pershing had more to think about than whether the German postwar army would number 100,000 or 450,000, with fortifications on two frontiers. Aboard the *George Washington*, which carried Woodrow Wilson to the Versailles Peace Conference, was nine-year-old Warren Pershing.

Colonel House was not alone in thinking of Pershing as a presidential aspirant. Pershing's former classmate, Lieutenant General Robert L. Bullard, wrote: "The lack-scandal and lack-discontent of this war as compared to others will make Pershing one of the two most successful Americans and would probably make him President if he had but a little more 'mixing' ability. He inspires no enthusiasm ever; respect, yes, but respect doesn't generally elect a President."

"The boys will never call him Papa Pershing," wrote Heywood Broun. "The sympathetic touch which makes a popular hero, even though severe, is lacking." Private Charles MacArthur, who was later to co-author *The Front Page*, recalled doughboys swearing that Pershing had lost their vote when he appeared hours late for an inspection.

From the Armistice until September, 1919, Pershing remained in France, absorbed in sending home the AEF. There was no more shipping available for this than there had been for sending the AEF to France. Pershing put it to his men: if they doubled up aboard the troopships, one half using the bunks by day, the other by night, they could get home twice as fast. To which the soldiers shouted, "Aye."

Pershing was also a nominal member of an American commission that was helping plan the reconstruction of Europe. One day his auto passed a company of Yanks working as a road gang in a bombed-out village. Pershing demanded of a French colonel to know who had ordered Americans to be employed as laborers. The colonel answered, "Marshal Foch." After some vigorous table-pounding by Black Jack, Le Maréchal called off American participation in reconstruction.

Though he might deny it to himself and tell intimates he was not interested, the growing prospect of his candidacy kept impinging on Pershing's consciousness.* In the spring of 1919, Senator Charles Dick of Ohio announced the formation of the Pershing Republican League. It was one of those ploys that commands newspaper space by virtue of its novelty rather than its consequences. No more was ever heard of the league. Pershing asked Dawes what he should do about leagues he hadn't authorized. Dawes advised him to ignore rumors if he didn't want to run.

To the chairman of a Republican delegation in Pennsylvania Pershing wrote that he was not a candidate, that his soldier's duty took preference over personal ambition—which is not really convincing to a state Republican chairman. Pershing was certainly thinking about it; even William Tecumseh Sherman had *thought* about it.

*For some of the subsequent material, I have drawn upon Lawrence L. Murray's, "General John J. Pershing's Bid for the Presidency in 1920," *Nebraska History*, Summer, 1972.

Colonel George S. Patton wrote to Pershing about the presidential candidacy of General Leonard Wood. Patton insisted that Pershing's organizational skills were far superior, and that Pershing was a more famous and worthier war hero. If anything beyond his own ambition and appetite inclined Pershing toward active political commitment it was the prospect of Leonard Wood as President and commander-in-chief and himself out of a job.

The event that made Leonard Wood's nomination a likelihood was the death of Theodore Roosevelt in January, 1919. The split in the Republican Party in 1912 between Roosevelt's progressives and the party regulars had been healed. The diligent, resourceful, and canny Roosevelt had virtually assured himself of the nomination in 1920. His demise, however, did not leave a vacuum. Roosevelt's reputation had been revivified by the Preparedness Campaign of 1916, in which Leonard Wood had been a chief instrument. Now he became Roosevelt's political heir. Wood was a still-remembered hero of the Spanish-American War and had accumulated considerable sympathy as a victimized political casualty of World War I.

One of the means Woodrow Wilson and Newton Baker used to victimize Wood was John J. Pershing. When these two Democrats announced Pershing's commission as Commander of the AEF, they came under heavy criticism for not naming Wood, who had been right about the war when they had been wrong, and who had a devoted congressional following. Critics of the administration charged that Wilson and Baker had sold the country short because Wood was a Roosevelt protégé. Baker stilled this incipient controversy by pointing out that, far from trying to diminish Roosevelt's influence, they had actually named another Roosevelt protégé, Pershing, to the important command.

Roosevelt caused Democrats headaches no matter how artfully they tried to control him. Upon the declaration of war, Roosevelt immediately offered to recruit a division of eminent men to serve in the trenches under his leadership. To deny Roosevelt was politically risky, so Baker and Wilson asked Pershing to discourage him. Pershing wrote to Roosevelt saying that to approve his request would open the door to many similar requests; that the creation of a Roosevelt division would cause a disproportionate loss of the best officers who would want to serve in it; and that the hardships of trench war demanded young men in the best of health. Roosevelt recognized the wisdom of the decision. In reply to Pershing he asked only that his sons Theodore and Archibald be included in the first contingent to go to France.

It remained for the administration to dispose of Leonard Wood, which Baker did by assigning him to train the Eighty-ninth Division at Camp Funston in the Southwest. But Wood proved an inspirational and competent commander, and in the fall of 1917 he went overseas with several divisional generals to acquaint himself with trench warfare, the better to train troops. In fact, Wood was wounded at the front when a German shell landed amidst his party, killing several French officers. Though Pershing was made a lieutenant general shortly after his arrival in France, Wood was still the senior major general of the United States Army. Once he brought his division overseas, it was reasonable to expect that he would have a corps command.

When the Eighty-ninth Division embarked for France in the spring of 1918, the President detached Wood from its command, a cruel and obviously vengeful political decision. Republican congressional leaders complained, and Republican newspapers excoriated the War Department. Wood stormed to Washington to see Newton D. Baker. He argued that the men of the Eighty-ninth had a right to go into battle with the general who trained them.

Apologetically, Baker told Wood that General Pershing did not want him in France and that the War Department was constrained to back him up. The incredulous Wood asked if Pershing was determining the lists of the United States Army, and the hard-pressed Baker said the War Department had no choice. President Wilson saw Wood and confirmed Baker's information. He ordered Wood to the command of the Western Department. Wood asked for another division, and the President complied.

It is, of course, possible that Leonard Wood might have been killed in France, It is possible that he might not have distinguished himself. But the chances are that the Wilson Administration cut short his chances for fame. Woodrow Wilson, no more than William McKinley, who kept William Jennings Bryan in Omaha, was not in the business of enhancing the reputation of an old political enemy and possible opponent.

Pershing may well have decided that he didn't want Wood in France. Wood, who never stepped softly, disagreed with Pershing's policy of waiting in order to create an American military entity for the front. Wood made no secret of his conviction that the American Command stubbornly refused to profit by the experience of the British and the French, that there was something to be said for the amalgamation of American with Allied units, and that the American Front itself was poorly organized. Generals have been replaced for less, but it is doubtful that Pershing insisted that Wood was not to serve with the AEF. A general is apt to lose the good graces of his commander if he says that he cannot control a subordinate.

At least one figure in the small drama saw Woodrow Wilson's hand—Theodore Roosevelt, who wrote Wood in July, 1918:

> I am sure that the political phase of the matter was what decided the action of the President in your case. As you say quite truly if General Pershing did object, he did so only under pressure. As I told you, in the case of Colonel Malone, they promptly overrode Pershing's recommendations (for his promotion to brigadier) when they think it desirable. They have used him merely as a shield tool.

An old friend who helped incline Pershing to the race was Charles G. Dawes, who soon felt a grass roots veneration for the Commander of the AEF. While Americans never held Pershing as dear as their fathers had held Grant, or the French held Pétain, still they accorded him great respect. In July, Wilson asked the Congress to reward John J. Pershing and Chief of Staff Peyton C. March with promotions to the permanent rank of general, Pershing's appointment to take precedence. Congress responded by reinstituting the rank of General of the Armies for Pershing, and by a thumping majority, Congress also voted to make Pershing Chief

of Staff, a resolution Woodrow Wilson and Newton Baker ignored.*
When Pershing came home in September to lead several victory
parades, he was immediately inundated with thousands of requests
for appearances and speeches on behalf of organizations as diverse
as the University of Nebraska and the newly formed American
Legion.

Dawes told Pershing that, whether he willed it or not, he was
now in the race for the presidential nomination, and that he would
have to show himself to the people and take advantage of his
military accomplishments to make a good showing. "Your strength
with the people," wrote Dawes, "lies in the fact that you are above
and beyond timidity in everything. No sincere and wise counsellor
will suggest to you, in my opinion, any attitude of deference to
former sentiment." Dawes, who had returned to his Chicago banking interests, laid out the strategy for Pershing's campaign: he was
to run as an undeclared candidate, a "dark horse" to whom the
convention would turn in the event of a deadlock.

There was no dearth of Republican candidates in 1920. In fact,
there was no dearth of dark horses, among them subsequent Presidents Herbert Hoover and Calvin Coolidge. The frontrunners
were Leonard Wood, an unquestionably competent administrator,
clear on the issues, and an ardent Republican; Frank O. Lowden,
the reform governor of Illinois; and Senator Hiram Johnson of
California, who drew support from old Populists by attacking
Woodrow Wilson's plan for the League of Nations and by con-
demning the usurious money interests of the East.

Dawes suggested that Pershing enter the Nebraska primary in
April, 1920, as a favorite-son candidate. To this end Dawes went
to Lincoln, where he recruited Mark Woods as Pershing's campaign manager. Mark Woods was not a professional politician, but

---

*The grade General of the Armies was created March 3, 1779, but was not men-
tioned in the Act of March 16, 1802, which determined the peacetime military
establishment. Congress had not authorized the design of six stars at the time, but
clearly the grade is senior to the five-star General of the Army. March did not
get his promotion to four-star General until he was retired in 1930.

a well-known, well-respected, overactive businessman. He soon found that Wood and Johnson supporters had already established statewide organizations and lined up delegate slates. Woods determined to counteract this by an intensive mail, advertising, and publicity campaign. He made political capital out of Pershing's purchase of the Lincoln home where Warren had been living with his aunts. Before the Lincoln Kiwanis, the general said, "I have always considered Nebraska at least one of my homes, but today I confess it is the most important of all."

Pershing's dark horse campaign was not unattended by criticism and discouraging advice. Washington professionals who had committed to the frontrunners took pot shots at the general. Representative Thomas Schall of Minnesota promised to do what he could "to thwart the ambitions of a man absolutely unfit for the office," who had "systematically eliminated any officer who ranked him or showed ability." Representative Isaac Sherwood of Ohio said that he was still trying to find out "when or where Pershing ever visited the battle front. Safety first for a war hero has no appeal to me."

Senator Francis Warren warned Pershing that it was unlikely the Republicans would settle upon a military man for President. There was a growing disappointment in the war and, moreover, there were too many professionals sure that 1920 was a Republican year to hope that a man who had spent most of his life out of the country could succeed in winning the nomination as a reluctant candidate.

At first Wilson and Baker helped Pershing's campaign by dispatching him on a military inspection throughout the country. But, because that inspection took him to the Panama Canal at a time when he should have been stumping, it is obvious that neither the President nor his Secretary of War had lost their touch.

In March, 1920, at a Washington reception of the Nebraska Society held in his honor, Pershing allowed that, if called upon by the people, it would be his patriotic duty to accept. It was a circumscribed announcement that did little to annoy or amaze either

Leonard Wood or Hiram Johnson, both of whom had entered the Nebraska primary and were campaigning for the sixteen delegates.

It snowed heavily in Nebraska on April 20. Fewer than 200,000 Nebraska Republicans went to the polls. Hiram Johnson carried the state with 63,262 votes; Leonard Wood polled 42,385; and Pershing 27,669. This effectively ended his candidacy, although it is true that Pershing continued to hope, because it is an American citizen's patriotic duty to hope somehow he will become President.

Leonard Wood came near winning the nomination in July, but lost it when he refused either to bribe delegates or to trade three appointments to Boise Penrose in return for the support of the entire Pennsylvania delegation. It is a military man's nature not to trade or compromise with standards and plans, and Wood proved once again that a man cannot be one-half general and one-half politician and get anywhere.

The Republicans of 1920 did, indeed, turn to a dark horse, Ohio's Senator Warren G. Harding. In the smoke-filled room the state bosses agreed on "Everybody's second choice" in order to break the deadlock between the three frontrunners. "What do you know?" remarked Harding, in his one memorable utterance. "We drew to a pair of deuces and filled."

Pershing cabled Dawes his pleasure at Wood's defeat: "Could anything be better? The victory is ours. I die content." Perhaps he was vindictive after all.

In retrospect, however, it was hardly Pershing's victory. He did not cost Leonard Wood the nomination by denying him the Nebraska delegation. What is important historically is that, after the greatest war America had ever fought, the politicians, given the choice of two military men for President, chose neither. It had hitherto been habitual for the people to seek in a victorious general a political savior who would smooth over the dislocations occasioned by the war. The American public had not really abandoned the tradition. Pershing and Wood failed to win nomination chiefly because of organizational problems, and chiefly problems on the politicians' level.

Pershing's campaign was afflicted with amateurism. Having determined on a dark horse campaign, it was to Pershing's interest to discover what warring factions his nomination would unite. But neither he nor Mark Woods was ever alert to the divisive fight that transpired in Ohio between Columbus and Cleveland politicians; nor did they realize that the less industrialized West had benefitted not at all from the war effort; nor did they grasp that long-denied Midwest Republicans, who held the whip hand, wanted a candidate of their own. Most likely, Pershing would have been better advised to seek favorite-son designation from the Missouri Republican caucus.

Pershing entered a primary where he was supposedly strong, only to lose—which is to compose himself the handwriting on the wall. The mail and advertising campaign was aimed at enlisting the support of the professional and business communities in a state that still had a populous agricultural constituency. When Hiram Johnson came to Nebraska, his campaigning touched not at all on the League of Nations as an issue, or the need to restructure government, but instead promised farm relief to rural voters who had weathered a crash in crop prices the year before.

Mark Woods expended too much energy in securing the endorsements of the eminent and important. Pershing needed to appeal to the average voter who, after all, has more votes in one small town than all of the university presidents, state legislators, and bankers put together. Asked for his support, Senator Warren said a quiet, underground campaign made no sense with a prominent Senator drumming up support for his son-in-law. Pershing should have been ringing doorbells in Nebraska instead of shaking hands in Washington.

Lastly, Mark Woods and his co-workers did not trust that the general had any personal appeal. In a letter to Dawes, Pershing himself worried that his campaign was not personal enough. His publicists, including two professionals recruited in Washington by Senator Warren, concentrated on portraying the general as "a kind, generous man, a human soldier." In their campaign biographies—George MacAdams's series ran in *World's Work* at this time—they succeeded in minimizing Pershing's toughness, so that he seemed a humdrum village-green polemicist instead of a hardened soldier who had made some weighty decisions. They did not understand that an inflexible disciplinarian, a determined aggressor in his own pursuits, a brave man who can gauge risks, has his own special virtues. General Leonard Wood's publicists were no better: every photograph of him showed the general in civilian clothes.

Pershing was at a political disadvantage as a soldier, but the disadvantage was not all of his own making. The euphoria of victory had passed. The war had, however, spurred inflation, strikes, race riots, unemployment, especially among returning soldiers, and Prohibition—and Prohibition was beginning to spur crime. Small-town America was stampeding to the cities, which resulted in a country of native-born aliens and produced severe dislocations in values, economics, and politics. There was a growing estrangement between the educated and the uneducated, between the industrial laborer and the middle-class clerk, and consequently a growing disillusion with the quality of American life. This disillusion was already evident in the novels of Sinclair Lewis and the poetry of Carl Sandburg. There was an overriding anxiety about the emerging role of America in the world, an anxiety that found expression in the acrimonious debate over the League of Nations and the need for universal military training.

Yet given the chance, the voters probably would have opted for Theodore Roosevelt, who liked to boast he was something of a soldier. To this extent, Pershing and Wood were instinctively right in depending upon the tradition of electing a soldier after a war to guide tumultuous readjustments. This tradition did not play Pershing false; what played him false was the nature of the war and his own concept of soldiering.

When America joined the Allies, the war was more than half over. It was another year before American forces were committed to the front lines, and during that year Pershing was subordinate to French and British generals. This was not the customary heroic role of the American military man. Pershing established a strict censorship over the AEF, lest Americans at home believe anything other than that the army was an army-in-becoming. He sent home the correspondent who headlined AMERICAN PILOTS CLEAR SKIES OF GERMAN ACES on the grounds that the man was a liar: there weren't five thousand American pilots in France; outside of the Lafayette Escadrille there wasn't one. This also militated against a heroic role.

Within three months of Pershing's producing an army-in-being the war was over. The image his countrymen had of him, therefore, was that of no-doubt a perfect soldier, but of a perfect soldier who kept company with kings and prime ministers and other superbly dressed perfect soldiers. Photographs revealed him in front of palaces and ornate halls. A public who had always hungered after heroes did not associate Pershing with the anxiety and hardship and ever-present death of the trenches. His face never betrayed the strain always evinced by Ulysses S. Grant in his field headquarters, or the telling inflexibility of expression on William Tecumseh Sherman. Pershing had projected another image as the leader of the Punitive Expedition, but it was not that image the public cherished. The image of the Commander of the AEF was of a general remote from the battle, a characteristic image because he was a man neither willing nor able to dramatize himself uncharacteristically. That image made him seem remote from heroic duty.

Americans responded to the image of Washington in prayer at Valley Forge, or crossing the Delaware; to Zachary Taylor at Buena Vista, contemptuously spurning the offer to surrender; to Franklin Pierce leading Vermont volunteers into Mexico City; to Ulysses S. Grant in enlisted man's blouse and muddy boots at the marble-topped table in McLean's parlor.*

"The American effort in the World War," wrote James G. Har-

---

*It is worth footnoting that the wartime image of Pershing's protégé, George C. Marshall, was always that of a general behind a Pentagon desk or at ease in a White House suite, while the images of Dwight D. Eisenhower and Douglas MacArthur were those of front-line generals. Marshall flew back and forth across the Atlantic to various fronts with the abandon of an early stunt pilot. Eisenhower was such a competent staff man that before the Normandy invasion Roosevelt proposed to bring him back to the States as Chief of Staff. MacArthur took three practice wet-runs onto the beach at Leyte before letting army photographers film the event, and this took place three days after the beachhead was secured.

bord, "took little root in the imagination of our countrymen. The censorship did its work thoroughly and well. It was a war of another age than the war our fathers fought. It was fought far away and in a foreign land. It furnished no legendary heroes, no Jeb Stuarts, Phil Kearnys, Custers, Hancocks, or Phil Sheridans. The purple mists of song and story have not yet begun to lend their generous inaccuracy to its deeds."

Pershing did not receive any votes at the Republican national convention, but he did at the Democratic convention in San Francisco. That convention, too, was deadlocked. Democrats did not nominate James M. Cox until the forty-fourth ballot. But on the twenty-seventh ballot one delegate put in nomination the name of John J. Pershing.

A political realist would have seen that, if Pershing wanted the presidency, the sure way to nomination was as a Democrat. A victorious general is virtually a member of the wartime administration and becomes a champion among party regulars. This obtained in the dark horse candidacy of Franklin Pierce. It obtained in the case of Ulysses S. Grant and all the generals who succeeded to the White House after the Civil War.* It was true of George C. Marshall, who enjoyed a lengthy second career as a cabinet official in the Truman Administration. And curiously it was true of Dwight D. Eisenhower, who recorded his amazement in 1945 when Harry Truman at their first meeting promised him the Democratic nomination in 1948.

On July 1, 1921, Warren G. Harding made John J. Pershing Chief of Staff. Harding also appointed Leonard Wood Governor-General of the Philippines. The two soldiers never exchanged another pleasantry.

---

*The one Democrat elected was Grover Cleveland, who had not served in the Civil War, but made his reputation as a reformer.

EPILOGUE

The fall of each one of your soldiers was a stab in the heart of his general, and the impassive expression under which you hide your feelings masked constant and unremitting grief. As an old friend and comrade in arms, I feel my thoughts dwelling on those who did not return and, like you, I think of them with infinite sympathy.

John J. Pershing
My Experiences in the World War

21

Peacetime in
the Company Town

Pershing's tenure as Chief of Staff—from July 1, 1921, to September 13, 1924—was hardly anticlimatic. These years were both frustrating and satisfying. They were frustrating because, as the senior United States Army general, Pershing had to preside over the dismantling of the great World War I military machine. He had noted to Secretary Baker that the United States Army had distinguished itself in engagements against an exhausted and depleted enemy; that by November 11, 1918, the army had only begun to learn the intricacies of modern military detail and organization; and that the soldiers needed training and experimentation with the new weapons that had emerged at the war's end. But in every session Congress appropriated less for a standing army, less for weaponry, and paid less attention to the need for a policy of military preparedness.

They were satisfying years for Pershing because Warren Harding was, by his own option, only a nominal Commander-in-Chief. The reorganization of the army and the creation of the new General Staff proceeded the way military men wanted it to proceed. This process had one notable mishap in the court-martial of General Billy Mitchell in 1926, but Pershing had retired two years before.

Though peace and prosperity were heady prospects for the country in 1921, it was still hard to call Washington "gay." It was a town with a transient population, and therefore no permanent social hierarchy; and a town that had to take Prohibition seriously. It was, and is, a company town, and one that dotes on celebrities. During his first tour of duty in Washington, in 1903, Pershing had been a minor celebrity. Now he was a lion. Now they gossiped about rather than delighted in him.

He bought a house in a fashionable area, a house in which no one presumed he would live alone. He was seen often in the company of Mrs. Louise Cromwell Brooks, a twenty-six-year-old divorcée, the daughter of Mrs. Edward Stotesbury. Mrs. Brooks was beautiful, gracious, and the heiress to a $150 million fortune. Mrs. Brooks did not marry John J. Pershing, but chose instead the forty-two-year-old Superintendent of West Point, Douglas A. MacArthur. The nuptials took place in January, 1922, and in February MacArthur was ordered to the Philippines. Washington gossip-mongers said that Pershing had threatened as much. Mrs. MacArthur said, "Jack wanted me to marry him. When I wouldn't, he wanted me to marry one of his colonels. I wouldn't do that. So here I am, packing my trunks."

It is more likely that Brigadier General MacArthur, who had been introducing educational and military innovations at West Point, opening it up, admitting sunlight, distressed the alumni, who judged he was well past due for an overseas tour. But the gossip that a jealous Pershing had banished MacArthur to Manila grew to such rancorous proportions that Pershing tried to clear the air in an interview with *The New York Times* bureau chief. "If I were married to all the ladies to whom gossips have engaged me," he said, "I would be a regular Brigham Young."

Eventually, Mrs. Cromwell-Brooks-MacArthur, who had danced the nights away in silver shoes and gossamer wings in Paris, Philadelphia, and Washington society, found the mosquito-infested boondocks provincial. Six years later she packed her bags again and sailed for the United States and Reno. She was to find lasting happiness with Lionel Atwill, an English character actor famed for his portrayal as the wooden-armed police chief in *Son of Frankenstein*.

More urgent personal crises occupied Pershing. In 1922, his good friend Charles Magoon died. He willed Pershing the gold cuff buttons he had received as his best man, as well as a gold-headed walking cane, a gift from the people of Panama. Two years later Pershing learned that Professor Charles E. Chapman of Stanford was about to issue a history of Cuba that detailed Magoon's dishonesty while Governor-General. Pershing's letters to Dawes and others were excited. He stated that Magoon had made a small killing in Washington realty *after* his Cuban residency, and that *before* it he had accumulated a modest estate in Nebraska land and municipal bonds. Pershing asked friends to remember how modestly Magoon had lived, and he insisted that Magoon had died heartbroken because the Harding Administration would not give him an appointment.

Shortly thereafter Pershing caught up with Professor Chapman, who told him, "You do not have to defend Magoon from me, but from the Cubans." The Cubans charged *every* American with gross corruptibility. It was to lay these charges to rest that Chapman had undertaken his study. He was, in fact, anxious to include testimonials to Magoon's honesty, two of which Pershing collected from General J. A. Ryan and Robert Leck, who had worked with Magoon in Cuba.

Though not a doting father, he delighted in his son, Warren, who had a mind and spirit of his own. Bad eyesight kept Warren from West Point and the boy went to Yale. On one occasion the youth refused to walk Pershing back across the campus when his visit was finished. "Too much swank," he told his father. At the beginning of World War II, Pershing promised Warren he would have him attached as an aide on George S. Patton's staff. Warren Pershing said his father would do no such thing: he intended to enlist in the army as a private, which he did, later going on to Officer Candidates' School, ending up on the Elbe as a major in an engineer battalion.

Upon retirement, Pershing's rank entitled him to a salary of

$18,000 a year and an office in the War Department, and left subsequent assignments up to his Commander-in-Chief. Calvin Coolidge appointed him as a delegate to the Tacna-Arica Conference, which convened in Arica to settle a bitter territorial dispute between Chile and Peru. When the conference was unable to resolve differences, Peyton C. March remarked that it was no surprise; Pershing was never noted as a diplomat.

Congress consented to his appointment as director of the Battle Monuments Commission. State legislatures, the American Legion, and patriotic groups had begun to spatter monuments throughout France attesting to the American presence. French farmers did not like the usurpation of their land, which was valuable for growing crops, and the unlimited spread of monuments seemed to suggest Americans had done most of the fighting on the Western Front. Additionally, the monuments had no perspective: those honoring a regiment dwarfed another commemorating a division. Pershing and the commission gathered the bodies of fallen Americans into cemeteries on the sites of the main American battlefields and, with care and thoroughness, sought designs suitable for monuments in the spirit of the whole

Pershing lived in France for several months out of every year, but when in Washington, he reported to his office every day. He interested himself in several philanthropic causes and proved an indefatigable correspondent. To say he mellowed is gross sentimentality. He received the following letter:

Tilden Gardens
June 20, 1928

You have been given as a reference by Major General B. A. Poore who has subscribed to purchase one of our co-operative apartment houses. We require that our purchasers be Gentiles who can furnish proper social and financial credentials.

Please inform us whether the applicant is a Gentile and accustomed to living according to the standards of a first class home community. This information will be regarded in strict confidence and you will of course realize the importance of such information both to us and to your friend, our desire and intention being to gather together a congenial group of home owners which in itself creates a priceless asset to any home community.

Pershing replied:

Gentlemen:
Referring to your letter of June 20th, it seems to me almost inconceivable that anyone with the standing of my old friend and comrade, Major General B. A. Poore, should be required to furnish recommendations. I can only say that I would consider that Tilden Gardens or any other community should be congratulated upon having him as a member of its group.

From the time of his retirement in 1924 until 1930, Pershing dutifully plugged away at his memoirs of World War I. It was a labor that many of his friends felt would bear no fruit, but *My Experiences in the World War* was published in March, 1931. It took Pershing longer to write the book than it did to create the new General Staff, though the book has less literary excellence than the staff has military utility. Yet, for all that, it remains what the French call a *quelle*, a source, which, however imperfect and graceless, remains the unique report of the events it describes. Such history as the book discloses has been facilely assimilated by subsequent military authorities, but it is an account to which every serious student of the war must sooner or later repair. It has, therefore, an instrumental value. And in many respects it is revelatory.

Before publication, *My Experiences in the World War* was widely syndicated in the major newspapers. In that version, Pershing described dining at Buckingham Palace with American Ambassador Walter Hines Page and King George V in June, 1917. The night before, German zeppelins had bombed London. From a high window, the king showed Pershing the palace garden which, instead of growing flowers, was producing a crop of potatoes. Pointing to a statue of Queen Victoria in the midst of the spuds, His Majesty exclaimed bitterly to Pershing, "The Kaiser, God damn

him, has even tried to destroy the statue of his own grandmother."
Thousands of Britons wrote to Pershing that their king did not use
such language, and in the published book Pershing deleted the
epithet.

Visiting an American field hospital, Pershing asked a young
soldier where he was wounded. "Do you remember, Sir," the
soldier asked, "just where the road skirts a small grove and turns to
the left across a wheatfield and then leads up over the brow of the
hill? Well, right there, Sir!" Pershing, who wanted to know the
personal nature of the wound, added, "He was clearly describing
the advance south of Soissons which pierced the Château Thierry
salient. It touched me that he should feel I must have been very
close to him."

Too often, however, the prose is lifeless. "Our troops behaved
splendidly and suffered but slight loss in the actual attack," is
anything but an inspiring sentence. His prose is much more vigorous and descriptive when he details the magnitude of a great supply depot. But, of course, that is what his book is precisely
about—managing the detail of modern war and managing it efficiently, because valor and sacrifice alone are not enough for military success. *My Experiences in the World War* is an algebra of
military detail that lists the formula for acquiring 25,000 draft
animals from Spain, which has embargoed horses, to explaining
what is needed by Walter Damrosch, commissioned to provide the
bands for the AEF.

Publication of *My Experiences in the World War* provoked controversy because Pershing was unremittingly critical of the General Staff in Washington, D.C. This controversy made *My Experiences* a lively news topic as old generals refuted Pershing's charges
point by point to newspaper reporters. In outrage, Peyton C.
March himself wrote a book bitterly critical of Pershing. The
controversy probably helped *My Experiences in the World War* win
the Pulitzer Prize for history in 1932. What also helped the book
win the award was the support it received from Nicholas Murray
Butler, President of Columbia University, who presided over the
prize committees. Butler was a devout admirer of Pershing and

later proposed him for membership in the National Institute of Arts and Letters.

It is worth remarking that, although war throughout history has proved a congenial and important topic for poets, writers, and historians, only Ulysses S. Grant and William Tecumseh Sherman among victorious American generals have been able to capitalize on their experiences for the advantage of literature. The lasting literature of World War I and II belongs to avowed literary men like E. E. Cummings, Ernest Hemingway, Norman Mailer, James Jones, Irwin Shaw, and Herman Wouk.

22

Day Is Done

As restless in retirement as he had been on active duty, Pershing moved from the fancy home in Chevy Chase to the Carlton Hotel and finally to the modest Metropolitan Club, where he lived when he was in Washington. The club maintained its cuspidors because he still chewed tobacco.

He spent twenty years of his retirement fostering the career of George C. Marshall. With Marshall, Pershing attended graduation exercises at VMI, where he remarked that the Brother Rats marched as well as the Mr. Dumbjohns. He was best man at Marshall's wedding. When Marshall's career was stymied by then Chief of Staff Douglas MacArthur, who appointed him senior instructor of the Illinois National Guard, Pershing visited his protégé's Chicago offices. With MacArthur's retirement as Chief of Staff, his successor, Malin Craig, brought Marshall back to Washington as assistant chief. On one of the occasions that he saw Franklin D. Roosevelt, Pershing suggested that the President would do well to look over Brigadier Marshall. Roosevelt did, and found Marshall more congenial than Hugh Drum when the time came. In September, 1939, Marshall became Chief of Staff. It was probably Marshall who suggested that Pershing might lend his prestige to the administration's decision to turn over moth-balled destroyers to embattled Britain. Pershing complied, making a nationally broadcast radio address in May, 1940, urging that, "By sending help to the British, we can still hope to keep this war on the other side of the Atlantic where the enemies of liberty, if possible, should be defeated." Certainly neither Roosevelt nor George Marshall thought the war would exempt America; the General Staff, in fact, had carefully detailed plans for American participation.

But these were perilous political times. As many Americans wanted "isolation" from the European conflict in 1940 as wanted neutrality in 1916. The speech marked the end of Pershing's public career. It was a paradoxical conclusion. Throughout his life Pershing had been a staunch Republican conservative. He had enjoyed an intimate and sympathetic relationship with Theodore Roosevelt, William Howard Taft, and, one supposes, Warren G. Harding. Yet Woodrow Wilson's Democratic Administration had made him. He knew Wilson hardly at all and had little to say about him until the ex-President was long dead. Actually, Wilson shocked Pershing by not visiting the battlefields or the graveyards of the AEF when he went to Europe after the armistice. The ground had shifted under the staunch Republican soldier in the twentieth century. In 1900 William Jennings Bryan, the Democratic candidate, campaigned to end the American adventure in the Pacific. In 1940 Republican stalwarts like Senator Arthur K. Vandenberg and Representatives Bruce Barton, Joe Martin, and Hamilton Fish were working as hard to keep America out of Europe.

Pershing survived a serious illness in 1938, but his health began to fail in 1941. He entered Walter Reed Hospital, where he spent the last seven years of his life in a small suite in continuing physical debilitation. His mind never failed or played him false. He charted the progress of the war on War Department maps pinned to his wall. In October, 1942, Major General George S. Patton came to say goodbye before leaving for Africa. "I like Generals so bold they are dangerous," Pershing said. "When I left," wrote Patton in his dairy, "I kissed his hand and asked for his blessing. He squeezed my hand and said, 'Goodbye, George, God bless you and keep you and give you victory!'"

On July 15, 1948, in his eighty-eighth year, Pershing died in his sleep at 3:30 in the morning.

The plans for his funeral, which had been kept in a Pentagon file marked "Top Secret," were a credit to staff work and planning. They provided that the commanding general of Walter Reed Hospital, Major General George C. Beach, personally announce Pershing's death to President Harry S Truman. At 0830 hours the President would pay tribute to the general and at 0930 hours the State Department would issue the presidential order for a period of national mourning "upon all public buildings and at all forts and military posts and naval stations, and on all vessels of the United States" until after the funeral services.

It went off like clockwork. The Pentagon had an operations center working by mid-morning which promptly dispatched three thousand already worded telegrams to public officials and service personnel (three thousand because that was roughly the seating capacity of the Memorial Amphitheater where the Episcopal service was held). The only change in the preordained plans was made by the Pershing family, which requested that his medals not be displayed in the Capitol Rotunda, where Pershing's coffin rested upon the Lincoln catafalque.

On a caisson, followed by caparisoned horse and the colors, Pershing moved through Washington, past 300,000 onlookers, to Arlington cemetery. He was buried in a plot he had selected himself. It was on a slight rise overlooking a section where many of the men of the AEF were buried. His resting place was marked by a simple white headstone. Soon the gravesite was known as "Pershing Hill."

Twenty years later, Pershing's remains were joined by those of his grandson, Second Lieutenant Richard Pershing, who died of wounds received in action in Vietnam on February 17, 1968. Outside the gate near Pershing Hill, on the Memorial Drive approach to the cemetery, is the statue of The Hiker, honoring the fallen of the Spanish-American War. In campaign hat and slung bandolier, the Hiker raises a beckoning arm.

Bibliography

I relied extensively on *Guerrilla Warrior*, by Donald Smythe (New York, 1973), a detailed and exhaustive account of Pershing's military career through the Punitive Expedition. Though I admired Smythe's book, I cannot help but feel the title is a misnomer. Pershing himself was never a guerrilla. Fr. Smythe has assembled a bibliography of sufficient inclusion to make the history departments of four universities happy. It made me happy, too.

Black Jack Pershing, by Richard O'Connor (New York, 1961), is an objective and comprehensive study of Pershing's life and career. *John J. Pershing*, by Frederick Palmer (Westport, 1970), a correspondent who first met Pershing in Korea and who later served as chief of the correspondents in World War I, is often rhetorical and fulsome, but on occasion insightful and includes many anecdotes. "The Life of General John J. Pershing," by George MacAdam, *The World's Work* (Vols. 37 and 38, 1918–1919), while always admiring was the first biography, and MacAdam missed no living bets in his perambulations. The series included many early phototgraphs not only of its subject but of battle maneuvers against the Indians, Cubans, and Moros. *My Friend and Classmate, John J. Pershing*, by Avery Andrews (New York, 1939), is a personal if vainglorious account by a West Point classmate. *John J. Pershing*, by Frank E. Vandiver (Morristown, N.J., 1967), published by the Silver-Burdett Co. for high schools, is the only biography to contain extracts of Pershing's writings with appropriate commentary. An eminent Pershing authority, Vandiver is also the author of the inspirational *John J. Pershing and the Anatomy of Leadership* (The United States Air Force Academy, Colo., 1963), a lecture delivered to the cadets of the Air Force Academy. "A General in the Making," by Dorothy Canfield (Fisher), *Red Cross Magazine* (XIV, September, 1919), is the source for Pershing's years at the University of Nebraska.

Frontier Regulars: The United States Army and the Indians, by Russell Utley (New York, 1973), is perhaps the definitive work on the post-Civil War Cavalry. *Moon of Popping Trees*, by Rex Allen Smith (New York,

1975), is the most objective account of the Battle or Massacre of Wounded Knee. Many other works either glorified the Indian Wars or condemned them. Smith regards Wounded Knee as an accident, an accident made inevitable by the good intentions of the white man, who wanted the Indian to succeed but not to succeed as a red man.

There is no single text on the creation and the early work of the United States General Staff. But *Washington, Lincoln, Wilson: Three Wartime Presidents*, by John M. Palmer (New York, 1930), does much to explain the historical need for one in the context of American military history. *Military and Colonial Policy of the United States*, by Elihu Root (Cambridge, 1916), and *Elihu Root*, by Philipp C. Jessup (New York, 1938), reveal Root's thinking and politicking on behalf of the Staff's creation. "The General Staff," by Malin Craig, *Army and Navy Journal*, 75th Anniversary Issue (Vol. 75–76, 1938), is a history of staff work in armies. *The American Expeditionary Forces: Its Organization and Accomplishments*, by James G. Harbord (Evanston, 1929), and *Report of General John J. Pershing, U. S. A.* (Government Printing Office, 1919) explain the staff work of the AEF. *History of the United States Army*, by Russell Weigley (New York, 1967), complements these, in itself a definitive study.

Martial Spirit: A Study of Our War With Spain, by Walter Millis (New York, 1931); *An Army for Empire*, by Graham A. Cosmas (Colombia, Missouri, 1971); *The Splendid Little War*, by Frank Freidel (Boston, 1958); *Soldiers in the Sun*, by William Sexton (Harrisburg, 1939); and *American Imperialism in 1898*, edited with an Introduction by Theodore Green (Lexington, 1953), are critical analyses of American foreign policy in Cuba and the Philippines. All regard the Spanish-American War as a fiasco. *Schoolbooks and Krags*, by John M. Gates (Westport, 1973), though not an apology, views the American presence in the Philippines as beneficial.

Revolution and Intervention, by P. Haley (Cambridge, 1970), searches out the economic and political motivations for Woodrow Wilson's policy vis-à-vis Mexico, 1914–1917. It concludes that the policy was wanting and misdirected and essentially a failure. "Woodrow Wilson's Dirty Little War," by Jules Archer, *Mankind* (Vol. I, Feb., 1968), nails down the same point. *Wilson: Confusions and Crises, 1915–1916*, by Arthur Link (Princeton, 1960), is Volume 4 of the authoritative and definitive biography of Wilson's political career. Link does not draw conclusions, but his inclusiveness makes it easy for another to draw what he may.

The Great Pursuit, by Herbert Molloy Mason (New York, 1970), is the best-rounded account of the Punitive Expedition. *Blood on the Border*, by C. C. Clendenen (New York, 1959), is the history of American military involvement with Mexico. *Chasing Villa*, by Frank Tompkins (Harrisburg, 1934); *With Pershing in Mexico*, by H. A. Toulmin (Harrisburg, 1935); "General Pershing's Mexican Campaign," *The Century* (Vol. IC, Feb. 1920), and "Pershing's Lost Cause," *The American Legion Monthly* (Vol. XIV, July, 1932), both by Frank Elser, are first-hand accounts of the Punitive Expedition.

Causes and Consequences of World War I, edited with an Introduction by John Milton Cooper (New York, 1972), and *Too Proud to Fight: Woodrow Wilson's Neutrality*, by Patrick Devlin (New York and London, 1975), are perhaps the ultimate criticisms of America's entry into World War I. Historians are by and large convinced that America was the dominant world power whether she fought in World War I or not. Having fought for a policy of worldwide peace, which America could not secure and which a consequent worldwide depression would have doomed anyway, we were simply marking time while losing lives. Had Woodrow Wilson understood the rapacious capacity of the American consumer market, even he might have seen that European markets made little difference and Asian markets none at all.

The Real War, 1914–1918, by B. H. Liddell Hart (Boston and Toronto, 1930), and *The American Heritage History of World War I*, with a narrative by S. L. A. Marshall (New York, 1964), are consistently interesting and often profound accounts of the fighting and the strategy.

West Point: A History of the United States Military Academy, by Sidney Forman (New York, 1950), is as well an interpretive history of American education. *Twenty Years a Military Attaché*, by T. Bentley Mott (New York, 1937), is a justified complaint of West Point during Pershing's years there.

Appendix: Pershing's First Philippine Tour

(Reproduced from the collection of the Manuscript Division, Library of Congress)

In Command Corps Cadets—400 strong—University of Nebraska 1891–1895.

Graduated in Law, University of Nebraska. Class 1893.

In Command Troop D 10th Cav., September 1895 to October 1896.

Rounded up and took to Canada, Cree Indians in Montana, June to August 1896.

On duty Army Headquarters, December 1896 to June 1897.

In Command Company A West Point Corps Cadets as Tactical Officer, June 1897-April 1898.

In Battle and Campaign of Santiago, A.M. and Act'g Adjt. 10th Cav.

In Command of various troops 10th Cav. during Santiago Campaign.

On duty Army Headquarters August 1898.

Chief of Bureau Insular Affairs until August 1899.

Requested Duty in Philippines, sailed September 1899.

Adjutant General Department of Mindanao and Jolo, December 1899 to June 30, 1901.

In field under Gen. Kobbe Northern Mindanao, December 1900 to March 1901.

Collector Customs, Zamboanga, July to October, 1901.

In Command Iligan, Mindanao, October 1901 to March 1902.

Conducted Friendly Expeditions among Moros north side Lake Lanao, November 1901-May 1902.

Command Squadron 15th Cav., October 1901 to May 1902.

In Charge Moro Affairs entire Lake region, May 1902 to May 1903.

Established peaceful relations with majority of Moros Lake Lanao and made frequent visits among, June 1902 to May 1903.

In Command of Camp Vicars with force varying from 600 to 1200 men, June 1902 to May 1903.

Commanded following expeditions from Camp Vicars, punitive and otherwise:

Punitive Expeditions Butig Mountains, September 16th to 22nd 1902, force consisting of four Cos. inf., one of Cav. one of Art.

Battle of Gauan, September 18th 1902. Three forts reduced and taken, Moro loss eleven killed, American Casualties, none.

Battle of Bayabao, September 19th 1902, five forts reduced and taken, Moro loss fourteen killed, American Casualties, none.

Punitive expedition to Maciu, southeast shore of Lake Lanao, September 28th to October 2nd 1902, force four Cos. inf. one troop Cav. and one battery Art.

Skirmishes Maciu country September 29th and 30th, Moros routed with considerable loss, several forts taken.

Battle of Maciu October 1st, stronghold reduced and captured; Moro loss during expedition, 50 killed, many wounded, American loss 2 wounded.

Expedition across Lake Lanao by Moro boats to Marahui, thence to Iligan and return, November 26th to December 2nd 1902, visiting many Dattos en route.

Punitive and exploring expedition west shore of Lake to Marahui and return, April 5th to 16th 1903; total command 1100 men, six Cos. inf. four troops Cav. two batteries art.

Battle of Bacolod, April 6th to 8th 1903. Four Cos. inf. three troops Cav. and parts two batteries Art. engaged. After stubborn defense of two days, Moro stronghold taken by assault. Moro loss: 120 killed, several wounded, American loss: none killed, 9 wounded.

Battle of Calahui, April 9th 1903, same force as at Bacolod, strong fort taken. Moro loss: 23 killed, several wounded, American casualties: none. Expedition continued to Marahui through unexplored country, troops everywhere well received.

Punitive and exploring expedition around Lake Lanao by way of east coast, May 2nd to 12th 1903. Total command 1100 men, six Cos. inf. four troops Cav. and one battery Art.

Battle of Taraca, May 4th 1903, Four Cos. inf. three troops Cav. one battery Art. engaged; two main strongholds and eight flanking forts taken. Moro loss: 250 killed, 13 wounded, 65 prisoners, 36 castiron and brass cannon, 60 rifles. American loss: 2 killed, 5 wounded. Expedition continued through difficult swamps to Madaya, returning to Camp Vicars by west shore May 12th having subdued refractory Moros and established American supremacy throughout Lake country.

Index

337

DATE DUE